PRAISE FOR TIMOTHY BROWNE

Clever, fresh, and endearing. I love Andy!
—JPB, Amazon reader

I love his novels! Fans of both James Patterson and Nicholas Sparks will find themselves absorbed in the pacing and story line of all 4 books in the Dr. Nicklaus Hart Medical Thriller series.
—Julia Loren, Author of the Shifting Shadows

As was said about Hemingway's writing, Timothy Browne writes with vigorous language...so much with less, leaving out all that could be readily understood or taken for granted and delivering the rest with savage exactness! He beautifully delivers the essence of love, that of human love and God's forever love. Timothy Browne's books are page turners!
—L. Harrington

Wow! Just finished this 4th book in Dr Timothy Browne's 'Dr Hart Series'; not even sure where to begin; I've been thoroughly educated, & all I know is I'm ready for his next one.
—JCB, Amazon reader

I think this is Tim Browne's best book yet(The Gene). He has a way of putting twists and turns into the story that keeps you guessing. Keep writing Tim.
—D. Denfeld

This (The Gene) speaks to us in a very personal way and makes this novel a thought provoking read.

—J. Huie

This novel (The Gene) was riveting, thought-provoking and timely. The characters are well-developed and winsome and in the character of all great writers the important questions of life are explored!!

—M Ghormley

TIMOTHY BROWNE

the book of
ANDY

The Book of Andy
By Timothy Browne
Copyright © 2021 by Timothy Browne
All rights reserved
First Edition © 2021

ISBN-13:
978-1-947545-20-5 (epub)
978-1-947545-21-2 (pb)
978-1-947545-22-9 (hb)

The event, people and incidents in this story are the sole product of the author's imagination. The story is fictitious, and any resemblance to individuals, living or dead is purely coincidental. Historical, geographic, political issues, religious, or public figures are based on fact.

Every effort has been made to be accurate. The author assumes no responsibility or liability for errors made in this book.

Scriptures are taken from the KING JAMES VERSION (KJV): KING JAMES VERSION, public domain.
Scriptures are taken from the THE MESSAGE: THE BIBLE IN CONTEMPORARY ENGLISH™:Scripture taken from THE MESSAGE: THE BIBLE IN CONTEMPORARY ENGLISH, copyright©1993, 1994, 1995, 1996, 2000, 2001, 2002. Used by permission of NavPress Publishing Group.

Cover Design by Brett Pflugrath
Cover art by Mike Savlen
Book layout & design by Agape Orthopaedics, Inc.

Library of Congress Control Number: 2021938507

Printed and bound
In the United States of America.

*"This is for all the lonely people
Thinkin' that life has passed them by."*—America

To Dad...dry-fly fisherman

ACKNOWLEDGEMENTS

The Book of Andy flowed from my heart, but like all stories, it took friends and a touch from the Divine to bring it to life.

To my wife, Julie. Thank you for your constant encouragement and companionship.

To my Beta readers and proofreaders, Julie, Devlin, Colleen, Lynne, David, Michelle, Kim, Paula, Karen and Glenn. Thank you for diving into the story and helping to flush out areas that were not clear. And mostly, I thank you for your encouragement to continue to write.

To Mike and Donna-Lee Savlen. Thank you for the amazing artwork on the cover. So, so beautiful!!!
https://savlenstudios.com

To Brett Pflugrath. Thank you for designing the amazing covers that grace all my books. You are a true friend!

To my family, who means everything to me. To my boys, Timothy, Joshua and Jacob and their beautiful wives, Jamie, Sarah and Devlin. I love being your Dad. And to the growing number of grandchildren...my heart grows with each one! You all make the work worthwhile.

"A quiet and modest life brings
more joy than a pursuit of success
bound with constant unrest."

—Albert Einstein

ACT ONE

The Book of Job

Job was a man who lived in Uz. He was honest inside and out, a man of his word, who was totally devoted to God and hated evil with a passion. He had seven sons and three daughters. He was also very wealthy—seven thousand head of sheep, three thousand camels, five hundred teams of oxen, five hundred donkeys, and a huge staff of servants—the most influential man in all the East!

His sons used to take turns hosting parties in their homes, always inviting their three sisters to join them in their merry-making. When the parties were over, Job would get up early in the morning and sacrifice a burnt offering for each of his children, thinking, "Maybe one of them sinned by defying God inwardly." Job made a habit of this sacrificial atonement, just in case they'd sinned.

One day when the angels came to report to God, Satan,

who was the Designated Accuser, came along with them. God singled out Satan and said, "What have you been up to?"

Satan answered God, "Going here and there, checking things out on earth."

God said to Satan, "Have you noticed my friend, Job? There's no one quite like him—honest and true to his word, totally devoted to God and hating evil."

Satan retorted, "So, do you think Job does all that out of the sheer goodness of his heart? Why, no one ever had it so good! You pamper him like a pet, make sure nothing bad ever happens to him or his family or his possessions, bless every-thing he does—he can't lose! But what do you think would happen if you reached down and took away everything that is his? He'd curse you right to your face, that's what."

God replied, "We'll see. Go ahead—do what you want with all that is his. Just don't hurt *him*." Then Satan left the presence of God.

THE BOOK OF JOB 1:1-12
THE MESSAGE

THE BOOK OF ANDY

Sparkling water danced with the morning sun and the promise of a new day at the confluence of the Blackfoot and Clark Fork Rivers. The blue-ribbon trout streams split the valley, carved by glaciers through Paleozoic rock layers in the heart of Western Montana. Before Lewis and Clark's expedition, before the settlers came, and long before roughnecks and lumberjacks dammed the river and built a mill, the Flathead and Salish Indians had named my birthplace and home, *Aices'te 'm,* the place of more bull trout. A place that drips with history and fish stories.

The fragrance of sweet cottonwood resin mingled with the cool of the morning in the truck's cab as I took the last swig of coffee and turned down Riverside for the shop. Hopefully, work duties would end in time to dip a fly into the big Blackfoot.

Montana's northern latitude guaranteed for the sun to set closer to ten and twilight to linger for another hour. Tonight, with a full moon and a predicted bug hatch, eager fishermen and rainbow trout lurked.

One of the few lessons my father had taught me was that salmon fly nymphs spent three years underwater. By some mysterious force they'd crawl out along the banks of the rivers, break out of their shucks, and appear as ugly, three-inch-long brown bugs with bright orange bellies, irresistible to fish and men alike. He'd also showed my brothers and me how to use a fly rod, which he readily admitted was one of the handful of things he'd done right in life.

Over the last few weeks the salmon flies had mated, and if the stars aligned this evening, females would launch from the bushes, fly over the water, and smack their abdomens on the surface to drop their eggs—a life cycle prying the most stubborn monster rainbows out of their deep holes. Dry-fly fishermen who catch the epic hatch walk away forever changed. These were the summer days that I and the rest of Montanans lived for.

I pulled into the east side of the parking lot of Butterfly Septic and glanced through the windshield at the large sign nailed over the door. The Hellgate winds had further collapsed the metal cut-out wing of the Rhopalocera, a term I remembered from eighth-grade biology.

Alongside my Chevy, the boss skidded to a halt into his reserved parking spot marked: RESERVED FOR THE PRESIDENT. I fanned away the dust cloud that filled my cab. He ignored me when I nodded and squinted against his pearlescent Ford. I favored last year's black truck with the lift kit and wide tires, but the new white one became his latest purchase and how he siphoned off all profits needed for repairs to the sign and building.

I pointed to the decrepit sign. He returned an uncaring shrug and inserted a large cigar into his mouth that he would chew the entire day. His pale, saggy-eyed, hungover appearance foreshadowed the harbinger of another shitty day.

Marty fumbled with the wad of keys on a lanyard attached to his belt, as the leather strained to support his obese belly. He unlocked the building, and I turned off the ignition to my truck. When the engine spit and sputtered, Marty, his round frame halfway through the opened door, turned and glowered.

"Hey, turd for brains! Put some decent gas in my truck before you kill it," he said, then slammed the door behind him.

In reality, the 1977 C10 had done that ever since he sold it to me and legally, I guess in a way, he still owned the truck. He held the note. When the local Chevy dealership manager laughed at my application, Marty, in a rare moment of kindness, offered to sell me his old truck—rust and all. Of course, with an over-inflated price tag and 12% interest, Marty was, as always, the winner.

I'd attended first and second grade with Marty until I flunked second, then remained a year behind him, something he never let me forget. Later in life, Marty's parents purchased his first septic truck to keep him out of trouble—the secret that the entire 253 people of Milltown understood. Even with all the turmoil he'd stirred up as a teenager, he'd built the business to a reasonably successful ten-truck fleet. I never had the nerve to ask if Marty or his parents came up with the sickening slogan: *Your Poo is Our Sweet Nectar.*

To survive, Butterfly Septic served the greater Missoula area, a place made famous by the movie *A River Runs Through It*. I had to agree with Norman Maclean that the number of bastards multiplied proportionately to the miles removed from the valley, but even Norman could not have predicted that Missoula would become overgrown with so many.

My nine other coworkers arrived, and without looking at my watch, I knew the clock ticked a few minutes before seven. Marty never tolerated tardiness from anyone. I'd seen two guys fired in the last few years who tested him on this, but no one wanted to give the man an extra second of their life.

Before I creaked open the door to the truck, as was my custom, I flicked my finger against the bobblehead Mandalorian action figure stuck to the top of the dash. Perhaps today would be a better day and the universe would slip me a break, but when I stepped out of the truck, my boot landed with a soft squish. I lifted my foot, and a wad of pink bubblegum stretched between the ground and the tread. *I should have known better.*

"Oh, that's where I put my gum," one of my coworkers, with the greatest seniority and the worst attitude, said behind me. "You can keep that one, Andy." He pointed to his mouth. "I've got a new batch."

Two of the other workers who walked alongside him laughed.

"Come on, Mandoo, you'll be stepping in worse by day's end," another said, and slugged me hard on the arm as he walked by.

I scraped the goo on the bottom of my boot against a nearby rock and grimaced at the Star Wars character on my dash. I longed for the space traveler's courage and was still sore at the fact that one of the new guys recently asked me in our morning meeting if I had a nickname. Taken from the Mandalorian's own choice, I told him, "Mando." This elicited hoots and hollers from the rest of the team, and they quickly added another "o" to rhyme it with poo. Mando became Mandoo.

I slammed the door closed on the truck and wished I would stand up to these bullies. The silver helmet of the

Mandalorian bobbed in agreement with me. If only I had a laser blaster, I'd put it to good use about now. Better yet, the phase-pulse rifle the bounty hunter carried that disintegrates his enemies to dust. Mama always taught me to "love thine enemy," but she'd never met these men.

When I opened the shop door and limped in on the side of my boot, I ignored the look of disdain from Marty and the ribbing of the others. Marty would have said something as well, but he'd just filled his mouth with a powdered sugar donut, the type that lasts for years on the shelf and eaten in one bite. He took a sip from the Styrofoam coffee cup, placed the cigar back into the corner of his mouth, and spoke around it.

"Okay you honey-dippers, now that fecal face has graced us with his presence, let's get on with our day."

Because history often referred to septic trucks as honey-wagons, Marty applied the term of endearment for his team —if he stayed in a reasonable mood. His morning slang for me was a new one, and I have to admit the moniker was kind of funny.

"All the trucks are in good working order and I expect them to remain that way today." He then listed the assignments of the trucks to the matching driver.

Not sure why he did that, as it never changed unless a truck or two were on the fritz. I always got truck Number One. Which sounds good, but this was the original truck his parents endowed him with, and by far the most fickle that broke down often. The most senior guys drove the shiny new rigs. Yes, a pecking order existed even in the crapper business.

As Marty walked to the large map hung behind him on the wall, he took his cigar out, popped another donut into his mouth, swallowed it after two chews and replaced the stogie with robotic precision. He'd repeat the dexterous maneuver many times throughout the day, but no one would dare say a word about the shower of white powder that cascaded down the front of his shirt.

We would all get a sheet of assignments and addresses, but I think Marty envisioned himself as the chief of police in his morning briefings as he pointed to the map of Missoula.

"The knuckleheads of the county still haven't fixed the axle-breaker on Broadway," he said, and thumped his fat finger on the map. "Steer clear of that and Russell Street…it's a traffic nightmare with the new bridge project."

Marty didn't understand social graces, but was smart enough to know that time was money, and he wouldn't put up with anyone wasting it. He took a swallow of his coffee—another bit of skillful oral gymnastics—drinking from a cup with the cigar in his mouth.

He turned back to the map and thumped his finger on a street on the hillside overlooking the city. I swallowed hard.

"Heaven is calling for someone special today," he said. This brought a series of catcalls from the others. He pointed to Heaven's Gate, a private road where the largest and most elegant houses loomed on the south hills over Missoula.

"Ms. C.C. has made her yearly ask." He enunciated the initials with a slight sway of his hips from side to side.

Heat rose into my face, and my heart pounded. C.C. stood for Carrie Carver. A beauty, even in grade school, when Marty and I were too young to understand the stirrings of our immature bodies. She was striking now.

I held my breath. Marty threatened every year to give the choice assignment to one of the other guys.

"I'd give the client to someone more deserving if Carrie didn't request you." He glowered at me and shook his head in disgust as the others ribbed me.

He walked over, handed me a slip of paper with her address, and started a child's rhyme with a sickeningly sweet voice. "Mandoo and Carrie sitting in a tree…" It elicited more laughs. Maybe the universe favored me after all today.

The new guy pumped his arm and fist in an obscene motion. "Yeah Mandoo, make sure you pump her real well."

I slumped in my chair and swallowed the curses that rattled in the back of my throat. It would just egg them all on. But even Marty shot my coworker a frown—some lines you just don't cross.

The room quieted as Marty took his stance in front and sucked down another donut in one swallow.

Most of the guys sat up straight, ready to race to their respective trucks to get on with their day. The earlier they made it through their list, the sooner they finished their shitty job and could head to the local bar or whatever way they drowned their existence as honey-dippers.

"Otherwise, be careful out there," Marty said as he stared down his crew.

Two of the guys stood but plopped back in their chairs when Marty crossed his arms. His eyes lit with delight, and he cleared his throat for a final announcement.

"Uh-oh! Guess what day it is! Guess…what…day…it is!" Marty said, imitating the camel's voice on the Geico commercial.

Everyone groaned and slumped in their chairs.

"Oh come on, I know you can hear me. Andy, Andy, Andy! What day is it, Andy?"

I shook my head, trying not to encourage him. We all knew what he implied—the monthly, sickening chore of washing out the tanks on the trucks. After the last client and dump at the sewage treatment plant, we'd don protective gear, climb through the manhole on top of the tank and spray out the inside, removing chucks of excrement, baby wipes, and anything else disgusting that one can imagine. Even with the hog boots, plastic apron, mask and goggles, the smell would linger in your nose hairs for days. I couldn't imagine the stink on the rest of my body.

So much for catching a break or the bug hatch.

2

SEPTIC

My septic truck and I left the shop last, followed by a large plume of black smoke. The diesel of ol' Number One had fired up like the first of January rather than the end of June, but it now hummed along nicely as the morning sun warmed the engine and the cab. My favorite meteorologist, the perky blonde with the shapely figure, predicted the temperature to hit ninety-five today. Perhaps, because of the heat, the bug hatch would hold off for a day and I could hit it tomorrow. I dreaded the disgusting business of climbing into the truck's tank this evening—the heat making it that much more intolerable. *I'm sure no one could talk the chief into postponing the task.*

I turned right out of West Riverside toward Missoula on Highway 200 behind an empty logging truck—the reason for the tiny communities nearby. Rich in timber resources and water, the great barons of Montana built a sawmill, and thus the settlements, in the late nineteenth century. The industry grew to where it supplied lumber around the world and secured jobs for the locals until 2008. Sadly, all that remained of the great mill was the log yard with acres of timber they shipped elsewhere for processing. This logger had just dropped his load.

Along this six-mile-long, two-mile-wide stretch of land, squeezed between the rocky crags and tree-lined mountains, are four towns: West Riverside, Bonner, Piltzville, and my home, Milltown. With a population of less than a few hundred in each, I suppose most city dwellers wouldn't even acknowledge them except as spots on a map. But in my mind, if it had a post office and at least two bars each, the designation as towns was legit. Milltown sat at the junction of the two great rivers, Bonner extended up the Blackfoot River, Piltzville up the Clark Fork River, and West Riverside toward Missoula. Each a stone's throw away from the other.

An outsider would assume they coexisted as one quaint community, but the locals knew exactly where the boundary lines ran that separated different ethnic groups. Not that the communities bore any animosity between each other, people just preferred their own kind. Finns established Milltown around 1903 when the landowner divided the confluence into lots leased for $1.25 per month. The Finnish were so populous, some of the oldest occupants still call it Finntown instead of Milltown. The Swedes and Norwegians spread out through Riverside and Bonner.

Number One followed the road through the valley and around the bends of the Clark Fork. I'm not sure who decided that the combination of the two rivers would continue west as the Clark Fork. I'm sure the Blackfoot was none too happy about it, but it was the Clark Fork that rippled and swirled through the Hellgate Canyon, then Missoula Valley, and eventually dumped into the mighty Columbia River. Lewis had explored this valley after the two split up on their journey home and Clark turned south at Travelers Rest, only to meet up again at the Missouri. For some reason, Lewis preferred his partner and named it after him, otherwise it should be the Lewis Fork.

As much as I fantasized about becoming a futuristic Mandalorian, I so much more dreamt of the past as one of the mighty men following the captains on their expedition. *I'm sure to have loved Lewis' Newfoundland dog, Seaman.*

As the mountains shielded the sun, I entered the Hellgate canyon that connected Missoula to our community. It was a funny way for Captain Lewis to describe God's handiwork. On his return trip home, Lewis followed Clark's river and described the Hellgate as a "narrow, confined pass." I swear Mama would cross herself through the dark canyon, and Dad would laugh and say it had nothing to do with the devil. The name came only because of the skirmishes between the Blackfeet and Flathead tribes—a sure-fire spot for an ambush. I suppose as a settler in a wagon, the place was surely the gate to hell.

Glacial activity cut the canyon between Mount Sentinel and Mount Jumbo. Apparently, God started his construction of my valley seventy-five million years ago when the earth heaved and pushed the Rocky Mountains up from the depths. He carved them down with erosion for a few million years, then brought about another upheaval a short thirty million years ago. Not satisfied, He formed huge glaciers that carved and ground out the valleys, laying down the tracks for the mighty Blackfoot and Clark Fork Rivers. I wonder what purpose He held in the next event two million years ago when He caused a massive ice sheet to form in the Hudson's Bay area that grew and extended into Western Montana, further sculpting out valleys. Whether it was an accident, which I doubt God makes, or further creativity, an ice dam formed to the west, trapping two thousand feet of water—now named in modern times as Lake Missoula. When the dam gave way fifteen thousand years ago, the water, about the size of Lake Michigan, surged through Washington State and into the Pacific Ocean. *What a sight that must have been.*

Mama told me four thousand years ago, the good Lord took six days to form the earth with one day of rest. I guess either way, a few days or a million, it doesn't change God or His creation. I suppose anything worth building takes a while and the beauty of the area deserved every second.

As I exited Hellgate canyon into the city limits of Missoula, the sun illuminated the striated shoreline marks from Lake Missoula across Mount Jumbo on the right and Mount Sentinel on the left. The University of Montana, the home of the Grizzlies, sits directly under the shadow of Mount Sentinel—the only school in the nation with a mountain of its own.

I motored down Broadway and swerved around the pothole Marty warned us about. It took me through downtown Missoula where the drivers are crazy. So much so, there was a term for them around the state. They'd sometimes pull a U-turn in the middle of a busy street or turn right from the left lane, so we affectionately coined the term, "Doing a Missoulian." I always take it slow through the city because my septic truck doesn't stop on a dime, especially fully loaded. I'd always thought we should use a flashing sign on the front of the truck to warn other drivers, but somehow, when people see us coming, they think they should pull out in front of the crapper guy so they don't have to follow behind. It's led to many close calls.

I soon turned off Broadway onto Mullan Road, toward the first customers of the day. The city had situated the sewage treatment plant out west Mullan, along the Clark Fork, so it made it handy to empty the truck after the first few jobs. I don't know exactly how it all works, but the plant treats the sewage enough to dump it back into the river. Something I feel bad about, but they tell me you could practically drink the water when it's gone through the process. I don't think I'd want to try.

Mullan Road quickly turned rural after it left the city, and I always wonder when I'm out here if the road truly follows the old Mullan Trail laid down by Lieutenant Mullan in the mid-1800s, the first wagon road to cross the Rockies. *I'll have to look it up one of these nights.*

Many of the developments on Mullan were not on the city sewer system, so each house had their own septic tank. A godsend for Butterfly Septic.

A house's septic system consists of an underground cement tank that connects to a drain field. The wastewater from the house dumps into the tank where heavy solids settle to the bottom. Here, bacterial action produces digested sludge and gases. The lighter solids such as grease, oils, and fat float to the top to form a scum layer. Liquids flow to the other side of the tank and into a drain field and back into the earth. Instead of "Ashes to ashes, dust to dust," Marty liked to say, "Shit to Shinola."

Our job as Butterfly Septic is to open the lid of the septic tank and suck out the sludge and scum. Something required every few years. Marty, of course, recommends to everyone to have it done annually at the very least.

Our trucks basically work like huge vacuum cleaners, able to hold over two thousand gallons of poo. A pump creates a powerful suction with negative pressure in the truck tank, so when we stick a three-inch hose down the honey-hole it sucks everything out of the underground tank. It's less disgusting than it sounds, if you can stand the initial smell of opening the tank and are fastidious about keeping the hose and equipment clean. Most guys don't even wear protective gear. I, at least, like to wear safety glasses. The worst smell is on the other end, when we open the outflow valve and dump it at the sewage treatment facility. Okay, I take that back—the worst is when we have to climb into the tank once a month to spray it out.

Marty pays us twelve dollars and fifty cents an hour for the privilege of doing this. At two thousand dollars a month, twenty-four thousand a year, the income puts us at the poverty line. Marty loves reminding us we make a dollar more an hour than the EMS guys driving the ambulance. It shows where the world's priorities lie. Because I barely made it past the eighth grade, I guess I'm fortunate to have the steady job.

3

C.C.

Near the end of the day, as Number One labored up snob-nob hill above Missoula toward Carrie's house, I decided the ribbing the guys gave me in the morning was worth every minute. They were jealous, is all.

I shifted down a gear when I hit the steepest part of the road and a large black diesel cloud shot from the tailpipe. Even with an empty tank, I reached my lowest gear at the top of the hill. I turned the corner and admired the panorama of Missoula. Late June, the city appeared as a sea of green, like an emerald placed in a mountain setting, bathed in the royal-blue, big sky. No wonder people wanted to live here. If you could tolerate winter's dreary months of cold and gray, this beauty blossomed as your reward. The view was spectacular. Overlooking the city lights, friends rumored the hill to be the best place to take a girl at night. I wouldn't know, since a guy like me doesn't get those kinds of chances.

I followed the road across the hill before it turned north to Carrie's house that sat on the edge of the bench over the city like a grand estate. It was quite the talk of the town when

Carrie and her husband, Willie Gray, built it. Like Marty, Willie succeeded off the shoulders of his parents, but Willie that much more so. Willie's parents were upright church-going folks and had built the successful Gray Insurance business. They handed their son a silver spoon and the business. I'm sure God blessed the business only because of his parents' righteousness, as it sure in the hell wasn't for Willie's. But somehow he'd grown the insurance business into financial planning, and supposedly that's where their money came from. Not sure I'd trust a money guy who lived in such a mansion.

Along with that silver spoon came superior good looks and physical prowess. Every school seemed to have that one boy who matured three years, and a foot taller, ahead of any other kid. As captain of the basketball, football, and any other ball team you could think of, and with his thick, wavy blond hair, blue-eyes, and muscular build, he was king. No wonder he got what he wanted and whatever girl he desired... including Carrie Carver. They'd been sweethearts since seventh grade, and rumors swirled that they "did it" on the day of eighth-grade graduation.

After high school, Willie excelled as the champion quarterback for the University of Montana Grizzlies. Something I'm sure that helped his business.

On the other hand, the girls always elected Carrie the captain of the cheer squad from sixth grade on through college. If I closed my eyes, I could picture her in a tight sweater, bouncing her pompons. Probably the same image that many guys pull up from their mental Rolodex in their private time.

Everyone agreed Carrie was a beauty. One of those rare, straight out of the box, natural splendors. Whether she wore holey jeans and a t-shirt, with no makeup and her hair pulled back into a ponytail, or all dolled up in full formal regalia, men and women alike would take notice—men normally doing a double take. Since we looked eye-to-eye, I figured she stood close to my five-foot, six-inch height, if not slightly over. She was thin and full figured at the same time, with shiny sandy-blonde hair and stunning cobalt-blue eyes. It surprised no one when they voted her Miss Montana 2005, but shocked everyone when she didn't win the national competition.

When Willie and Carrie married, I breathed a sigh of relief when she decided to go by her maiden name. Somehow, Carrie Gray didn't fit her.

It's funny now, thinking back to grade school, I don't remember her as an awkward middle-schooler. Carrie was always Carrie. Maybe I didn't notice, or perhaps by some quirk of the universe, she existed like that since first grade.

There were only two things I disliked about Carrie Carver. The first is that she went through life painfully naïve and especially didn't understand blonde jokes. The second was Willie. Perhaps I could overlook both if the day ever arose when she finally came to her senses and professed her undying love for me.

I laughed at my joke and pressed the brake on Number One. The Mandalorian's plastic head bobbed in agreement, and I nodded back. Unlike the figurine in my Chevy, this Mandalorian wore the rusted helmet from before he reclaimed his armor, a fitting tribute to the rust bucket I drove.

I willed the fantasy from my thoughts and centered the truck through the log-arched gate with the gigantic sign. SHADY ACRES is what Willie and Carrie had named their ten-acre plot. Snarky folks like to reverse the names and call their place on the hill Gray Acres and his business Shady

Insurance. I doubt they said it to Willie's face, as they knew him for his hot and reactive temper. I found it humorous, as Willie and Carrie always reminded me of Eva Gabor and Eddie Albert on the old sitcom *Green Acres*, and even now my foot tapped out the show's tune.

Willie and Carrie had built their home as a beautiful white Victorian mansion with a wrap-around porch. I imagined Willie with a large cigar and Carrie wearing something light and frilly, sitting on the porch swing, sipping gin and tonics, looking down at the city and wondering what all the poor people were doing.

I drove around the circular driveway and backed up toward the garage. The septic tank sat near the pool, and I carefully maneuvered Number One around Carrie's white Lexus to the rear of the house.

I pulled within inches and thought I'd better check my clearance before going any further. I placed Number One in park, pulled the yellow tab on the dash to apply the parking brake, opened the door, and slipped down from the cab. As I did, a magical sight appeared. Carrie Carver emerged from around the corner with nothing on but a pink bikini. My eyes instantly focused on the asphalt and heat rose up my spine. I thought I might have a case of the flu, because my head spun like I had a fever.

"Hey, Andy. Good to see you." She bounced up to me.

"Oh…hey…Carrie," I said, and tried to look but not stare at the same time.

She got close enough that I thought she might reach out and give me a hug, but I could feel her examine me up and down and choose not to. In an act of pity, she extended her hand. I shook it, but afterwards noticed her holding it away from her body like she'd just touched something disgusting.

"Thanks for coming today," she said sweetly, trying to make up for it. "That time of year again. How've you been?"

"It's good to see you, Ca...Ca...Carrie," I stammered, my mind and tongue tied in knots. Embarrassment flooded my brain that I'd said, 'see you'. I couldn't 'see' and think at the same time. The peripheral vision of the pink bikini seared itself into my brain. "How's Willie?" I asked, trying to get my mind to refocus.

"Oh, he's on one of his adventures with the guys. Fishing in Mexico, I think." She frowned and waved it off.

A hint of sadness crossed her face as I stole a glance at her when she looked out over the city. I wondered how she balanced the luxury of her life versus the pain of living with a guy like Willie.

"I was sure sorry to hear about your mom," she said. "She was a gracious lady."

Afraid to study her for sincerity in case my eyes went rogue, and I looked at her chest instead, I diverted my gaze. "Thanks," I murmured, wondering if she actually remembered my mom.

"Willie and I couldn't make her funeral. We were hunkered down in the Caribbean," she said, like they had hidden in a bunker from the Nazis.

I nodded.

"Anyway, I sure never understood how she could have eleven kids. God, I can hardly keep my two little brats in line."

Heat flooded my face at the mention of my mother's reproductive abilities. "Dad always told us, 'After the first six, I stopped counting and caring,'" I said, trying to cover for my embarrassment.

She pacified me with a quick chuckle, but then said,

"Sorry, I parked the Lexus in the way. I'll move it." She smiled and walked away.

I couldn't help but look. Her bikini bottom covered little of her toned behind. The shutter of my mind camera clicked away, but I died a thousand deaths when she turned and caught me admiring the view. I quickly climbed into the truck with my face on fire and watched in the rearview mirror as she moved the car beside the four-car garage.

A wave of loneliness washed over my mind, wondering why the universe had dealt me such a crappy hand. People like Willie and Carrie seemed to live in a different universe. Not sure they even realized it or saw it. Perhaps this was how it'd been since the beginning of time—the people who have and those who can only dream.

My stomach rumbled, either from the pain of being one of the undesirables in life or from the fact I hadn't eaten lunch today. I tried ignoring both. I definitely needed some time in the river where life's injustices seem to drift away.

Backing up along the side of the house onto a graveled pad next to the Lexus, I stopped well short of the lawn, since the truck held plenty of hose to reach the septic tank. Normally, Willie parked a boat on the pad, but I'm sure it now floated at their place on Flathead Lake.

Again, I put the truck in park, engaged the parking brake, and slid out of the cab. The large diesel powered the vacuum pump, and when switched on, it revved the truck's RPM. I slid my safety goggles in place and opened a small compartment above the pump where I stored my elbow-length gloves. Then I unwound the three-inch hose and stretched it to the honey-hole, protected in the yard by a six-inch concrete cover. I knelt down in the grass and pried the top off. Here contained the secret that all my other friends didn't know about Carrie Carver. Her crap stunk as much as everyone else's.

Threading the hose into the darkness, I inserted it past the scum layer. If the top layer of grease plugged up the system right away, you'd have a real mess on your hands. I walked back to the truck and opened the hand lever, which put suction to the intake valve where the hose connects. There's a specific order to sucking out a septic tank, one that you only break once if you're lucky. You don't want the sewage moving the other way.

As soon as I attached the line, it jumped and wiggled as Willie and Carrie's last meals filled the hose and gushed into the tank. I grabbed the honey-stick from the rack on the truck. I used it to stir the tank, helping remove the bottom layer of sludge. By the end of the hot day the pole reeked, and with the freshwater washer on Number One broken I had no way to clean it.

As I stirred the pot and moved the hose, a splash came from the swimming pool, and I glanced over my shoulder. Carrie's daughter broke the surface with more splashing and swam to the edge of the pool. She pulled herself up and ran to the diving board to do it again.

How nice that must feel on a hot day like today. I took a double take and realized Carrie, partially obscured by the landscaping, reclined on a lounge chair at the side of the pool. She had pulled the straps of her bikini top down to prevent the dreaded tan lines. I hadn't remembered Carrie being so busty growing up, but she sure was now. I tried not to linger, but tell any man that. A shapely figure held an invisible power that most seemed helpless against.

I fantasized that Carrie would sit up, smile at me, wave me over to join her poolside—maybe offer me a cold drink and shade under the cabana. There she'd confess her long-held crush for me and rejection of her scoundrel husband. "Move in with me," she'd say as she lightly stroked my cheek.

And like my mind willed her, Carrie sat up, adjusted her straps in one smooth motion, and looked my way. Then, like watching the graceful Bo Derrick exiting the ocean, my mind turned her movement into slow motion. She waved, stood, and walked in my direction.

"Attt, attt, attt, attt!" a childish voice startled me from behind and back to reality.

I turned to see Carrie's youngest, her nine-year-old son, dressed in full army regalia, holding me at bay with a plastic machine gun.

"Attt, attt, attt, attt!" He imitated a gun sound again at my chest.

I smiled and grabbed my chest like he'd just riddled me with bullets. "Got me," I croaked.

He didn't return the smile—laser-focused on me and the hose in my hands. "Hands up, crapper guy," he demanded.

I guffawed. I'm sure he'd learned the slang from his father. Even so, here this little nine-year-old taunted me. I tried to think of something smart to say to the boy, when his attention looked past me toward the pool. I followed his stare. Carrie trotted over to us. All I could see was her pink bikini moving gracefully with her body. She yelled something, but I couldn't hear over the loud suction of the hose and the roar of the truck.

Was it to me or her son?

Maybe she came to rescue me from the little turd.

She now sped to a gallop, her pompons bouncing.

I smiled.

Suddenly my ears awoke to a high-pitched squeal of the suction pump at the truck.

"Andy!" she yelled. "Something's wrong with your truck!"

I dropped the honey-stick and hose and ran to the truck.

"Oh God! Oh God!" I yelled as I reached it. The pump screamed. The system had plugged. And as I reached to turn it off, the entire system blew.

Ka-pow!

My ears rang, and my nose burned. Like getting hit in the face with a hard right cross. Everything went black, and for a second, I wondered if the explosion had knocked me out or killed me.

Neither transpired, but I soon wished it had.

Carrie screamed.

The smell was overwhelming.

Thinking I'd gone blind, I reached for my face and removed my stool-covered glasses. Poop coated everything.

Sludge had backed up into the pump, blowing a hose.

I slowly turned toward Carrie's scream. As my mind cleared, I realized the object of her frenzy. Her son had followed me to the truck and stood frozen in sludge, like a monument to the great turd god.

"You stupid, stupid man!" Carrie screamed, along with a mouthful of obscenities—words that surprised me she knew. "Look what you've done to my son. You imbecile!" She gritted her teeth. "Look what you've done to my house!"

I tried to say something.

"You've always been the stupidest person I know, Andy Strobel."

4

PARTS

The masked bandit, my reflection on the stainless-steel tank of one of the new trucks, stared back at me as Marty repeated each curse and insult that Carrie had spewed. Dried sewage covered every inch of me, except for where my goggles had protected my eyes. In her anger, Carrie chased me off without allowing me to apologize or clean up my mess, including myself—not even letting me use a hose that hung from a bracket on the house. I simply climbed into my truck and drove back to the shop, gagging the entire way. Now, both me and the cab smelled rank.

I didn't understand why Carrie screamed, "You always ruin everything!" Not sure I'd ever had an ounce of power over her life, nor could I recall having interactions enough to do that kind of harm. The one time I could remember occurred in second grade when I acted out and the entire class had to skip recess, but that seemed dumb.

"You're not even worth the powder to blow yourself up with!" Marty screamed at me.

The sewage had dried into a solid cast over my clothes, and I stood frozen like a statue.

"Are you even listening to me, turd-head?"

The other guys laughed in the background.

"You ruin everything, you little son's-a-bitch."

There it was again. *Not sure how I did that for everyone around me.* Even Pop had accused me of the same when my brother and I were playing catch in the living room, and Larry failed to grab a particularly well-thrown ball. BAM—it hit smack dab in the middle of the TV. We went without entertainment for an entire year until Mama and Pop could afford a new one.

"My parents gave me that truck and now you've ruined it. We'll never get the stench out of it!" Marty screamed. "You're going to pay for this."

I tried to apologize, but hard poo caked my mouth shut.

"Carrie already called me and threatened to call her lawyer next. I didn't know that woman had such a mouth on her, but dammit, Andy, you're a miserable dumbass. I don't even know how your shit-for-brains managed this one."

He'd screamed long enough that he'd lost his cigar and nearly his voice. I wanted to remind him I'd told him about needing to replace the pump for over a year, but that would only inflame him.

"Since you smell and look like one big turd, you might as well climb into the tank and spray it out. By morning the entire truck better sparkle like new or I'm going to kick your ass from here to Missoula."

Marty walked back into the shop, but I could hear him cursing well after he slammed the door.

I looked at the remainder of the crew who stood at a safe distance.

"Well, that's as intimate as you'll ever get to Carrie," one guy said, making the others laugh.

"At least get it off your face, it'll make you plenty sick otherwise," one of the old guys said, taking pity on me and handing me a bucket of water and a rag.

"Thanks," I murmured.

I did the best I could to clean my face with the water and rag, but once contaminated, it only smeared the sewage. There remained nothing I could do but back the truck up to the pit and wash out the tank.

The pit meant the empty lot next to the shop. I'm sure the neighbors loved it when we rinsed the tanks. Thankfully, the junkyard stood as the closest business to us, so maybe it mattered little, unless the wind blew east toward Bonner.

After putting on the goggles, face mask and plastic apron, I started the engine for the pressure washer, climbed the ladder with the hose, and opened the access hole on top of the tank. You'd think sitting in sewage for the last hour would burn every single olfactory nerve from inside my nose, but I can guarantee that there were some survivors. Even through my mask, it smelled terrible.

I suppose going into the tank felt much like bungee-jumping or cliff-diving. If you don't just leap, you'll stand at the edge thinking too much, and soon your brain will tell you all sorts of reasons why you shouldn't do it. I took the first step into the tank and lowered myself down.

Another manhole at the back of the tank, which I had already opened, let some light filter in so at least it wasn't pitch black. The tank is just that—a big empty space, except for two steel cross bars stretched across to keep it from collapsing in on itself from the negative pressure. The suction comes from the top, and just like a huge shop-vac, a large ball valve keeps the sewage from getting into the pump. Herein lay the problem. The valve had gotten stuck open with baby wipes, the scourge of honey-dippers. I guess like me, they ruin everything.

I try not to ponder my life too much or else I'd be one bundle of discouragement. But at a time like this, when I sprayed the scum off the inside of the tank, it became impossible not to think about things. I guess I'd heard about the rare person who rises out of their lot in life and builds a simple thing called a computer in their parents' garage to become one of the richest men in history. But those stories are as real to me as the ones about unicorns. For the rest of us, poverty begets poverty. It's hard to rise up when you're born at the bottom of the totem pole with the heaviness of your family's social and economic status, mixed with a batch of bad luck, weighing your down.

One part of me tells me I'm okay with who I am and the way God made me, and yet other parts of me—especially burdened with the voices of the nay-sayers around me—remind me of all my faults and shortcomings. It's kind of like there are different people inside of me—one who knows all sorts of facts and figures and another who is "dumber than a fence post," as my older brother would often swear at me, and also a part of me who wants to be a fearless Mandalorian and another who is as meek as a mouse.

I wished I could get all these different parts of me into the same room and calm them all down. It might go a long way to still the voices in my head telling me I'm no good.

For now, all those parts of me were smack dab in the middle of a stinky, dark and dank sewage tank lined with sludge, and the ones with the loudest voices reminded me I was not the sharpest drill in the toolbox. Only one faint voice whispered that beyond flunking second grade, I actually did pretty well in school. At seven, I either couldn't read or wouldn't read, and they sent me back a grade. Something that didn't exactly instill confidence in me. But whatever the stumbling block, my brain finally caught up, and I earned mostly A's in eighth grade. Once I learned to read, I discovered the ability to lose myself in a good book and the universe opened up to me. Our family never traveled out of Montana, but Mama gave me a ticket to the world when she'd take me to the library.

Perhaps I would have made something of my life, but fate dealt me a bad hand, making it hard to recover. Mama and Pop had eleven of us, and there might have been more if Pop hadn't up and died during my eighth-grade year. But by the time Pop passed, he'd already buried four of his sons. His second son succumbed to the flu at the age of one. Then his first-born died in Vietnam at twenty, and two of his other boys died the day I was born. Killed on the road between Milltown and Missoula, coming to see me in the hospital. Even I have a hard time forgiving myself for that one.

5

RESIGNATION

The faded white sign with red lettering, HAROLD'S CLUB, hung innocently on the old Milltown bar, but stirred emotions I'd rather not feel. Twenty-two years ago our family and friends held my father's funeral here, and I hadn't set foot in the place since. Before he died, Pop had told his best buddy that he'd spent the majority of his life here, so they might as well eulogize him at the club.

"Harold 'Stubby' Strobel was a good man," they'd all agreed.

His friend stood and said, "He started his faithful service to the Champion Lumber Mill at fifteen and put in forty-eight years until the saws went silent in 1993. We called him Stubby because that's all the saws left of his first two fingers, but he could pull from the green chain faster than men half his age."

I turned the key to the truck, and the engine stubbornly idled down. Anger boiled in my belly. "A good man," I scoffed. Maybe a good man to the guys at work or his friends at the bar, but certainly not to his sons. Pop held a tender spot for his daughters but treated us boys like an afterthought. "They have to figure it out on their own," I overhead him yell at Mama as he left the house after they'd argued about spending time with his sons. Most nights entailed a fight, a door slam, then Pop holding down a barstool at Harold's for the remainder of the evening. It wasn't until my teenage years that I realized the club's name came from Harold Herndon, the long-time proprietor, and not my father. It might as well have been his namesake for all the Hamm's beers he drank into oblivion until my older brother retrieved him.

Five years after they had laid him off from the mill, the alcohol caught up to Pop, and he died of cirrhosis of the liver. "Lord, rest his soul," Mama's voice echoed in my head. Part of my heart resented him and now, twenty-two years later, the rest longed for the man. The deepest of yearning to love and be loved by him.

I checked my phone—9:35 p.m.—and decided that entering Harold's was a terrible idea, even though my boss insisted I meet him here after washing out the septic truck. I reached for the ignition, but before I turned the key, Marty pulled in beside me. The big man replaced the stub of his cigar with a fresh one and exited the new Ford with a decisive slam of his door. Marty had not revealed why he wanted to meet me here. *Most likely*, I thought, *he would belittle and then fire me.* But why not just send me home permanently after I'd finished cleaning up my mess?

Marty paused at the door, and for the first time acknowledged me with a tilt of his head to follow him. I glanced at the Mandalorian figure on my dash for guidance, but the silver helmet stood still.

What would the Mandalorian do? With his face hidden behind the T-visor mask and his body shielded with Beskar armor, he'd nonchalantly stroll into the bar with his blaster pistol holstered and Amban phase-pulse disruptor rifle slung behind his back. His mere presence would silence the room, Mando's code of honor and warrior toughness triggering the most hardened man to envy.

"Why can't I be more like you?" I asked the figurine and flicked my finger against the silver helmet. Mando's head bobbed in a circular motion, asking the same question.

I blew out a deep sigh. Might as well get the butt-chewing over with. I got out of my truck and willed one foot in front of the other to the door. The half-empty parking lot suggested a small Wednesday crowd and not the popular Tuesday night Karaoke gathering. Guys at the shop talked about a more rambunctious college horde from Missoula that filled the place on the weekends.

The door creaked as I yanked it open, and the stale smell of beer and cigarettes transported me to age twelve when I stood at the entrance with Mama and my six remaining siblings for the awkward handshake from well-wishers. Nothing had changed—the same grimy floor and greasy gray curtains covering the windows. Red vinyl barstools still supported husky men with full beards and chiseled features under dirty ball caps. The wooden bar braced their elbows, like it had for a century of patrons since Fred Thibodeau had built the place.

Even the music emanating from the jukebox in the corner remained the same and played America's "A Horse with No Name." A fitting memorial to the working men and women who sought solace here. I glanced over my shoulders at the mountain goat and bighorn sheep mounts with empty dead eyes under plexiglass domes that stared back at me from both corners of the room. Yup, nothing had changed.

The sour men at the bar ignored my entrance. I cut a beeline to Marty, who had plunked down at a corner table and harassed the barmaid trying to get his order. She gave me the once-over and flashed a welcoming smile.

"You want anything?" she asked.

I looked at her and then down at Marty. "I, uh…"

"Septic boy will have a burger and a beer. Same as me," Marty said.

I cleared my throat to protest, but Marty cut me off. "I'm buying." He sliced his hand through the air above the table to end any argument. It was not the burger I protested, but the beer. I didn't drink. I thought it best to accept my last meal graciously and sat down.

The barmaid nodded, then grabbed the ketchup and mustard caddy advertising Bud Light from the adjacent table and placed it between us. I wished for a reenforced brick wall of protection from Marty's ill-nature, but he ignored me and spit a speck of cigar tobacco from the tip of his tongue. Then he saluted in approval as he watched the back-pocket jewels of the barmaid's jeans sway as she walked to the bar. He finally spun his attention to me, and his expression soured.

"What am I going to do with you, shit-head?"

But instead of the usual onslaught of insults and abuse, Marty went silent and shook his head in disappointment.

The barmaid interrupted his thoughts by plunking down two generous glasses of beer with foam spilling over the top. His eyes lit with delight, and he emptied half the glass in three large swallows.

"Might as well bring us a pitcher," he encouraged the woman.

I forced down a taste of the bitter brew that killed Pop, then shielded my face from my executioner with the glass.

Marty drained his beer and wiped the back of his hand across his mouth. His shoulders relaxed.

"I got Carrie settled down finally," he said with a scowl. "I drove to her house to assess the damage. Damn, Andy, you exploded a real nuclear bomb. Her new white Lexus looks like she went mud-bogging, and her son was still whining after a thorough dousing with the hose."

Marty cleared his throat, and I prepared for the worst, but a smirk cracked the corners of his mouth and spread across the rest of his face.

"Probably the funniest damn thing I've seen in a while." His laugh started as a chuckle, then erupted into a full belly laugh. His usual steadfast cigar dropped from his lip, rolled down his shirt, and hit floor.

I thought he would explode from the mishap, but it made him roar all the harder. The men at the bar glowered back to see what was so funny.

"I've never seen Carrie so mad in all my life." Marty slapped the table. "And that bratty kid of hers still smelled like we fished him out of the septic tank. When I got there, she had shaved him bald. He looked like Baby Yoda," Marty hooted louder. "That kid has some ears on him."

His frivolity shocked me. I sat frozen, waiting for the other shoe to drop.

It never came.

"As far as I can tell, no physical damage occurred to the car or the house or, thank God, the kid. Probably be a different end to the story otherwise." His expression turned serious. "I promised her you would be up first thing tomorrow to clean off every speck of poo, even if it means you're on your hands and knees for a week with a toothbrush." A fat finger thump on my chest and a low growl accentuated the first sign of harshness, but his hostility gave way to a laugh once again.

"I told her I have insurance that would cover anything and everything, but she reminded me that Willie would use

their homeowner's policy and would probably come away
smelling like a rose from the transaction. She even laughed at
the irony of her own joke. You're lucky we're all friends,"
Marty said, as if they spent weekends together at the lake.
"Besides, that ass, Willie, will be home tomorrow, so having
to deal with him will be punishment enough for you."

"I'm sorry," I said.

"Hell, I guess it's good for the Richie Riches of the world
to know what the rest of us poor shmucks endure."

I studied him. It may have been the first time that Marty
lumped me in with his own people group.

The barmaid brought the pitcher of beer in one hand and
balanced two plates with burgers and fries in the other and set
them down in front of us.

"You boys need anything else?" she said, then looked
toward the door when three boisterous young men walked in.
They were wearing t-shirts that sported some Greek letters on
the front and plaid shorts.

Marty stuffed three fries into his mouth and waved her
off. His mouth slacked open and steam came from the just-
out-of-the-fryer potatoes. He fanned his face and reached to
pour a beer. "Holy crap, those are hot!" Marty said, but
shoved in two more.

Marty slathered the condiments to overflow the bun. I
waited, then grabbed the mustard and swirled it on carefully
before applying the onion and pickles.

Marty had already taken three bites into his burger when
he asked with a full mouth, "Andy, how old are you?"

The rhetorical question irked me, as he knew full well that
we were the same age. Even born in the same month of July.

"Aren't we both thirty-four?" I shot back with irritation.

"Right," Marty said around his beer glass. "Old enough to
know that what's we got, we got. There ain't no more." He

toasted Andy with a tip of his glass and set it down. "Hell, I remember you telling everyone in second grade you wanted to be an astronaut." He snickered. "Isn't that the year you flunked?" He laughed hard, and a dollop of ketchup landed on his shirt as he stuffed another bite of the burger into his mouth. "I bet NASA keeps calling you, huh?"

White-hot anger shot up my spine, and my ears burned with heat. Little kept me from storming off.

"You've been a daydreamer from day one, Andy. Guys like us aren't given much of a chance. We just have to accept our lot in life and get on with it as best we can." He finished his burger in two more bites. "Look at these dudes." He thumbed at the three young men who racked the billiard balls on the table and chalked their pool sticks. "Probably college pukes living on their daddies' trust funds."

One boy smacked the cue ball hard into the racked balls, and they scattered with a clatter. The yellow one-ball flew from the table, bounced along the concrete floor, and stopped at the side of my foot. I bent over, picked it up and tossed it to the closest boy, who fumbled it with drunken incoordination. *Obviously not the first stop of their night.* I ignored his curses and tried to refocus on Marty's advice.

"Your daddy left you nothing but a butt load of siblings and a kick in the ass out of the house," Marty said.

I had enough of his lecture and measured my words to blast back at him. The problem with it all—he was right. I'd just finished paying off the rest of Mama and Pop's debts.

"I know you didn't dream of working for me, but whatever else you hoped for, you need to let die and become the best honey-dipper you can be." Marty slugged me on the arm with his meaty fist. "What else could you do? I pay you well enough, don't I?" He reminded me who held the power.

Unfortunately, he was right again. Hard to find much of a

job with an eighth-grade education. The multiple parts in my brain argued with themselves. Part of me wanted to stand up and walk out, but the practical part knew rent came due in a few weeks and living paycheck to paycheck didn't help persuade the courageous part.

"I tell ya what, I'll think about giving you a twenty-five cent raise this year, if there are no more screw ups," Marty said.

I shrugged and settled in resignation when the door of the bar creaked open and Marty followed my gaze.

With the subdued lighting of the club, I couldn't see the woman's face, but I recognized right away it was Abby Arnold, the local mail carrier. Cerebral palsy caused Abby's distinctive walk. To step forward with the left leg, she swung it around as if the leg hung too long. If the music wasn't playing from the jukebox, her swoosh-clunk, swoosh-clunk gait would have been audible.

Whatever brain insult she sustained at birth affected her entire left side, so besides the limp, she had an atrophied arm —flexed at the elbow with her thumb tucked under her fingers—that she held against her chest. Her right side had developed completely normally. Since we'd all grown up together, that's just how we've always known her. Even enduring teasing from other kids, she matured into one of the funniest, smartest, and nicest people on the planet.

Her plump behind gave the walk more swing, something even she would joke about. Only mean people said things like, "With all the miles she walked every day delivering the mail to Bonner and Milltown, I'm amazed she's not as skinny as a rail." How she bore those miles carrying the heavy mailbag over her bad arm amazed me.

Abby wore her USPS uniform, which surprised me as she

walked to the bar and greeted the men with a smile. She then handed the barmaid an express envelope.

"I'm sorry to get this to you so late. I saw it back at the office and thought I'd bring it to you on my way home. It got stuck in the wrong place. Again, I'm sorry."

"No worries, Abby. Can I pour you a beer?"

Abby smiled and waved off the offer. "Oh, no thanks. It's been a long day."

She turned to leave and spotted Marty and me at our table. She smiled and waved, but before she took two steps, the college boys had her corralled.

"Hey, we were just getting another beer. Let us buy you one," the taller one said.

"You boys are sweet, but I'm headed home," Abby said.

"Oh, come on," the guy with a backward ball cap said. "Don't be a party pooper," he slurred. "Pour us all a beer," he shouted to the barmaid.

Abby shook her head toward the bar, then took three more steps for the door before two of the college boys stepped into her path.

I looked at Marty, who poured himself another beer, and then back to Abby. Between battling the Montana elements and the local dogs, I'm sure she could take care of herself. But the boys' attitude fueled my already bubbling anger, and I stood.

"You better sit down, before you get your ass whooped, Mandoo," Marty scolded me.

The third frat boy, who had remained silent until now, reached out and held the Postal Service patch over her left breast between his fingers. "I love a girl in uniform," he said, making his friends laugh.

Abby tried to pull away as a scowl creased her face, and more rage welled up in my chest.

By some unseen force, my legs propelled me forward. As my body leapt into action, my mind registered that all three of the college boys were a foot taller than my five-foot-six frame, and I figured they were not only from the university but probably jocks as well.

That didn't stop my legs from charging the guy that still had a hold of Abby's shirt. I hit him hard, and we tumbled to the floor.

Pride in my nimbleness swelled when I somersaulted and came upright on my feet. That is, until the sight of a pool cue arched toward my face.

6

LEMONS

After spending the entire night in the emergency room and getting no sleep, my mind and body dragged like I had the flu. I lingered in the moment with the summer sun warming the Missoula morning as my truck idled a safe distance from Willie and Carrie's house.

A frenzy of activity swirled around the blast zone from yesterday. Already three hours late, my spirit lagged—in no hurry to get another tongue-lashing. Apparently Willie got home last night, but I planned on tuning him out. Carrie's harsh words still stung on old wounds of loneliness. We'd known each other since grade school, but I understood I'd never experience the affections from someone like her. She'd always been pleasant to me, and that was enough. Her anger from my screw-up bit at my heart and reverberated with the messages of worthlessness from Pop and many of my teachers.

And now I showed up looking like a raccoon. "Pool cue one, Andy zero," I said nasally to the Mandalorian after inspecting my face in the rearview mirror. If I could see behind the silver helmet, he would probably smile at the adventures of last night.

Not sure I'd ever been that brave in my life, charging into the fray and tackling that kid. The jerk's advances on Abby injected my rage with jet fuel after Marty's insults. It happened without me thinking it through—something Pop often accused me of.

After the college kid knocked me cold with the pool cue, I guess all hell broke loose. "The sight of blood woke the weary men at the bar like smelling salts to a prizefighter, and them boys received a good old-fashioned ass-whoopin'," Marty described. "They were lucky they could leave of their own accord, but I doubt they'll ever set foot in Harold's again. Good thing Abby stopped me before I took a turn at 'em," he added to justify his non-involvement in the melee.

I remember nothing after the blur of the stick swinging toward my face, but afterward it entertained Marty to no end. He sat with me in the emergency room and retold the story at least four times, each telling more exaggerated than the last. At least Marty was kind enough to take me to the hospital, where they straightened my nose and stuffed it with cotton. Something I painfully remember.

I gingerly pushed at the cotton pledgets that hung out of each nostril and blinked. The black and purple bruising swirled around each eye and across my nose. Not sure how much blood I'd lost, but by the looks of my shirt from last night, it seemed to me that my system should be half empty.

"Well, I might as well get this over with," I said, and put the truck in gear. Marty originally scheduled me to be here at seven, but I left the emergency room about then and had to go home, clean up, and change clothes.

I parked in the circular driveway next to two white vans with red crosses, overlaid with large yellow letters: RESCUE

SERVICES. Willie, dressed in red shorts over blue stretch pants, directed a crew from the restoration business. His bare chest glistened with sweat. Three men scrubbed the side of the house with brushes, while another man sprayed the roof with a power washer. Willie must have decided that professional help surpassed what I could do and hired the company. Carrie's Lexus sat nowhere in sight, and if I was lucky, she had left for errands.

Walking toward the house, I forced down a chuckle, thinking Willie looked like Jack Black's wrestling character in *Nacho Libre*, but more muscular. He'd probably just finished a yoga workout, but a sense of embarrassment rumbled my gut for his ridiculous attire. Like a bull in a china shop, Willie was painfully unaware of his effect on the world around him.

"Oh God, here comes trouble," he said to the other workers without looking directly at me. "Boys, the collective IQ just dropped twenty points. Watch out in case he has more turd grenades in his pockets."

The men afforded him an obligatory chuckle but continued to clean. Tiny particles of toilet paper and wipes covered the entire area. As the crew scoured and sprayed the house, it rained down and accumulated over the landscaping rock like dirty snow. I couldn't tell if I just imagined it, but a septic odor wafted from under the heavy bleach and industrial cleaner.

"What a frickin' mess you made, Andy," Willie said without turning to look at me.

"I'm really sorry, Willie."

I didn't know what else to say.

Willie blew out a sigh of resignation. "I'm submitting a claim to replace the siding, gutters, and shrubs," he said, and pointed to the pathetic greenery decorated with grotesque tinsel. "The body shop picked up Carrie's Lexus to see if it's salvageable. I'd been really pissed if the boat was sitting there."

"I'm sorry," I said again.

He finally glanced at me, but only a slight furl of his brow acknowledged my injuries. His signature charm and glisten in his eyes replaced any concern. "Gonna cost my insurance a butt load, but I've wanted to redo the landscaping on this side of the house anyway." He shrugged. "I'll collect the money and then see what else needs fixing." He winked at me.

I thought about asking, "Isn't that fraud?" but it wasn't my place to question.

He looked out over the city, raised his arms, arched his back, and opened his chest to the sun. Impossible to not notice the outline of his well-endowed manhood, my face flushed, and I joined his gaze over the city. He then pushed back his wavy blond hair with both hands. His biceps flexed and abs tightened like he posed for a bodybuilding magazine. Then he released a loud moan. "I hate to go to work on such a glorious day, but someone has to do it."

Without another word to me or a thanks to the cleaning crew, he disappeared around the corner of the garage.

Turning to the man who led the team, I said, "I'm sure sorry about the disaster. I've been telling the boss for months about that old pump."

The man shrugged. "This is what we do, son."

I figured I should at least help the men clean up my mess, so I headed for my truck to get my equipment and gloves. Somehow it comforted me, knowing these guys ranked on the same level of the totem pole as us honey-dippers.

I had almost reached the truck when a crimson-faced Carrie charged out the front door of the house, wearing multi-colored yoga pants and a neon-green sports bra. I hoped a workout caused her appearance, but feared she was still furious with me. The way she stomped down each step, it had to be the latter. Her hands found her hips, and she opened her mouth to speak, but pulled up short after seeing my face. Her anger melted like chocolate in a hot car, and her eyebrows softened from a scowl to concern.

"Andy, are you okay?" She reached my side in two more steps, stretched out her hand and cradled my chin, turning it from side to side for inspection. "Oh Andy, you poor thing. Marty didn't tell me you were hurt."

"I...uh..."

"Andy, you look terrible. It looks like someone took a two-by-four to you."

I looked at the sidewalk, trying to decide what to say. "I...uh..."

"Here I walked out like a mad, wet chicken, and here you are with all that trauma to your face."

A smile cracked across my lips because of her misuse of the cliché. She didn't do well with those either.

"I'm sorry I didn't get up here earlier," I said, finding my words. "But I sat in the emergency room for most of the night." I looked at my shoes again and realized how innocent white lies start, even lies of omission. The explanation of how my appearance had nothing to do with the accident formed in my brain, but before I got the words out, she interrupted me.

"Oh Andy, that's terrible. You could've gotten killed. Now I feel rotten. Willie told me you were out here but said nothing about your injuries. What a jerk." She waved an exasperated hand toward the house.

"Please come inside and have some lemonade," she said, grabbing me by my arm and pulling me toward the house.

My shoes stuck to the cement. "I shouldn't, Carrie.

Besides, I need to help these fellas." I pointed to the cleaning crew.

She pursed her lips and waved her hand again. "That's what we're paying them for. You need some rest."

I tried to protest, but with surprising strength, she broke my inertia and led me to the house.

"I feel awful that I chased you off yesterday after the explosion, not realizing how bad it injured your face," she said, and squeezed my arm.

"Well, it was quite the blast…but my face will be okay."

As Carrie led me to the house, I thought, *True, true and unrelated.* Knowing the real truth about the difference between the accident and bar fight—not exactly coming clean on how my face got banged up.

7

LEMONADE

As I drove my truck home, I realized the entire time I sat in Willie and Carrie's house I felt like a cat on a tin can. *At least that's how Carrie would say it,* I thought, and laughed. But sitting at their breakfast table my heart had pounded, and my voice and breath were labored.

Carrie hadn't shown me the entire house, but what I saw of it left me speechless. A spectacular entryway with a green marble floor inlaid with cherry wood led to a curved staircase to the second-floor balcony. French doors on the left opened to Willie's office and library, and to the right a columned arched entry opened to a formal dining room. Carrie escorted me through the expansive kitchen with cherry cabinets and granite countertops, to the breakfast room above the sunken and massive living room.

She had poured lemonade as her kids ignored us and watched cartoons on a large-screen TV in the living room. Her son, with his shaved bald head and large ears truly fit Marty's description as Baby Yoda. I'd forced back a chuckle. Carrie's eleven-year-old daughter, on the other hand, with curly blond hair and blue eyes, was the spitting image of her mom.

Carrie had retrieved an iced gel pack from of the freezer and insisted I put it across my eyes. Not sure if she tried to be helpful or just shield my banged-up face from her view, but I complied. Every second with her made me so nervous that now I can't even remember what she blabbered on about, but nodded often to let her know I was listening.

I never did tell the truth about the injuries to my face, and that's why I now turned into St. Ann's church. Four months had passed since I'd attended Mass, and over six since I'd gone to confession. Filled with enough guilt, regret, and sorrow, it was about time.

I used to take Mama to Mass every Sunday. The pattern didn't escape me—except for last night I hadn't been in Harold's since Pop's funeral. And until this morning, I hadn't set foot in the church since we buried Mama four months ago.

I parked, exited my truck, and stood in the near empty parking lot. Only two other cars were parked near the entrance. I looked at my watch and thought that morning Mass should be over by now. Perhaps since I hadn't attended in a while, I noticed for the first time in my life that the modern rock-faced, wedge-shaped church seemed slightly out of place in the lumber-built community of Bonner. The Catholic church had served all four communities since 1905, but the parish erected this third building after growing out of the first in 1939, and the second white clapboard structure burned in 1985.

Mama spoke with pride about being on the new building committee, but in private she wished for a more traditional style architecture. The Strobel family were regular fixtures on Sunday mornings, but Pop stopped attending after he got laid off from the mill and his anger toward God fumed.

I opened the front door to the church and breathed in the comforting smell of burned candle wax, incense, and a woodsy, ancient fragrance of what I can only describe as holiness. Father Papadopoulos, still dressed in his Mass vestments, stood in the nave in lively discussion with two elderly ladies, Mrs. Jarvi and Mrs. O'Reilly. Behind them lay the simple wooden altar and lectern. Bluish-green stained-glass windows on the far wall glowed with the morning sun. The church was as simple and unitarian as the communities it served—the hardworking, down-to-earth souls that filled the four towns of Milltown, Bonner, Riverside, and Piltzville.

Father P, a bear of a man, roared with laughter that echoed around the sanctuary and bounced off the heavy wooden pews and simple, spacious interior. I slipped into the last row of pews and gingerly sat down, but the dark oak creaked under my weight. The trio turned and smiled at me.

"Dang it," I said under my breath, hoping that the ladies wouldn't notice me. Confession always felt to me like I should sneak in under the cloak of darkness to reveal my deepest regrets and sins—sure the ladies, along with God, read every misdeed on my bashed-in face.

I gave an awkward wave, and they returned to their conversation. I made the sign of the cross toward the life-size crucifix at the front of the church and the one person who Mama said would understand every hurt and pain I felt. Growing up, the agony the artist sculpted into Jesus frightened me. Today, looking past the hands and feet nailed to the cross, the crown of thorns, the prominent ribs and tortured body, I saw something I'd never noticed—Jesus' face reflected peace. Maybe this is what Mama found here. As Pop found solace in the eye of the beer bottle at Harold's, Mama found it here at the church. The thought brought a deep longing for her. With an alcoholic husband and eleven children, there was not much attention to go around. But whatever I received, she filled with kindness and love. She'd lived to ninety, but sadness rose in my heart thinking that I never asked her once about where her strength or source of peace came from. Especially since six of her children's deaths preceded hers.

I reached under the pew in front of me and quietly pulled the kneeler down. It also squawked, so I quickly knelt, closed my eyes and crossed myself once more, hoping the ladies would pass me by without comment.

With my eyelids pinched together, I heard Father Papadopoulos escort the two women down the aisle. He'd taken over the parish three years ago, but with his Franciscan generosity to the poor and commitment to contemplative prayer, he continued to be an enigma to the community. The Jesuits had founded and directed the church for the last one hundred years. Mama told me that because of his advanced age and adherence to a different Catholic stream, the bishop and the search committee hadn't even considered Father P's application until no other applicants came forward after two years. She'd said, "Few priests want to dedicate their lives to a handful of Catholic families left in a community of sixteen hundred people."

"I'm sure God will forgive us for using the white and gold vestment today," he said to the ladies in his strong Greek accent and emphasized his faith in God's forgiveness with another belly laugh.

This was the other thing that Mama told me drove the elderly women of the parish particularly batty—his informal style and lackadaisical adherence to Catholic formalities. Something the church ladies guarded with fervor.

"Yes, but using the wrong vestments makes my skin crawl," Mrs. O'Reilly said.

"I will make sure the green ones are back from the cleaners for tomorrow morning's Mass," Father P reassured as their voices moved down the aisle.

I thought I was in the clear, when I heard Mrs. Jarvi clear her throat at the end of my pew. I opened my eyes and turned, and her normally stern, motherly look turned to compassion.

"Oh dear," she gasped, and put a hand to her mouth.

I smiled and decided that I should get hit in the face more often.

"Hi, Mrs. Jarvi."

"Andy, dear…are you okay?"

"I had a little accident," I said. My heart fluttered. Repeating the lie again.

"I'm glad you're okay." She fanned her face with a hanky. "I'm glad to see you back in church. It would make your mother very happy."

I managed a smile.

"Morning Mass is at ten, you know," she said, as less of a suggestion and more of a command.

"Thank you," I said, then closed my eyes and bowed my head, hoping she would move on. Because she lived next door to me, I would hear about it again.

As Father P escorted the ladies through the door, heat rose up my back, and I wiped a bead of sweat from my upper lip. I hated confession—it always seemed like I performed it wrong, like everything else in my life.

I sensed the priest's presence, and I turned and nodded.

A wide smile spread across his face. "You should see the other guy." He laughed.

His comment surprised me, and an involuntary shiver

quaked through my body. Did he already know about the brawl, or just cracking the old joke to ease my tension?

He yanked at the front of his ornate vestment robe. "You mind if I slip this off? The ladies had me on the hot seat."

Without waiting for a response, he slid the heavy garment over his head, folded it carefully, laid it on the arm of the pew, then smoothed down his thinning hair and straightened his glasses.

No wonder he sweltered, I thought as I scanned down the heavy brown friar habit. His habit, snugged at the waist with a rope belt, and his sandal-clad bare feet reminded me that his differential dress from the black Jesuit slacks, shirt, and priest collar remained the subject of much conversation, an occasional joke, and wonderment of what he wore under the robe.

"Whew, that's better," he said, and sat next to me, the oak complaining under his weight.

His aura of pipe tobacco and slight body odor wafted over me; not offensively, but with comfort.

He settled onto his seat, extended his arm, and laid a hand on my shoulder. "It's good to see you, Andy. What can I do for you?"

I wanted to say, "Isn't it obvious?" but I blew out a long sigh while he waited patiently.

The church had no confessional booth. Maybe in the confines and diminished light of a true confessional, this sort of thing came easier.

I stuttered out the opening of confession when he squeezed my shoulder.

"You know, I had a man give confession the other day," he said with seriousness. "The elderly man said, 'Forgive me, Father, for I have sinned. I'm 80 years old and have been happily married to the love of my life for 60 years, but last night I slept with two twenty-one-year-old bikini models.' I asked how long it'd been since his last confession. The man looked at me with surprise and said, 'I've never been to confession. I'm Jewish.' 'Then why are you telling me this?' I asked. The old man replied, 'I'm telling *everybody!*'" Father P emphasized the 'everybody,' and broke out in loud laughter and slapped his own knee.

I laughed with him and relaxed my shoulders. His slightly inappropriate jokes were another reason the community adored the priest, especially the men.

The opening words of the confession slipped my mind and anxiety built in my chest.

"I heard about the fight at Harold's," Father P said. The surprised look I shot him made him continue. "Joe Curser visited this morning and told me all about it. It was good of you to defend Abby." He smiled.

I decided Joe must have been one of the men at the bar who came to my rescue.

"Yeah," was all I thought of saying.

"Well, I'm not fond of fighting, you understand, but you're a good man, Andy. I know that about you." He gave my shoulder another hard squeeze.

Uncertain if it was the release of stress that had built over the last two days or the man's kind words, but tears flowed from my eyes and my chest quaked in sorrow.

"I fought...then I lied about it," I poured out. "And I've lusted over a married woman." I sobbed as the image of Carrie's breasts bounced across the screen of my mind. "It's been almost a year since my last confession. Bless me, Father, for I have sinned." The correct confessional words finally came to mind. "I'm sorry for these and all my sins."

In Father P's silence, a sorrow and grief deeper than any of my sins welled in my chest to the point where my bones ached, and I could not hold it in any longer. A great swell of emotions lapped over the walls of the dam in my heart.

"Why am I always getting the short end of the stick?" I blurted out through tears. "I'm so tired of everyone picking on me. Of life dishing out the worst to me. What did I do to deserve all this?" I said, wiping at the snot running out my nose. "I just don't understand! I have a shitty job and a shitty life," I blurted out, and then regretted my swearing. "I'm sorry." I looked at him. "I'm just so tired of it all. What did I do to make God so mad at me?"

The man didn't flinch from either my cursing or my outburst, but just nodded and smiled at me. Only when my cries subsided did he speak.

"Andy, how old are you?"

Great, there's that question again, I thought, but answered anyway, "Thirty-four." *Why do people keep asking me that?* I wondered as he reflected on my answer. *He probably thinks I'm too old or too stupid to not have my life figured out.*

"What do you want out of your life?" he finally asked.

I had to think for a moment, then answered, "I don't know, maybe what everyone else wants. A nice house and car and...I don't know...a family, I guess. A better job," I added quickly, thinking of Willie and Carrie and how easy and comfortable they had it.

"So if you had all those things, you would be happy?"

"A whole lot happier than I am now," I snapped back, but then apologized.

He again took it in stride gracefully. "And your lack of those things is because you've done enough bad things in your life for God to withhold those from you?"

"I guess," I said, wiping my hand across my face. "I can't seem to explain it any other way."

"You understand, as a Franciscan priest, we choose to give up those things."

"Does that make you happy?" I asked.

He smiled and turned to me. "Aw, I like a good chess match." He grinned. "And it's a good question," he added. "As a friar, we think of it more as a blessing of sacrifice. Our chastity toward possessions and our selflessness brings us closer to God, and in turn that brings us joy. We can then rejoice in our suffering and thank God for it."

This was not what I wanted to hear, and anger rose up in me. He didn't know what it was like to be raised by an alcoholic father and fight for every scrap of attention from so many siblings. He didn't understand what it was like to live alone in a dumpy little trailer in a lonely little town, and he certainly didn't know what it was like to be a honey-dipper.

8

THE BIG BLACKFOOT

"Man, I need some caffeine," I said under my breath as I stood in line at the grocery store, glancing at the half-liter bottle of Coca-Cola. "And why in the heck is Albertson's so crowded on Thursday at one o'clock in the afternoon?" I said loud enough for the person in front of me to nod.

I'd never understand the equation: twenty checkout stands, ten customers, and one checkout person. The entire line stood behind a large man who looked like he'd cleaned out the entire frozen dinner section and extended a handful of coupons for each item that the slow clerk rang in one at a time.

I still had a headache from my visit with Father Papadopoulos. After my confession and a discussion about suffering, which I took little comfort in, he gave me an act of penance. I recited the Contrition, then he blessed me with the prayer of Absolution—my right standing with God restored. Except for my pounding head, I guess I felt better after unloading my guilt. For my penance, Father P asked that I mow Mrs. Jarvi's lawn, something I did faithfully every Sunday afternoon anyway. She must have failed to mention it to the good father, or most likely she'd just plain forgotten with her ninety-two-year-old failing memory. Although she would never forget to wonder out loud every Saturday who might help her with her lawn. My true penance would come when she lectured me on the importance of going to church.

The line ahead of me finally moved up one person as the bagger loaded the frozen food fanatic's sacks and helped him wheel his stash out the door.

At least I'd catch the bug hatch this evening, my mind drifted while in line. I had stopped by Butterfly Septic and explained to Marty the situation at Willie and Carrie's house, but withheld the details of morning lemonade with Carrie. It would have just made him mad. The visit gave Marty one more chance to berate me then retell the bar fight story, which quickly turned into his own superhero story of rescuing Abby and me and beating the pulp out of the city dwellers. Fortunately, all working trucks were already out, and not having to pay my day's wages pacified him. Either that or he felt sorry for my bruised face. I'm sure it was the former, but a day off is a day off during the salmon fly hatch, and the trout wouldn't care if I looked like I'd escaped the morgue.

I glanced four checkout stalls over and a young man miraculously opened a second register. The opportunity tempted me to drift nonchalantly to the open line, but I had just gone through confession after all, so I told the people in my line to go ahead of me. A handful of them moved to the other line. Now, standing behind only three people with small baskets, I'd be wetting a fly in the Blackfoot soon enough.

I scanned my mental checklist for this afternoon. Fishing license, check. Fishing gear, check. Waders, check. Food? I looked down at the Coke and prepackaged sandwich in my hands. Check. I'd stopped at the fly shop a few weeks ago and picked up a handful of salmon fly imitators. The only thing left to do was to get through this blasted line and go pick up Max.

One more person ahead of me and I heard the dreaded announcement, "Price check, please."

Oh brother, I thought, and glanced down the row to see that the other line had grown to seven. "Be patient," I murmured under my breath.

Besides, Max would be so excited. He loved and lived for riding up to the fishing hole and sitting patiently on the bank, watching me cast the line. Maximus acted strange this morning when I got home from the hospital. At first he behaved like he wanted nothing to do with me, but after sniffing out my horrendous appearance he'd barely left my lap, his mongrel eyes steeped with worry.

A box boy spun around the corner. "A dollar ninety-eight."

Apparently, that is the price of one jar of Aunt Nellie's whole pickled beets. I breathed out deeply.

The checker smiled and handed the woman her receipt. I thought he'd reach for my two items, when the man placed a sign on the conveyer belt. NEXT LINE PLEASE.

I protested, but he disappeared in a flash. A collective groan rose from the three people behind me.

My oldest brother's words echoed in my head as I made my way to the other line. "Hell, Andy, if you didn't have bad luck, you'd have no luck at all."

I took my position in the other line. "So much for making things right with God," I muttered.

Standing on the bank of the Blackfoot River, I blinked as if taking a snapshot of the glorious splendor. The deep, crystal clear water drifted silently over the rocks—the spring water had collected at the Continental Divide then flowed a hundred thirty-two miles through wilderness and farmland. Towering ponderosa pines cast patchwork shadows across the stream, lined by green willows and jagged rock. Boulders had tumbled from the surrounding cliffs and squeezed the Black-foot into deep emerald pools. All backdropped by a sapphire blue sky.

I loved this spot. I wasn't sure if it was the fond memories of the few times Pop taught us boys how to fish or the picnics we'd occasionally enjoy with the entire family; those who had survived, of course. But here I felt whole. Like every broken piece of me repaired by a master of Kintsugi, welding those parts together with gold. Mama would say, "God's Spirit hovers here."

I slowly breathed in the earthy pine fragrance, not wanting to disturb the solitude, but the screech of a red-tailed hawk overhead broke the silence. I shielded the sun with my hand and found the raptor soaring high above. Perhaps he knew of the hatch as well and waited for his prey to rise to the surface.

The stress of the last two days melted off my shoulders like wax. Actually, it started the minute Max and I drove out of Milltown and headed up Highway 200 to Johnsrud Park, but now I could finally breathe. For Max, it probably started the minute I rolled down his window in the truck. With his paws gripping the frame of the door, his snout facing into the wind, and his mug in a perpetual smile, he caught every scent between here and Milltown.

"You having fun?" I looked down at Max. His entire body wagged, and he nervously pranced. At a whopping twelve pounds, he feared only two things: being left behind and water. I'd found the flea-bitten, mange-covered, scraggly gray-haired pup with sad copper eyes three years ago. The pound had named him Tater-tot. It was love at first sight. Not much had changed in his appearance, except he no longer had fleas or mange. But with exuberant energy and endless affection, Maximus was my rescue dog. Everyone knows the rescue went both ways.

Max let out a yap, urging me to get the river crossing over with.

"Okay, okay, let's get to the other side." I pulled the straps of my waders over each shoulder and snugged them tight.

I glanced up and down the river. Upstream, lines of two anglers flashed in the sun as they arced across the river. At three in the afternoon it seemed unlikely they would be successful, but you never know in the course of the hatch.

During the golden hour, when the sun set below the horizon, the water cooled a few degrees and the female salmon flies hopped along the surface of the water, the monsters of the deep ventured from their lairs. I wanted to get across the river well before then.

I slipped on my dry fly vest. Well-worn, it had belonged to Pop, and I always felt an unusual closeness to the man when I wore it. My oldest surviving brother, Larry, had inherited it when Pop died. But last year, when Larry succumbed to a massive heart attack at age forty-one, the family handed the vest down to me. The older girls had no desire or use for it.

When I stepped into the river, the sixty-three-degree water filled around my waders as a shocking reminder that even in the middle of summer, the stream filled from snow-capped mountains and was not something to be taken for granted. If I flipped with my chest waders on, they would fill up like lead balloons and drag me to the bottom with no way to escape. The river had taken two dumb and drunk college kids this year alone.

I plopped the innertube between two boulders, looped my fishing bag strap around my neck, and sat down with a small splash.

"Okay, Maxi-boy, come on."

His little feet danced in the sand for a moment of indecision, and then he launched himself onto my lap with a perfect swan dive.

"That a boy."

He twirled two turns, curled into a ball, and tucked his face under one paw like he knew my propensity for disaster.

I snugged my ball cap and pushed us out into the current. The water swirled us in a circle until I reached behind with my arms and stroked us diagonally to the opposite shore. As anyone with knowledge of surviving a fall into the river will tell you, swim with the current. Allow the powerful river to assist you. Otherwise, it will quickly overwhelm the most stubborn pride.

Fortunately, I'd done this crossing many times throughout the years, so my launch, angle, and backstroke placed me in good stead to dodge the dangerous boulders and eddies and would place me safely on the other side before reaching the real hazardous waters.

Three-quarters of the paddle across the Blackfoot, the object of my desire landed on my leg. A two-inch, beady-eyed, articulated orange-bodied, six-legged, large membranous vein-winged, probing-antennaed creature...Pteronarcys California—the salmon fly. Looking like she'd just emerged from an alien spaceship, it gripped onto my leg, and I had to wonder if it had any clue of the excitement she stirred. By some primeval rhythm she'd exited the river where it had existed in nymph form, crawled onto the surrounding boulders, split from her exoskeleton, and emerged ready to mate. And in this process nourishing the big Bull, Brown, and Rainbow trout that called the river home.

A few more paddles and I crossed the forty yards of crystalline water. I stuck my landing perfectly.

"Okay boy, we made it safely," I said, and gave Max a nudge. He leaped from my lap to the closest boulder, spun circles, and barked with joy and relief.

I pulled the innertube onto a large rock, held on, and searched for solid footing. That was the other hazard of the mighty Blackfoot: the moss-covered rocks were slipperier than stepping on wet ice, even with felt-bottomed wading boots. One misstep and in a nanosecond I'd find myself on my backside, then under water.

I climbed up the bank and smiled. I loved the north side of the Blackfoot—the wild side. There were only two ways to access the land that opened into the Rattlesnake National Wilderness—how I'd just crossed over or by driving upriver seven miles and hiking back five and a half. Which I found rather humorous, since for thousands of years this had worked as the business side of the river until private land ownership pinched off access. The Nez Perce, Salish, and Shoshone Indians traversed the *Cokahlarishkit*, the Road to the Buffalo, with horse and dog travoises, carving deep ruts in the earth as they crossed the Continental Divide into buffalo hunting grounds. It was this side that Captain Lewis and nine of his men nervously navigated during the summer of 1806 to meet up with Clark on the Missouri, and where the Big Blackfoot Railway laid tracks in the early 1900s.

I loved to fantasize about exploring the future with the Mandalorian, but I equally dreamed of sitting here on the bank of the Blackfoot and watching history march by. The proud Native Americans mounted on their paints, or even Lewis with his massive Newfoundland drooling at his heels. I looked down at Max, who pranced. "Seaman wouldn't know what to do with you."

Max spun a circle and barked.

I closed my eyes for a moment and thought I smelled the oily locomotive and heard the airy whistle, full of the rough-necks who harvested millions of board-feet of lumber from these mountains and loaded them on the train or floated them downriver bound for the Anaconda Mill in Bonner.

I reached up and gently pinched my nose between my fingers. Still packed to prevent any more bleeding, it remained plenty sore. It reminded me of how life tends to smack me in the face most days.

"Dear Lord, if you see fit, I could sure use a break."

But for now, I sat on the wild side, the salmon fly hatch bloomed, and all seemed a bit more right with the world.

ACT TWO

My Servant, Andy

In the land of the Big Sky, there lived a man whose name was Andy. Life had beaten him up and he lived in fear. But the man feared God and tried doing the best he could. He had no wife and no children, and others considered him one of the least among all the people of the West.

Even though everyone knew Andy, he had few friends, except for his scraggly mutt, Maximus. He ate alone in his rundown single-wide trailer that had a leaky roof. Mrs. Jarvi lived next door and would yell at Max when he pooped in her yard. Before his mama died, he attended Mass at the local Catholic church with her as often as his job allowed, praying, "Perhaps I have sinned and cursed God in my heart." This was Andy's regular custom.

One day when the angels came to report to God, Satan, who was the Designated Accuser, came along with them. God singled out Satan and said, "What have you been up to?"

Satan answered God, "Going here and there, checking things out on earth."

God said to Satan, "Have you noticed my friend, Andy? There's no one quite like him—honest and true to his word, totally devoted to God and hating evil."

"Does Andy fear God for nothing?" Satan replied. "He *is* nothing. He is like a minnow that should be tossed back. Yet, have you not put a hedge around him and the little he owns? You have protected him from the trappings of the world, so all he has is a mongrel dog and trailer. But now stretch out your hand and bless everything he has, and he will surely forget you."

God replied, "We'll see. Go ahead—do what you want with all that is his. Just don't hurt *him*." Then Satan left the presence of God.

9

A WHOLE LODE OF BULL

In Montana, fish stories, legends of epic huckleberry patches, or finding gold often assume a life of their own. You're never quite sure if the yarn spinner is pulling your leg or exaggerating to fill their ego. But the Blackfoot River corridor dripped with tall tales.

I savored my time at the river, in no hurry to disturb my favorite fishing hole until after supper. As I sat on the boulders, I rested, knowing that I'd satisfactorily staked my claim. Not that others dared attempt the crossing, but I wanted to clarify that for at least tonight the spot belonged to me. Even though the deep emerald pool where Gold Creek entered the Blackfoot was nearly impossible to reach from the other side, it hadn't always kept some out-of-stater from trying. Directly across from the hole, the roadbed lay a good forty feet above the river and dropped off at such a steep angle that you'd need climbing ropes to access the river's edge. One night last summer, I watched a guy from California toss a large number-three Mepps spinner from the road. Darned if he didn't hook a huge rainbow that he dragged and bounced up the bank and into his cooler. That poor fish—that ain't fishing.

Not that I blame the fella for trying. Where Gold Creek pours crystal clear water from the Rattlesnake Wilderness, this fishing hole was as good as it gets. Even Captain Lewis mentioned the prominent twenty-foot-wide stream in his journal as they crossed it following the Road to the Buffalo. Big enough, a person could fish the creek outright if they were looking for fry-pan-sized brookies. The tributary enters the Blackfoot at the crux of an elbow bend, cutting into the land above it and forming the pool where monster trout wait for nutrients and bugs as the waters merge. I didn't know for sure, but if the bank above indicated the depth, the hole sank probably thirty feet deep or more. I had to wonder if the Indians stopped to fish this spot, too.

Max stretched and yawned at my side, enjoying the last of the sun before it dipped below the cliffs that pinched the Blackfoot into this fish haven. The surrounding mountains would cast the river in peaceful shadows for hours before the sun officially set at 9:46 p.m. With Summer Solstice in two days, the evening glow would linger for another hour after that, and with a near full moon, many hours of fishing remained possible. I expected to fill my limit well before then and the reason I sensed no urgency. I'd rather sit and let the calming babble of Gold Creek mix with the sweet fragrance of the towering ponderosas and the rivers-edge willows—filling the air with grace and damping the recollections of my cruel world. If Heaven truly existed, it had to look something like this.

I took the last bite of my sandwich and swallowed it down with a swig of Coke. Max looked up with sad eyes, even though he'd gotten his fair share. When I pulled the Honey-crisp from my bag, he sat up and wagged his tail.

"Aww, your favorite." I held the apple in front of his face, and he licked his jowls.

A squirrel in the pine above us chattered an alarm, perhaps wanting some of the fruit, but I glanced around just in case. Plenty of bears roamed in this area, but none were in sight.

I looked back at Max, who hadn't taken his eyes off the treat and wagged his entire body in anticipation. Telepathically, he willed a piece into his mouth.

I flicked open the blade of my knife, cut off a slice, and gave it to Max. He swallowed it down without one chew. When I sliced a section and ate it, Max looked at me, highly offended.

"Sorry, boy; you have to share."

The squirrel's shrill alarm intensified as a stone tumbled from the cliffs above the hole. A small herd of bighorn sheep meandered through the patchwork of grassy slopes in the rock. Two rams tussled at the brink of the crag.

My family referred to these rocks as the Strobel Cliff, thinking that Pop owned it. We all knew better. Pop didn't own the land, but he held the mineral rights, something that the guys at the bar and the mill loved to rib him about. As a sixteen-year-old, some jokester at work had convinced Pop that there was gold here. "Why else would they call the stream Gold Creek?" he'd taunted him. "Nuggets as big as your fist."

The man told Pop so many stories that Pop finally went down to the courthouse, and with all the extra money he scraped together, filed a claim on the twenty acres in and around the cliffs, something that even today a person has a right to do, according to the 1872 governing law. Pop based the lode claim on a ribbon of quartz that ran across part of the rockface. The law required that he 'prove up' the claim by showing he'd worked it within five years. This meant he'd tie a rope around his waist and lower himself down the face of the cliff with a shovel and pick. All he received for his efforts included a rattlesnake bite from a den the man at the mill knew about, a broken leg from the fall, and a severe willow lashing from his father for being so gullible and stupid.

Year after year Pop continued to make the annual lease payment, something we couldn't afford. But the worst part, even with all the ridicule he endured, he died believing in his dream of finding his gold here. I truly believe he held on to those hopes for us kids. It was all he had. After Pop's death, and per his instructions, we scattered his ashes at the base of the cliff by a huge ponderosa pine that shaded his favorite drinking spot.

I guess I was no different, fantasizing about being the Mandalorian, or one of Lewis and Clark's exploration party, or a proud Native American with his family traversing the land to hunt the mighty buffalo. Probably my way to escape the reality of my life. Who wants to feel that much pain? Like I told Father P, I wished for a family of my own and a pleasant home to put them in. Someone to love and be loved by. Even I had to laugh, remembering Marty's ribbing about wanting to be an astronaut in first and second grade. I hadn't thought about that in a long time. Now, I could hardly afford to fill my gas tank. I sensed the familiar companions of depression and loneliness join me by the river.

"I'm afraid this apple didn't fall far from the tree," I said to Max, who perked his ears with the word 'apple.' I cut him another slice and tossed it in the air for him to catch. I shook my head, hoping to make sorrow fade, as the two rams ground their horns together up on the rockface.

Max lay his head on my lap. I looked at him, patted his head, and smiled. "It's okay, boy; we'll figure it out."

I took a deep breath and pushed the air out of my lungs

through my lips as a tremendous splash sounded from the middle of the fishing hole. So large, I thought some idiot had tossed a rock from the road. Then it happened again. This time I saw the tail fin of the massive fish going after a salmon fly.

It was here. All that I'd waited and hoped for all year had arrived. I saw them now, the female salmon flies launching themselves off the surrounding willows and dancing across the top of the water as they laid their eggs. Another splash. The dorsal fin of a gigantic trout cruised just below the surface. Even Max saw it and stood up, looking between the fish and me, asking with his eyes, "Aren't you going to do anything about that?"

My hands shook with excitement as I tied the foam salmon fly imitator on my leader. I couldn't help but think of my father's instructions for the improved clinch knot to connect the fly to the tippet. "The line through the eye of the fly," he'd said. "Always go from the bottom up." Later in life I found out this was one of his many superstitions and made no difference, but I still did it the way he taught me. And yet another superstition: "Make seven, not one more or one less, twists of the fly. Push the tippet through the loop between the hook eye and the first wrap, then lock by pulling the end back through the last wrap. Moisten with spit and snug the knot down to the eye, and trim the end with your teeth, always giving a final tug to make sure the hardiest trout won't untie the knot."

I stood and secured the fly to the hook holder on my rod, an Orvis 1856 handmade bamboo, the first year the company produced these fly rods. My great-great-grandfather bought it originally for less than twenty dollars, a small fortune at the time spent on a luxury, but now worth over three thousand bucks, and ceremoniously passed down through the generations. So, before I assembled the rod, I'd been careful to oil the joints of the three pieces like Pop had taught me by rubbing the male end at the crease of my nose. "Just the perfect amount of grease," he'd said.

I stepped into the water and almost had my foot slip out from under me. "Slow down," I told myself. "Not going to do my fortune any favors by ending up at the bottom of the eddy," I said to Max as he sat and watched me move into the river.

I carefully waded out a few more steps. It dropped off quickly, and the current tugged at my legs. The depth of the pool ensured the glorious fishing. Willows and the ponderosas stood far enough from the water's edge to make a backcast relatively simple, and I could spool out enough line to reach the principal part of the deep hole as the Blackfoot rounded the bend. The most efficient cast placed the fly into the exiting current from Gold Creek and let it float naturally into the Blackfoot, like the Almighty delivering the bug from the wilderness.

I let fifteen feet of line unwind from my reel with the river's pull, whipped the rod to eleven o'clock and shot it forward, then released the line. Thankfully, it landed nowhere close to the hole as it hit the water like a hunk of buckshot.

"Settle down; relax," I told myself, like Pop would have said.

I spooled out fifteen more feet in front of me then repeated the cast, this time settling it gently on top of the water and in the current. The fly bobbed and fluttered in the ripples as Gold Creek joined the Blackfoot, then floated elegantly to the edge of the deep hole.

With a splash, my rod arched severely, and my reel squealed as line shot out with the pull of a fish as it defensively dove to the bottom. I lifted the rod high to set the hook with my right hand and slowed the spool of the reel with my left. These fish were smart. You had to keep the exact amount of tension using the rod or they would shake off the hook. Too much pull easily snapped the line.

Max barked and pranced with excitement.

"It's a nice one, Maxi-boy," I said, and coaxed the fish from the hole with a few winds of the reel. As soon as I gave the fish tension, it pulled hard and almost yanked the rod from my hands. The fight ensued, and I let it take more line.

The reel whizzed, and the handle rapped my knuckles as it spun.

"Holy cow."

The junction between my float line and backing shot through the last eye of the rod. With little slack to give, I slowed the reel again with my palm.

And just like that, I thought I had lost him. As the line went slack and my rod straightened, a sick feeling plopped in my belly.

"Oh, come on!" I shouted and reeled like crazy. When I'd retrieved half my line, I decided the fish had escaped. But like so often with these native Blackfoot trout, the monster swam right toward me. I took a step back and almost fell as my feet slipped.

The fish popped its head above the waterline. As soon as it saw me it flipped, splashed, and dove for the deep again, nearly yanking the rod from my hands. The fish was enormous.

I didn't know what the record trout pulled from the Blackfoot weighed, but judging by the old mounts lining the walls of the local bars and restaurants, it had to be well over ten pounds and perhaps pushed fifteen. That's a whole lotta fish when you consider they're all muscle. But that was then, and people considered one- to two-pounders a decent-sized fish now.

The struggle continued, with Max coaxing me from shore —unsure of who would wear out first. My wrist ached holding the tension, but the pressure on the line lessened a degree at a time. Each time reeling in more line than the fish would pull back.

Twice, the fish broke the surface and danced on its tail. Yes, this was a big fish.

I readied my net as the battle neared the end, but as I pulled the fish toward my feet, it fought hard and splashed my face with cold water.

In a moment, the trophy fish finally surrendered and slowly swam against the current, opening and closing its mouth, panting. A beautiful bull trout. "No Black, Throw It Back." The Montana slogan read for the protected fish, referring to the lack of black spots on its dorsal fin. A magnificent fish: dark green on top, fading to a golden hue with reddish-orange spots on both sides.

How big? Well, its size might increase with every retelling of this story from here on out, but if I had to guess, it weighed a good ten pounds. I'd never know for sure, and it really didn't matter. I used a barbless hook for just this reason, as bulls and cut-throat were catch and release only.

I reached down and pulled the fly from its jaw.

The fish hesitated for an instant, and then with another splash swam away.

Standing in the river, on the far side...the wild side, I took a deep breath of the piney, clear air. The golden hour had come. The rest of my pitiful life didn't seem to matter. Right now was important. The fading light, the coolness of the air and water, the soft babbling of the streams. This was the best of Montana, and I was grateful to be alive.

10

SINGLE-WIDE

The air horn of a train blasted, and I jumped. You'd think after living here for the last year I'd be used to it by now, but with the railway crossing twenty yards from my trailer, the ground shook as it rumbled by. I waved to the conductor from my porch, where I cooked a plump rainbow trout I'd caught earlier in the evening.

The engineer blew one more blast of the train's horn for good measure for the people of Milltown. I'd wondered how the few hundred occupants of the town endured the round-the-clock intrusion all these years, but when I'd asked folks about it, they'd shrugged like the trains were part of the rhythm of their lives. Most said that the sound of the railway brought comfort and stability to the blue-collar, hard-working men and women of the town. It certainly kept the non-train-savvy dogs and cats to a minimum.

Milltown encompassed a forty-acre piece of triangular land bordered on one side by Montana Highway 200, another by Interstate 90, and the third by the Blackfoot River. Then split right down the middle by the train tracks. Except for the beautiful river, it wasn't exactly picturesque. I'd heard the term, "From the wrong side of the tracks," but Milltown *was* the tracks.

Mrs. Jarvi, the owner of two permanent homes, had squeezed my compact single-wide between them. She lived on my right and rented the house on my left, with frequently revolving tenants. Currently, a young couple occupied the rental who fought and loved at the same volume. But my trailer held a free front-row seat to the fifteen freight trains that came through town day and night. The most deafening being the coal trains delivering heaped coal from the Powder River Basin to export terminals in Washington State to meet China's demand for energy.

The train thundered through with authority, causing the fish on the barbecue grill to jiggle. I salted and peppered the salmon-colored fillet, closed the lid and glanced up, thanking the waning gibbous moon that lit the evening sky. Like Pop's fly-tying superstitions, fishing the moon cycles held their own legends and stories and made for fierce academic arguments. The truth is that the fish will bite when they're hungry, but the near full moon seemed to bring about mystical qualities.

My stomach rumbled in anticipation of the glorious meal of trout. "It's almost done," I said to Max, who stayed glued to my feet in case a nibble fell from the grill.

The hatch lived up to its reputation. After the excitement of reeling in the monster bull trout, I caught and released a near creel-full of nice-sized cut-throats, but only kept two large rainbows. Pop always said, "Limit your catch, don't catch your limit." The fish tasted best fresh out of the river anyway, and I'd hope to return soon. On nights like tonight, it was almost hard to keep fish off my hook. When my stomach had growled, it reminded me that I wanted to get back across the river well before dark, so I abandoned the fishing hole.

The train's clickity-clack faded over the bridge of the Blackfoot as a pair of headlights bounced over the rail crossing and another car turned onto the dirt road between the tracks and houses. It pulled to a stop in front of my trailer.

A sinking feeling soured my gut, and a thought popped into my head: *Am I in trouble?* My mind made up a story that the Missoula boys had filed a complaint with the sheriff, and they'd come to question me. "Just my luck," I murmured.

In the dark I couldn't tell who drove, but when the headlights clicked off, I blew a sigh of relief that it wasn't a patrol car.

In the moonglow and my flickering porch light, I saw the distinctive gait of Abby Arnold. She limped up the driveway, then the five steps onto the deck. Max barked once, but his body wagged.

"Hey, Abby. What are you doing here?"

"Hi, Andy. What'cha cooking? It smells so good."

I opened the lid of the barbecue and a large plume of fragrant steam escaped. "The catch of the day. I just got back from Johnsrud."

She eyed the cooking fillet. "Man, that looks tasty—" She looked up at me and lost her train of thought. "Oh my gosh, Andy." A tear flowed from the corner of her eye. "I am so sorry."

"Do I look that horrible?"

"Yes, worse than terrible." She smiled. "Does it hurt much?"

"Actually, I kind of forget about it, except that I sound like Rudolph after his dad puts a cap over his glowing nose… all stuffed up." I exaggerated my nasally tone.

Abby laughed, then said, "Well, I feel awful because it was all my fault. In fact, I brought you this." She held out a plate of chocolate chip cookies.

"Abby, you didn't have to do that. Besides, those jerks started it." I took the plate. They looked just like the Nestle Tollhouse cookies that Mama used to make. "Thank you," I said, and smiled, deciding once again that getting hit in the face might be one of the luckiest things that may have happened to me in a while.

"What'd the doctor say?"

"Those boys busted my nose, so the doctor straightened it in the ER. Now it's just a matter of letting it heal, but he said the bruising might be around for a few weeks."

"Well, thank you for coming to my defense. Not sure anyone has ever done that for me before. I truly appreciate it."

I smiled at Abby, looked down at the fish then back at her, not having seen her out of uniform and wearing street clothes in a long while. Heat filled my face as a moment of awkward silence settled between us.

"Uh…have you eaten? You want some fish?"

"Oh, that's okay, Andy. I didn't mean to interrupt your dinner. I just wanted to stop by and say thank you."

I hesitated, wanting Abby to join me but afraid of how the inside of my trailer looked. "Really, I have plenty. This was a nice-sized rainbow." I motioned to the fish. I hoped she'd decline. I hadn't had company since I'd moved into the trailer, and my place was a mess. But I wanted her to say yes. It was a long time since I'd had any companionship.

Max leapt to put his front paws on Abby's leg and yipped.

She bent down and scratched him behind his ear with her right hand. "I guess I can't refuse such a warm welcome."

"Great," I said, and tried to hide my anxiety. I used a large spatula to pry the fish off the grill and placed it on a plate.

I turned, opened the door to my trailer, and realized I'd been blind to my living conditions. Embarrassment flooded my mind as I looked at my life through the eyes of a visitor. Part of me wished I could rescind the invitation.

I glanced at Abby and grimaced. "I'm so sorry, it's such a mess. I only clean the place up on the weekends," I murmured.

I stood frozen in the entry as Abby walked up beside me. The mobile home manufacturer designed the single-wide for one occupant—one bedroom, one bath, and an efficiency kitchen that shared space with the living room and small dining table. My carvings, in various stages of completion, covered the table along with all my carving tools. Living alone, I typically sat on the couch to eat, watch TV, or play video games on my PS4—my one and only splurge in life. I had paused the Mandalorian video game, *The Bounty Hunter*, but the background music continued in repeat. Stacked boxes from Mama's house that needed sorting filled the empty spaces.

"Yo-ho, yo-ho, the bachelor's life for me," she sang her version of the Pirates of the Caribbean anthem. She laughed and broke the tension. "It's okay, Andy; I grew up with brothers, remember? Let's clear a spot at the table. It'll be fine." She pushed past me and waded into my disaster of a living space, moving my carving tools to the middle of the table.

Queasiness bubbled in my belly, and I quickly realized what a fussy bachelor I'd become. Someone touched my stuff.

"You have any chairs, Andy?" Abby asked, breaking my trance.

"Uh...uh—"

She reached for the plate of fish. "You go get us some chairs and forks and we can just share this feast."

"I'm so sorry, Abby; I didn't plan on eating anything else but the fish."

She took the plate from my hand. "Just what the doctor ordered for my Keto diet." She laughed.

I did what she suggested and snapped open two metal folding chairs that leaned against the wall and placed them at the table, then took out two clean forks from the drawer.

Seeing how pitiful the lonely plate of fish looked, I reached into the pantry and pulled out a box of Cheez-It Hot and Spicy crackers. I opened the refrigerator. "I'm afraid that all I have to drink is grape Fanta."

She laughed again. "Then grape it is."

Abby and I sat in the soft candlelight, the flickering fluorescent bulb from the kitchen, and the blue glow of the TV. Before dinner, Abby had spied one of Mama's candles on the coffee table and suggested we add to the ambiance of the evening.

"How much do you suppose someone in New York City would pay for a feast of freshly-caught rainbow trout out of the Blackfoot?" Abby asked. "That was the best meal I've had in a long time." She smiled. "Thank you."

"Yeah, crackers and all," I said, and laughed.

Abby picked up my latest carving from the table and twisted it back and forth to inspect the six-inch figurine.

"The Mandalorian?" Abby asked, put it down, and then picked up another. "Who is this?"

"Captain Lewis and his dog, Seaman," I said.

"Andy, these are fantastic. Do you sell them?"

I shook my head in embarrassment.

"How long have you been carving?"

I bobbed my head from side to side. "Forever, I guess."

Abby followed my gaze to the hundreds of carvings that lined the tops of the cabinets in the kitchen.

She stood to examine the collection. No one else besides Mama had seen it, and my back instantly dripped with sweat and vulnerability. I hoped she'd just sit down.

"Oh my gosh, Andy, I had no idea. They're unbelievable…fantastic."

"It's simply a hobby," I stated, deflecting her praise. "Did you get enough to eat?" I asked, changing the subject.

"Yes, but remember, we have freshly-baked cookies," Abby said, grabbed the plate from the counter, and limped back to the table. "You have so much talent. You should think of selling your art."

I ignored her suggestion, and Abby caught me looking at her deformed arm as she placed the cookies in front of me.

My cheeks flushed with heat, but Abby addressed it square-on like everything else from the evening. "It's because of my cerebral palsy."

"I've always wondered if it hurts," I told her.

She sat down and used her good hand to pry open her fingers. "No, just stiff and about as helpful as a headless spatula." She shrugged. "My left side gets tight when I sit too long. It's why I love my job and all the walking."

"What happened?" I asked.

"When I was born, I guess I got stuck in my mom's birthing canal and my brain didn't get enough oxygen for a while. It affected my entire left side, but fortunately not my speech or cognition."

I nodded in understanding, as Abby had consistently scored high on all our grade school aptitude tests, so the teachers always boasted about her smarts. They even awarded her the top honor at eighth grade graduation out of pure academic achievement.

"The worst part is my balance. I've taken a tumble or two."

"How did you get stuck?" I asked, embarrassed that we were discussing reproduction.

"I guess it just happens sometimes. I was a big baby, and my mom inherited my grandma's narrow Chinese hips."

"Chinese?" I asked, eager to change the subject. "You're Chinese?"

"Well, one-eighth. My great-grandmother on Mom's side came from China."

I'd never considered that anyone in our area would be anything other than Finnish, Swedish, or some other Nordic heritage. I'd never paid much attention, but now, looking at Abby with her shiny black hair and deep dark eyes, I noticed the ancestry. "Chinese. Wow. Do you speak Chinese?"

"Oh, yes: Kung Fu, Chop Suey," Abby snorted. "I think the last person to speak Chinese in my family was my great-grandmother. No one in my family really wants to even talk about it now. Her story is a bit sordid, but I've explored some of my legacy with my therapist."

"Therapist?" I asked. I always thought only crazy people went to therapy, and Abby seemed the furthest thing from that.

"A counselor," Abby explained. "I've seen her for a year. It's been super helpful."

"Why did you start?"

Abby looked at the flickering candle flame and sadness darkened her usually perky affect. "You know, life can be diffi-cult for all of us." She paused, and tears instantly filled her eyes. She wiped at one rolling down her cheek. "Uh...sorry; I didn't mean to have stuff bubble up like that." She chuckled.

"My therapist is teaching me how to access those feelings and live with that discomfort."

"I'm sorry, Abby; I didn't mean—"

She raised her hand to cut me off. "Really, it's good. We've waded into my psyche and brought healing to some of those parts of me that were stuck with burdens of the past." She smiled. "The highlight is finding what my therapist calls the Self, with a capital S. She says it's the true self…the one God first made us to be…the one given everything we need: wisdom, creativity, leadership, joy and so much more. I'm seeing beyond this girl with cerebral palsy to who I really am."

THE ACCIDENT

The morning sun burned bright when I turned out of the parking lot in Number One, but an uneasiness of dread weighed heavy on my heart—the kind that's hard to explain or easily shaken off. All the peace I'd found on the Blackfoot yesterday had evaporated.

The septic truck seemed to contain a similar lack of zest for life this morning as I pointed it down Highway 200 toward Missoula. A red Camaro ripped up to my rear bumper, swerved, then passed by with a middle finger flashing me out the window. I waved an apology, unable to coax more horsepower out of the sluggish diesel.

I couldn't say that it thrilled me to be back in Number One, but at least Marty allowed me to return to work, so my paycheck wouldn't be any more dismal than usual. Marty had replaced the pump all right, but installed another old pump destined to fail. I'd need to mind my p's and q's with this one or else end up with another major mess.

As Marty handed out assignments this morning, he

stopped in front of me, powdered sugar cascading down his shirt, and asked, "Does your face hurt?"

I should have known he wasn't extending sympathy when he answered his own question. "Well, it sure hurts me," he roared, evoking an avalanche of insults from the crew.

But I doubted this fueled my dread, nor did the morning greeting from my neighbor Mrs. Jarvi. She'd tottered out in her worn pink robe for the newspaper and hollered that she prayed for me as I got in my truck for work. I chuckled that my unusual late-night visitor would fuel the gossip pipeline this morning.

I honestly didn't care. Having a friend over satisfied a lonely part of me, and I had to laugh. I supposed some might consider her pretty, but someone with her smarts would never think of dating someone who had flunked second grade and barely made it through eighth. I removed any hope from my mind of a romance with Abby, or anyone else, except for unrealistic fantasies about Carrie Carver, of course.

"What a dumbass." I heard the words of my old Phys-Ed teacher as he tossed me across the gym that ended with a knee-splitting skid on the wood floor. Anger boiled in my gut, remembering the willow lashings Pop provided as a reward. The school, on the other hand, recognized the teacher as "Educator of the Year" despite his history of abuse. Life seemed so unfair.

I shifted the diesel into fourth. The engine warmed and picked up speed, coasting along the road that followed the Clark Fork River on my left. The sun sparkled off the water that would overflow with floaters and rafters later in the day. Perhaps I could fish the Blackfoot over the weekend and regain some peace.

I had plenty of issues that I could discuss with a therapist. But when Abby told me it cost over a hundred dollars an hour, for me it would be a matter of choosing counseling or eating. Abby's government-provided insurance covered most of her tab, but for someone like me, having health insurance or therapy wasn't an option.

Abby had shared about her family's challenges—a narcissistic mother who desperately wanted a girl and how delivering a daughter with cerebral palsy dashed her mother's dream for an idyllic life. Abby's disability landed a death blow to her parents' marriage, something she'd worked on in counseling for the last year to remove this misplaced shame in her life.

When I shared my heartache and shame about my two brothers getting killed the day I was born, she cried tears that my own heart had locked away. She tried to get me to open up about it, but I found it too distressing. I'd agree with Mama about this one. "Some things are just too painful to bring up." But Abby disagreed and encouraged me to find someone to talk with.

Letting out any more of that troubled water from behind my emotional dam scared me, but Abby told me that these painful emotions have a way of leaking out on their own if ignored. Perhaps my unsettling dreams last night allowed my psyche to process some pain and were the reason for my melancholy this morning.

The dream that haunted my sleep was as weird as most, I suppose, but this one woke me up in a sweat.

An enormous roadrunner the size of a velociraptor, with fiery red eyes, chased me through an inescapable maze. The beast's relentless pursuit only equaled its desire to destroy me. It toyed with me, and every decision I made seemed wrong. I'd found a weapon but didn't have the strength to pull the trigger. An overhead loudspeaker repeated, "You're not safe."

In an instant the Mandalorian, flying under the power of his jetpack, swooped in and saved me. But as we reached the clouds, the Z-6 jetpack sputtered. Then we fell, faster and faster, for what seemed like an eternity. As I prepared for impact, I tried to scream, but nothing came out. I was certain that we would not survive.

The Mandalorian pulled me close and protected me as we hit the ground, and in the mystery and incongruity of dreams, I stood unscathed. I looked down as Mando gasped his last breaths. He needed his helmet removed, but under the Mandalorian code of honor he'd pledged to never take his helmet off in front of anyone.

When I finally removed the helmet, it shocked me to see my own bruised and battered face staring back at me.

"I'm sorry," I said.

"This is the Way," the helmetless man whispered with his last gasp.

Now, safely driving the truck, the fear felt as real as it did in my dream, and I could almost smell the putrid breath of the creature standing over me. I wiped my forehead with the back of my hand. "The shrink would have a heyday with that dream," I said and chuckled, reminding myself that the odor emanating from the cab still held a tinge of septic smell from the incident the other day.

I shifted the truck down to third as I approached the big bend where Marshall Ski Area Road entered the highway. Construction crews had worked all summer on the curve to shore up the steep edge leading down to the Clark Fork. The river's unyielding flow had eroded the bank. The curve had always been a dangerous intersection, especially in the winter. With a near-forty-foot drop, a plunge into the icy river was not survivable.

I glanced at the assignment sheet lying on the passenger seat.

When I looked up, an old Chrysler slid sideways and

drifted into my lane.

The sedan had taken the corner too fast and hit the mud sheen from the early morning construction.

"Easy! Easy!" I yelled, trying to coax the driver from over-correcting.

But they did just that, and the car spun and headed for the cliff above the river.

"No, no, no!" I yelled. The old automobile probably didn't even have airbags, and if it plunged over the edge, the occupants were as good as dead.

The front of the car hit an earthmover's tire, and the construction workers dove for cover. The vehicle missed the edge and ricocheted into my lane.

I slammed hard on Number One's brakes.

The sedan spun toward me, and now I could see a woman's panicked face.

I had to make a split decision. Praying to God that I'd make the correct one.

With construction equipment and workers to my right and the drop to the river on the left, there was nowhere else to go except through her.

I couldn't do that.

I jammed the steering wheel hard left and off the embankment. The only thing that went through my mind as the truck dove toward the water was, "Marty is going to kill me for this."

My face hurt.
My wrists hurt.
My head spun.
I had finally hit the ground.

But as cold water filled the cab, I understood this was not the Mandalorian dream. The dashboard of Number One lay crumpled around me and water gushed in. Death would follow if I didn't get out.

Oh God, oh God, what happened to the woman?

The chest-level water quickly rose as I tried to unlatch the seatbelt. It didn't give.

I panicked and ripped at the belt.

My pocketknife!

Awkwardly scrunched against the dash, I reached with two fingers, relieved to feel it attached to my pocket.

I stretched my chin as the water hit my neck.

Then withdrew the knife, flipped open the blade, and sliced through the nylon.

I gulped one last breath, wiggled from behind the smashed steering wheel, and fumbled for the door handle.

Underwater, I pulled on the handle and pushed on the door with all my might.

With too much pressure behind it, the door didn't budge. Unless I wanted to drown, I had to find another way out.

Smash the window, I thought.

I peeled the small fire extinguisher from its mount and thrust it at the window.

Once.

Twice.

The third time, the window crumbled. The force of the water momentarily pinned me to the seat. When the pressure relaxed, it was time to go. My lungs burned. I pushed myself out of the cab and into the current of the river.

The river threatened to suck me under, but I fought hard for the surface and gulped for air. Out of my peripheral vision, I saw people standing high on the rim of the embankment. They were screaming.

In exhaustion, I surrendered to the current and let it take me down river, paddling to the side. When I got to the shallows, I noticed the people continued to yell and point. Curiously, not at me, but further upriver.

"Oh, my God!" I screamed.

The woman's car must have followed the truck off the edge and into the river. It was upside down, with only the tires sticking out of the water.

I splashed to the riverbank and raced along the shore, hopping from one rock to another, thinking that by the time I got there she'd be dead.

The bystanders stood helplessly on top of the steep cliff, with no way to reach the automobile down below.

The wheels of the car spun with the fast-moving water. With no time to waste, I dove into the river and battled hard against the current to the vehicle. I gulped a deep breath and swam underwater. I could see the woman floating lifeless inside as I pulled at the door.

It gave way.

She wore no seatbelt, so I dragged her through the door and to the shore, coughing and gagging.

When I twisted her on her side, she vomited but then gasped the words, "My baby."

I instantly turned, dove back into the water, and took one last deep breath before going into the submerged sedan.

The silt blurred my vision, but I pushed into the back seat, sweeping my arms to feel for a car seat.

My lungs burned from lack of oxygen. My mind raced with anxiety, trying to force me to the surface for another breath.

Like a bad dream, my fingers brushed against the soft, fleshy, lifeless baby—strapped into an infant seat.

I had no idea what to do. *How does this thing work?*

"Oh, my God, oh, my God."

I pushed and pulled at every buckle.

Miraculously the straps released, and the baby floated free. Pulling it by one arm, I jettisoned over the front seat and out the door.

With no time to swim to shore, I hauled myself and the baby on top of the submerged car. Standing in six inches of water, I turned the baby around and compressed its chest like ringing out a sponge. Then flipped it back, placed my mouth over its blue mouth and nose, and gave it two quick breaths.

With its mouth full of water, I tilted the baby and squeezed.

Then turned it over and puffed in three breaths.

Nothing.

"Come on, little one!" I yelled and started what I could remember of CPR.

In Boy Scouts in the eighth grade, I received a First Aid merit badge for passing a basic lifesaving course. Pushing on the plastic baby's chest with two fingers felt nothing like this. Was I pushing too hard? Not hard enough? I remembered the compressions needed to come fast.

More water flowed from the baby's lungs. I drained its mouth, gave it a couple more breaths, and put two fingers on its chest.

But before I resumed the compressions, the baby sputtered and coughed.

"Thank God!"

Pink returned to its lips, and I brought it to my chest and patted its back.

A joyous cheer erupted.

The baby cried, and applause rang out from the witnesses above.

12

MIRACLE

My arms and legs rested slack and heavy on the bed—
my body unmovable. The crisp sheet pulled tight
around my neck. "Go away, morning," my subconscious said.
The rhythmic beeping aroused my brain one more click into
awareness, but I tried to will it back to sleep even though
bizarre dreams of danger and adventure awaited me there.

"Is that darn machine keeping you awake?" a voice startled my mind to consciousness.

I took a deep breath, moaned, then coughed. My ribs
ached like a MMA fighter had taken issue with them.

"Oh, were you asleep?" the nurse said sweetly. "Well, I
need to take your vitals anyway." She pushed a button on the
machine next to my bed and the beeping stopped.

I stared at the ceiling tiles and tried to focus my vision
and wake my brain. My head pounded and the overhead
lights stung my eyes. I covered my face with my hands.
Every muscle in my body rebelled against movement. I
walked my fingers down my eye sockets and nose. Everything felt in place, although I thought I remembered terrible

pain when the emergency room doctor replaced the packing in my nose.

"What time is it?" I croaked out through a desert-dry throat.

"It's almost noon," the nurse said, and swiped a temperature probe across my forehead. She looked at it and smiled. "Ninety-eight point three."

She pushed a button on the blood pressure machine, then held my opposite wrist to check my pulse, and I grimaced.

"The doctor said we could place your wrists in splints if they're still sore. He said you didn't fracture them, so it was up to you." She finished taking my pulse, and I rolled my wrists in circles and shrugged.

"You can go home this afternoon. The doctor just wants you to eat first and then we can get your IV out. You can see how your wrists do when you're up and around. Have you passed any gas?" she asked nonchalantly.

"Uh…" What an embarrassing question.

When a voice came from the corner, the room grew hot. "Yes, I can vouch for that."

I craned my neck to see Abby sitting in a chair, smiling, and holding a bundle of flowers.

"Oh, good," the nurse said, and nodded at Abby. "You're sure?"

"Unless Andy has a whoopee cushion under that sheet." They both laughed.

I let my head fall onto the pillow and moaned. "Great, two women talking about my bodily functions…just what I need."

The nurse recorded my blood pressure. "Your lunch should be here soon," she said, and left the room.

"Well, that's embarrassing," I said, gingerly pushing onto my elbows to sit up.

Abby's smile broadened. "Two brothers," she reminded me. She then stood and handed me a bundle of daisies. "I figure placing daisies on your nightstand is better than pushing daisies up with your toes." She laughed, but the strain of seriousness broke through her humor. "Andy, when I heard about the accident, I was beside myself. How in the world did you survive? It's a miracle."

"Everyone keeps saying that," I said. "It seemed to shock the medical staff in the ER that I hadn't broken every bone in my body."

"I totally understand. When I drove past the bend this morning, a huge crane had fished the truck and car out of the river. The fall destroyed the cab of your truck." Tears welled in her eyes. "It made me cry."

"What about the woman's car?"

Abby shook her head. "How you ever got that woman and her baby out..." She wiped at tears with the back of her hand.

"I've been afraid to ask..." I stuttered.

Abby's face lit with joy. "No one has told you? Andy, you saved both of them. The mom's in surgery as we speak. Apparently she has a broken leg and arm that they're repairing, but the nurse tells me they think she'll fully recover."

"And...the baby?"

"Oh my gosh, Andy. I'm sorry you don't know all this. The baby is perfectly fine. The nurse told me they're keeping it in the hospital for observation. You saved them both."

"Yeah, some stinking miracle, turd-for-brains!" Marty growled from the doorway. I looked past Abby as she turned. Marty marched into the room and slammed a newspaper down on the overbed table.

The paper read: MIRACLE ON THE CLARK FORK. Its front-page picture showed old Number One, pointed nose-first into the river, with the large butterfly logo and BUTTERFLY SEPTIC clearly visible above the waterline.

"They're calling it a frickin' environmental disaster," he said, emphasizing the words with grand arm gestures. "This here could destroy all that I've built, you dumb-ass." He rapped his knuckles against the paper. "There are rumblings the state might hold Butterfly Septic responsible for the cleanup, and our insurance company is already balking at covering the costs."

I picked up the newspaper, trying to shield myself from Marty's growing anger and crimson face.

"Well this is the last straw, turd-head. You're fired!" He slapped the overbed table hard, making Abby and me jump. "Don't even think about coming in for a last paycheck." He turned, walked to the door, and threw out one last demand. "Pay off your damn truck by the end of next week, or I'll repo it." He marched out the door but continued to curse down the hallway.

My stomach threatened to rebel as I stared at the front page of the Missoulian. It felt like a dream, a bad dream, one that grew worse with time. Why couldn't I remember much of the last twenty-four hours?

Abby reached for my arm and held it. "What an asshole."

Her cursing surprised me, and I looked up at her.

"It's going to be okay, Andy."

No words came out, but as I glanced back at the picture, I wished I hadn't made it.

A knock on the door interrupted my morose thoughts. An attractive woman stood in the doorway, holding a laptop.

"Andy...Andy Strobel? I'm Helen Morley from NBC. May I come in?"

The woman wore a royal blue silk blouse with a colorful floral scarf tied around her neck.

I looked up at Abby, and she shrugged. The woman took that as an affirmative and entered the room. A man holding a large camera on his shoulder stood behind her.

The woman walked to the bedside and extended her hand. "Hi, Mr. Strobel. I'm Helen from the local NBC news station. Could we interview you?" She waved her hand at the cameraman. "This is Brett." Then introduced herself to Abby.

The woman was quite pretty, and her face seemed familiar.

As if she read my mind, she asked. "Perhaps you've seen me on TV?" She beamed a white-toothed smile. "I do the morning show."

She seemed a bit disappointed when I shook my head, but continued anyway.

"This morning we filmed the crews removing the truck and car from the river, but we have some other remarkable footage that we'd like to show you and get your comments. Would that be all right?"

She paused and examined my face. "You really got banged up. You doing okay?"

I glanced at Abby, who knew the truth behind my bruised face and bludgeoned nose and didn't know what to say. Fortunately, the newscaster didn't wait for an answer and placed the open laptop in front of me on the overbed table.

"We got this footage from two sources. With the construction of the highway at Marshall Canyon, there's a webcam set up for folks to track the progress of the work. The other is from a bystander who filmed the entire rescue."

She started the video on the computer. A low-resolution image of the construction site emerged. The video played, but it appeared to be a series of still photos taken every few seconds. Construction workers repairing the erosion of the steep bank looked like Charlie Chaplin figures in jerky, cinematic movements. Earthmovers and a large crane shuffled in the same odd stop and start motion. With no sound, the scene seemed serene.

From the east came the woman's Chrysler, and even in the odd syncopation of the video I saw she took the corner too fast. Just like I remembered, the car skidded sideways, over-corrected, bounced off an earthmover, spun, and headed right toward my approaching truck.

My throat knotted, watching Number One turn and fly off the lip of the road. It hit the water with the force of a breaching humpback whale.

What the video showed next brought tears to my eyes. The newscaster nodded to her cameraman and a bright light switched on.

"Can you rewind the last part?" I asked.

The Chrysler spun around my truck, missing it by a fraction of an inch, hit another piece of large equipment, and bounced over the edge of the steep embankment.

Tears welled in my eyes and overflowed.

"Mr. Strobel, can you tell me what you're thinking?" Helen asked.

The lump in my throat blocked my words. When they finally came, I said, "I thought I'd knocked her over the side." I tried unsuccessfully to stop my lower lip from quivering. "I thought I did that to her...I thought I caused it."

"Can I show you the other video?" Helen asked and started it on the computer.

This video played in clear, high-definition, and started in what appeared as the point of view of a person in their car. The image bounced as the person ran to the side of the road. The accompanying audio filled with screams and shouting at the truck stuck in the river on its front grill and the car upside down, steam erupting from its hot underbelly.

"Call 911!" someone screamed.

"Get me some ropes!" a construction worker yelled as he ran past the camera.

The surreal picture appeared like a mad artist had dropped the vehicles in the river for effect as the water swirled naturally around them.

Out of the corner of my eye, I saw Helen and Abby wiping tears from their eyes.

On the video my head finally broke the surface of the water, and I half-floundered, half-drowned my way to the shore.

"There's a person trapped in the car!" a woman in the crowd screamed.

"We've got to get down there!" another man said.

The background erupted in chaos and commands.

The videographer moved the camera between the sunken car and me. I could not comprehend how I made it to the submerged car, but I looked like Spider-Man, leapfrogging over boulders and scrambling across the bank until finally diving into the water and swimming to the car.

I felt Helen study my face as I watched the video of myself dragging the woman to safety. Then what seemed like an eternity of disappearing back underwater and reappearing with the baby, giving it CPR, and holding the baby to my chest when it revived.

Helen stopped the video, and I stared at the blank screen.

"The person captured the entire rescue of the mom, baby, and you—but do you mind if I stop it there?"

I didn't respond.

"Can you tell me what you think?"

I blew out a slow breath. For as long as my consciousness had returned, I'd thought it was all my fault. I had nearly killed that mother and child. Maybe my mind had grown so accustomed to gathering blame, it made it difficult to wrap my brain around any other scenario. "I thought it was my fault," I said again. "I didn't know how I would live with myself."

"Andy, did you turn off the road on purpose to miss that car?" Abby asked from behind the news lady.

I nodded involuntarily and looked at Helen, whose eyes filled with compassion and admiration.

"I didn't have a choice," I whispered.

"What a miracle," she said. "What a hero you are. Your boss must be so proud of you."

13

JOSEPH

True to his word, the doctor discharged me from the hospital after I ate lunch. As Abby drove past the scene of the accident, it seemed so surreal. The construction workers carried on as if nothing had happened. My fifteen minutes of fame had expired, and now I faced an uncertain future. Perhaps it would have been more humane if the seatbelt of the truck had trapped me underwater. Although that would have affected not only my life, but the mother and child would be dead as well. Their rescue was the only thing that buoyed my melancholic mood.

Before I left, my nurse told me the surgeons had finished repairing the mother's arm and leg and she convalesced comfortably in the recovery room. When I asked about the baby, the nurse reassured me he was okay. They were watching the baby's lungs carefully and so far, so good.

My nurse asked if I'd seen the noon news. When I shook my head, she told me I had become the talk of the town—a genuine hero. Everyone called it the Miracle of the Clark Fork.

"You okay?" Abby asked.

A shudder quaked my body as I remembered the feeling of the rising waters ready to entomb me. "Yeah, I guess. It doesn't seem real suddenly." I watched a group of young people on blow-up tubes, floating down the river, oblivious to the drama that had unfolded there hours ago.

"It's a boy," I said.

I glanced over at Abby, who drove the car with one hand. She looked past me and shrugged, not following what I meant.

"The baby in the river...it's a boy."

Abby nodded in understanding and smiled at me.

I looked away and back to the river. I'm not sure why my psyche processed this one fact. What a cruel way to start in life, a near-drowning. A thought popped into my head that sent a shiver up my spine. "He can save others, but he can't save himself." It rang true with me somehow.

"We never talked about it," I said.

Abby gave me another look of confusion.

"My brothers who died on the day I was born...we never talked about them or the accident as a family."

"I'm so sorry, Andy. What happened?"

I blew out a long breath. "My mom told me before she passed that during my birth month, Sam had just turned sixteen and Ernie twelve. Sam had recently gotten his license and drove Ernie to the hospital to see me. A drunk driver ended their lives on the freeway."

Like a simultaneous punch in my gut and nose, tears flowed from my eyes that no amount of willpower could stop.

Abby drove in silence.

Rage, fear, sadness, and anxiety threatened to overwhelm my system, like voices screaming in my head.

"It's okay, Andy. It's good to let those feelings out," Abby said tenderly.

My breathing came hard and fast, and I gasped for air—locked in the cab, drowning.

I squeezed my head in my hands, trying to force the emotions down, but they continued to bubble out like a spring in the desert.

"Why did I ever have to be born?" I blurted out.

Now embarrassment joined the other emotions. I heard my older brother teasing me after I'd fallen off my bike and scraped my elbow, then Pop's voice yelling at me to stop crying like a wimp.

I hated to cry in front of Abby and wiped my eyes. An awkward silence made my ears ring.

"You obviously were too young to remember…so how did you find out about your brothers?"

I thought about Abby's question until a memory came to mind. "Mama always said that her greatest sorrow was that she never had a picture of her entire family together. It took me a long time to understand the meaning of that. But I later realized that it distilled all the grief of losing her children down to that one statement." I pulled a hanky from my front pocket and blew my nose. "The two oldest boys were long dead when I was born—the oldest died in Vietnam at twenty, the second when he had just turned one. The next two to go were the brothers killed in the accident." I forced back tears. "Four pictures hung above our dinner table: Pop and Mama with the two oldest, ages seven and newborn; the largest with the two oldest girls and my two brothers who died; then a photo of me when I was eight with my older sister and brother, and two younger brothers; and a picture of Jesus, of course."

We drove in silence.

I finally started again, "It appeared as if Pop and Mama had three separate batches of children." I looked at Abby and shrugged. "A guy at Pop's work told me at the funeral that Pop's heart died the day they lost Jimmy to the war."

Abby nodded.

"I think I was five when I inquired about the largest picture that included Sam and Ernie. Mama said they were killed on the day she delivered me and wiped tears from her eyes. Pop told me to stop asking stupid questions and eat my supper."

"That's all they said?" Abby asked.

I nodded and looked out the window. "It's why they never celebrated my birthday."

"My gosh, no wonder that little boy made up this story."

"What little boy?"

"You, silly. Your brothers getting killed in the accident was not your fault," Abby said firmly.

I didn't think I could allow myself to let the shame and guilt go, but had no idea why. I wanted to stop talking about it.

"You think you can stop here at the truck stop?" I asked as we approached the turn. "I could really use something to drink."

Abby took a sharp right into the parking area, swerved around two eighteen-wheelers making their way to the exit, and pulled to a stop in front of the store.

I felt for my wallet in my front pocket. "Uh…never mind," I said when I realized my wallet probably lay somewhere in the Clark Fork.

Abby opened her purse and pulled out a five-dollar bill and handed it to me. "No worries, Andy. My treat."

I begrudgingly took the bill. "I'll pay you back."

As I went into the store, I understood I'd have to face

some of my new reality. Everything in my lost wallet needed replacing, and I had to find a job. I'd lose my truck in a week. "What in the world am I going to do?" I murmured.

Walking straight up the aisle to the drink cooler, I pulled open one door and grabbed a can of the original green Monster drink—a caffeine boost.

I made my way up to the front of the store to the cashiers, with two long lines of people waiting to pay. Then I remembered on Friday afternoons, truckers, boaters, and weekend revelers filled up on fuel and snacks for the weekend. The digital sign above the cash registers gave the other reason for the backup. The Montana Powerball Lottery had reached twenty million dollars and the people at the counter purchased tickets, growing the lines by at least ten people or more.

"I just cannot catch a break," I said, and turned to put the can back in the cooler. I didn't want to inconvenience Abby more than I already had.

As I spun around, a woman walking down the aisle, wearing a Town Pump vest, smiled and stopped in front of me. "I'll get you over here." She waved for me to follow her to the other side of the store.

I felt guilty for bypassing the long lines, but at least Abby wouldn't have to wait and I could still buy a drink.

I placed the Monster on the counter and held out the five to the woman, conscious of her prolonged examination of me. Then I remembered how bad my face looked. She scanned the barcode, held the can out to me, then withdrew it.

"Hey, aren't you that guy?"

My first thought was that perhaps someone had recently robbed the store, and she thought I was the man.

"Yeah…you're that guy who saved the mother and baby in the river. I saw you on TV today."

I smiled and shook the bill for her to take.

She ignored it. "Wow, that was just amazing." She turned to another girl stocking cigarettes in a rack behind her. "Hey Martha, here's that guy we saw today."

The girl turned and a wide smile crossed her face. "Man, that was the most unbelievable thing I've ever seen." She glanced at the five I held out. "Dude, I don't know how you survived that crash. You're the luckiest man alive…you need to buy yourself a lottery ticket."

I looked at the money in my hand and almost agreed to her suggestion just to shut them up, but it wasn't mine to waste. "That's okay, just the drink."

The woman at the counter held her hands up and took a step back, like I handed her a snake. "Then the drink's on me," she said.

Never in my life had I faced this dilemma. I didn't know what to say.

Heat rose in my battered face "Uh, thank you," I said.

As I walked through the store toward the exit, the woman followed behind me, and the tenor of the store changed. As I pushed through the doors, out of the corner of my eye I saw the women pointing me out to everyone, and the collective stare of the crowd followed me.

"Everything okay?" Abby asked as I got back in the car.

I swallowed hard. "Someone recognized me from the interview the news lady did. Kind of embarrassing."

"You might have to get used to it for a while," she said, and pulled out of the parking area and headed toward my house.

"Thank you for the drink," I said, and snapped open the tab. "You want a sip?"

She stuck her tongue out and shook her head. "A little too sweet for me."

I took a drink. "Aww yeah…just what the doctor ordered." I smiled.

"I'm not sure they consider that health food," Abby said. She turned onto the dirt road, bounced over the railroad tracks, and pulled into my driveway.

She looked at me when we parked alongside a shiny new, midnight-blue Cadillac Escalade. A man dressed in a gray suit and red bowtie stood at the front door of my single-wide, pacing back and forth. Except for his spiked bleach-blond hair, he reminded me of Pee Wee Herman.

I exited Abby's car and waved at the man.

He put his palms on his hips. "Oh my God, you're perfect." He emphasized his enthusiasm with a wave of his hands and bow at his waist. "You poor dear, are you going to be okay?" He sashayed over to the car and thrust out his hand. "I'm Joseph."

We shook hands awkwardly, then he pulled a card from inside his suit coat and handed it to me.

"I'm a producer for the Oprah channel."

I examined his magical, spiky hair when he redirected my look to the card. "Yes, that Oprah."

I squinted at the thick white linen card watermarked with a cursive O and other letters that followed. Joseph's name was printed boldly in black across the top.

I tried to hand the card back to him, but he waved it off, "Oh no, you keep it," he said, like he'd just handed me a hundred-dollar bill.

"How can I help you, Joseph?" I asked.

"Aren't you the polite one?" he said. "How would you like to come to the network for an interview? My God, Andy. We've all seen the video. You, my friend, have accomplished a remarkable feat. The entire crew sat speechless. And these are all people who make their living by talking. We knew instantly that we had to meet you. Would you do us the pleasure of an interview?"

"In Missoula?" I asked. Then my stomach growled, reminding me I'd have to eke something out for dinner tonight.

"No, silly. In L.A."

Abby finally spoke up. "In Los Angeles?"

Joseph looked Abby up and down and especially lingered on her contracted and deformed arm. "Is this your significant other?" He held out his hand.

Abby and I both laughed.

"No, we're just friends. I'm Abby." she said, and shook his hand.

"Los Angeles?" I repeated. "I don't know—"

"Has some other network already been here?" Joseph said, looking around.

I followed his gaze, still suspicious of trouble, but shook my head, reassuring him we were alone.

"Oh, whew." He made a dramatic swipe across his forehead. "Oprah would kill me." He laughed. "Then it's settled, you'll come to L.A. for an interview."

"I'm sorry, sir. I have no way to get there."

This brought an even louder guffaw. "Andy, I am going to take you there."

I peered back at his sweet ride. "In that?"

He slapped me on the shoulder. "Oh Andy, you are so funny. You are just perfect," he said again. "This is my rental. The network's plane is waiting at the airport."

"Now?" Abby asked.

"Yes, time's a-wasting." He looked at his watch. "If we leave now, we'll have you back this evening. Or we'd be happy to put you up for the night at the Hotel Bel-Air. Either way, you will have a fabulous time."

My stomach growled loud enough for everyone to hear.

"And yes, we'll feed you." He turned to Abby. "And if you would like to join as well, you are welcome."

I'd almost forgotten why I was so eager to get home. I walked to the door of the trailer and pulled it open. Maximus came bounding out, spun four quick circles and leaped into my arms, furiously licking my neck.

"Yes!" Joseph shouted. "Please bring your dog." He lifted his hands into the air like he led a praise service and sang, "You all are perrrr-fect."

"You gather anything you need, and I will call the network and tell them we're coming."

I nodded to Abby for her to follow me into the trailer.

"Who is Oprah?" I whispered into her ear.

14

OPRAH

I'd never ridden in a plane or a limousine, nor had I even traveled out of Montana, but in just over two hours I'd done all three. On the airplane, Joseph told Abby and me that the network had a new series in mind called "Ordinary People, Extraordinary Events." The pilot episode was in early planning stages, but when the crew saw my story they all agreed I would lead off the series.

The stretch limousine had dropped us off in what Joseph referred to as West Hollywood. It disappointed me that the Hollywood sign stood somewhere else, but he promised he'd show it to me before we left Los Angeles. I'd whispered to Abby that Hollywood looked nothing like I'd imagined. They had plunked the Formosa South campus into the middle of apartment buildings, shopping malls, and the neighborhood of a busy city.

We first entered a newly-constructed five-story building covered in reflective glass. With irregular portions of the building jutting out, it seemed the architect had measured it incorrectly. Abby told me she thought they meant it to look that way.

Joseph then drove us in a golf cart to an enormous, nondescript, industrial-looking building he called Soundstage Two. We entered what looked like an abandoned warehouse, but once inside, a flurry of activity funneled down to one central area. Bright lights and cameras surrounded the pod. Joseph grew more and more nervous and animated the closer we came to the commotion.

He stopped us at a table piled high with food outside the center of attention.

"You guys are welcome to whatever you'd like," Joseph said. "I need to make a couple phone calls. We've thrown this all together in an afternoon, so we're still deciding on who will be the host for the show."

"Where do we pay for the food?" I asked.

Joseph laughed and walked away, dialing his cellphone. "You are a funny man, Andy."

I looked at Abby, glanced around the expansive building with its odd open rafters, then back at the feast. Max, who seemed right at home with all the attention, jumped and placed his front paws on my leg, then sat, wagged his tail, and licked his lips, as if they had set the table for him.

Abby whistled through her teeth. "Wow, what a spread."

There was so much food, I did not know where to begin. The layout started on one end with pyramids of fruit, some I didn't recognize. Then meat and cheese platters that led to perfectly arranged trays of shrimp surrounding a mound of crab legs. Vegetable platters with dips of all kinds separated the proteins from the desserts—stacks of donuts, cookies, and at least four fresh cakes and five pies. With so much, I thought it couldn't be real.

"Maybe it's just part of a movie set," I shrugged.

Abby plucked a grape from a bunch and popped it in her mouth. She gagged and spat it back out. "Ugh…plastic." She laughed hard and put it back in her mouth. "It's actually delicious. Oh my gosh, it tastes like cotton candy."

Looking around at all the people busy at work, it seemed strange that we were the only ones aware of the feast.

I handed Max a piece of beef that he swallowed whole, then I examined the other food. I hesitated to disrupt the perfectly spaced shrimp, but I pulled one from the circle, dipped it in the cocktail sauce, and bit it off to the tail. I took another and did the same.

I searched for a place to put the remains when Joseph ran up to the table. "Oh my God, oh my God, oh my God." He flapped his arms like an excited penguin. "You will not believe who is going to interview you today. Oprah herself!" He waved at his reddening face. "She's on her way to the lot as we—"

He didn't get the full sentence out when the thirteen-thousand-square-foot space went still.

I would have thought General Patton had just entered the room. Everyone around us froze in place and stiffened.

A group of men and women moved toward us, and I stuffed the two shrimp tails into my pocket. At the center, walked an attractive black woman dressed in an orange sweater who carried an air of authority. Her long curly black hair highlighted with streaks of brown bounced with each step. Her smile and presence lit the room.

"This must be the man of the hour," she declared decisively. She transferred the stack of papers she held to her left hand and walked with her right hand thrust out to shake.

Joseph practically fell over himself to introduce us. "Oprah, this is Andy Strobel. Andy, this is Oprah."

She stopped in front of me, and I hesitated. Looking at

her outstretched hand and afraid that shrimp juice still lingered on mine, I wiped my palm on my pant leg and took her hand. She mesmerized me. I could not take my eyes off her skin.

"Andy, you act like you've never touched a black person before," Oprah said with a hint of irritation.

"No…no, ma'am. I have never been this close before…" My voice trailed off.

Oprah glowered at Joseph, who seemed to shrink, and then back at me. I turned over her hand and inspected the back of it.

"Your skin is so—"

"Dark," she finished my sentence.

"Beautiful." My attention moved from her hand to her face.

Her expression shifted from anger, to shock, to a blush in a millisecond. She adjusted her thick-framed glasses and examined me for the first time.

The room went silent after a collective gasp, and heat burned in my cheeks. Where I'd felt Oprah pulling her hand away before, now she leaned into the handshake.

I just knew there must be a scolding coming, and her stare intensified. My knees weakened and sweat dripped from my armpits.

But when I searched in her eyes, they held no anger, but a tear formed in the corner of her right eye.

"Are there no black people in," she paused and studied the papers in her hand, "Milltown?"

Was this a trick question? I didn't want to get the answer wrong. I always got it wrong, and all I could do was shake my head.

If silence could be silenced, the hush in the room deepened.

Oprah exhaled a snort through her nose, and her mouth bunched at the corners. Her face contorted like she'd just tasted the sourest lemon until it erupted into a guffaw. A ripple of exhales ricocheted through the staff and back to Oprah who burst into a deep belly laugh. The chain reaction of laughter crescendoed through the room until happy tears flowed from Oprah's eyes and jiggled her chest. She first fanned her face with the stack of papers and then tossed them over her shoulder like a lucky horseshoe.

This display sent the crew into uncontrollable glee. Joseph held himself upright on the lip of the food table.

Still in her grip, she wiped tears from her cheek with her other hand and then pulled me to her for an embrace. She was warm and soft and smelled of some exotic flower, and her body quaked with laughter.

"Oh my goodness, Andy Strobel, you do not know how much we needed that."

Now it was my turn to pull away from the uncomfortable affection of a woman I'd just met. The worst part was, I had no idea why I'd stirred such a ruckus, but it wasn't the first occasion I ended up the butt of a joke I didn't understand.

Oprah released me, and this time used both hands to wipe under her glasses and examine the mascara on her fingers. "Now look at what you've done...you ruined my makeup."

That made her laugh all the harder. At least I'd fallen into my role of ruining everything—something I seemed to excel in. That familiar cloud of disappointment and shame pressed on my shoulders. *Why am I so stupid?* I wanted to slap the back of my head like Pop or my older brother would do.

I examined her dark eyes that glistened with life. She truly was one of the most beautiful women I had ever seen.

But I'd seen the news of the unbelievable tragedies inflicted on the black communities around the country, and here I appeared so dumb. Mama always said, "We are all equal in the eyes of God." She'd get so mad at the injustices directed to anyone.

"I'm sorry," I said in a near whisper.

The words sucked the oxygen from the room and froze everyone in place.

Oprah's joy instantly turned off, and she straightened her back.

"What?" she asked with an edge.

My throat went dry, but I croaked, "I'm sorry about what has happened…" I couldn't find the correct words.

For what seemed like an eternity, the woman stared back at me, penetrating me with her look and probing my soul. An involuntary cough exhaled through her nose, but instead of growing into a laugh, deep grief welled in her eyes.

I did something unexpected, even to myself. I reached out and hugged her again. As I did, her head rested on my shoulder and her body relaxed into mine as waves of anguish pulsed through her.

When her sobs subsided, she pulled away. She smiled at me and then looked around to the rest of the crew, who stood stunned.

"Well, I'm ruined for the day." She backhanded the air in a grand gesture. "Bring us some tea to my office." She wrapped her arm through mine. "And send makeup," she added over her shoulder.

It seemed like such a strange world I'd fallen into, but at least I had tumbled into my familiar role of ruining everything.

I fidgeted in the chair. If I didn't know better, the blazing fire next to us emitted enough heat to make me sweat. Actually, the fear of the unknown and the banks of intense lights caused the perspiration. Abby held Max out there somewhere, but I couldn't see anything beyond the sterile set. The only things that were real were Oprah and me and the chairs where we sat.

Oprah focused on a folder of papers as three people attended her, one for her hair, another for makeup, and Joseph, whose nerves seemed overloaded with caffeine, reviewed the information in the folder. Oprah had changed into an attractive gray suit and round glasses.

Our time backstage flew by and we mostly talked of Montana and fly-fishing. No one had ever made me feel so comfortable—like old, long-lost friends. But when Joseph announced the crew stood ready, I saw a switch flip to seriousness in my new friend.

A Grinch-green backdrop covered the entire area, even the floor beneath us. But looking at the TV monitor stationed on the floor, we appeared to be sitting in a very comfortable white living room, complete with the roaring fireplace.

I watched in the monitor as I slowly raised one hand. Then, like I made a shadow puppet, I opened and closed my little finger. Movie magic, I guessed.

"It's weird, isn't it?" a young woman said, startling me from behind.

"Sorry," I said, and tucked my hand between my knees.

She smiled, then dabbed my forehead with a cloth and applied powdered makeup to the spot. I'd wished they'd cover my bruised face. I still looked worse than a rabid raccoon with the packing in my nose hanging from both nostrils.

"You'll do great, Andy. Just be yourself. We all love you already."

"Are you sure I shouldn't change my clothes?" I asked, looking at Oprah.

"No, you look perfect."

At least I'd thought enough to put on a clean black T-shirt when we left the house, but my jeans had a small rip at the knee.

The staff walked off the green stage, and Joseph demanded quiet on the set. I felt myself shrink into the chair. Oprah flipped through the file one last time, mouthed some words to herself, and then slid the folder behind her and out of view. She closed her eyes for a moment and took a deep breath. When she returned, she looked at me with a warm smile.

"Andy, I know you see yourself as an ordinary person. It's what makes us all so fond of you," Oprah said. "But what you did yesterday was extraordinary. You have affected all of us deeply. The best part of meeting you is that you have no idea of the impact you have made."

I bowed my head in embarrassment, unaccustomed to the compliment.

Out of the corner of my eye, I saw Oprah's smile widen, and she raised her hands. "This is exactly what I mean." She then looked at the camera. "It is fortunate that all of Andy's remarkable sacrifices and feats were captured on film. Let's watch this together."

The footage rolled on the TV monitor surrounding us and I glanced from one to another, but paused when a closeup of my face appeared in the corner of the screen. I looked terrible.

The film stopped with me holding the baby to my chest.

Oprah blew out a long breath. "Just remarkable...remarkable," she emphasized again. "How did you do that?"

Fortunately she didn't wait for an answer, as I had none.

"You nearly sacrificed your own life for this mother and

child, who you didn't even know. Your poor face. What a beating it took."

Oprah had no idea. This lie of omission clung like gum on my boot and followed me everywhere. The production lights hid Abby, or else I would have looked to her for direction, but the time came to confess.

"I...uh—"

Oprah didn't let me finish and continued, "Andy, I understand that life has not always been easy for you. Both your parents are deceased, as well as over half of your eleven brothers and sisters. You were telling me you flunked second grade and ended your education after eighth grade to provide for your mother. For the last ten years you've worked on a septic pump truck. You called yourself a—"

She paused, waiting for me to fill in the gap. "A honey-dipper," I said.

I thought she might laugh, but she looked at me with such sincerity that I choked down a chuckle with a cough.

"Where do you think that kind of bravery comes from, Andy?" She pointed to the screen frozen on the picture of me giving the baby mouth-to-mouth.

I shook my head. I honestly didn't know, and my mind swirled. I hated being put on the spot and suddenly I felt like I had returned to second grade and stood in front of the class trying to read out loud. The surrounding kids snickering.

"Your father must have instilled this kind of courage in you."

I crossed my arms over my chest. "Pop told me about my oldest brother, Jimmy, who died in Vietnam when he saved some fellas in his platoon. He threw himself down on a grenade. The Army awarded him the Medal of Honor posthumously."

I swallowed hard and thought I'd end it there, but Oprah's eyes pleaded for more.

"Pop told me I'd be lucky if I ever amounted to anything…that I'd never be half the man Jimmy was."

15

BACK HOME

I guess I should have been more careful. Floating on the innertube at the north side of the river, I rubbed my head and scowled at my bad luck. On Saturdays the traffic on the Blackfoot increased, and I should have looked both ways before I crossed, but the two girls in bikinis frolicking down-river on the south side at Johnsrud Park distracted me. I thought I had put the traffic jams behind me when we left Los Angeles, but here I'd gotten run over in the middle of the Blackfoot River. No matter what, I was happy to be away from the crazy big city and back to my peaceful place.

"You okay?" the guide shouted at me from the drift boat.

I waved, indicating I'd survived.

The wooden boat smacked the top of my head and almost knocked me off my tube. Hopefully, the guide just didn't see me or couldn't steer the boat away from me in time, as I'd hate to think he'd hit me on purpose, wrongfully deciding that I was one of the dumb college kids filling the river on the weekend. Either way, it was fortunate that I didn't lose Max, my pole, or fishing bag.

"That was a close one, boy," I said to Max, who lay curled in my lap, shaking from the near miss. When I glanced down at him, I saw the top front pocket of my fishing vest had popped open. When I smoothed it down, a sinking feeling of an empty pocket hit me—the collision dislodged whatever it contained. My heart sank even further when I realized the pocket held my bottle of Gink, the gel that makes a fly go from wet to dry. And worst of all, the truck keys.

Why I'd put the keys in my vest was a mystery to me and another poor decision. Just for this reason, I typically hung them inside the front bumper. But now they lay at the bottom of the icy Blackfoot River. I'd hurried too fast to get to the fishing hole, too darned excited to be back in Montana. Fortunately, I kept a spare in a magnetic box on the frame under the engine, but I hated losing all my other keys.

The truck didn't matter anyway, Marty would take it back in six days. I wouldn't have the money to pay him off by Friday. He'd dismissed me before, but this time he fired me for real. Since his visit to the hospital, I hadn't heard a word from him. I'd caused him so much trouble and made him so mad, I didn't expect him to change his mind about me.

I rubbed at my head again and watched the boat drift around the bend. The guides would always try fishing my hole, but because the river took a sharp ninety-degree bend directly after Gold Creek poured in from the north side, they'd frantically try one cast before the current took them downstream and around the corner. When I stood in the fishing hole, they could only look at me with envy.

After the bend, the river flowed a quarter of a mile before ducking under Highway 200 at McNamara Bridge, turned again and raced to Bonner and Milltown. Johnsrud Park lay on the opposite side. From where I sat on the north side, they prohibited access through the McNamara's place. Now owned by some distant relative, most still called it McNamara Landing. Bought by Mike McNamara in 1889, the Big Blackfoot Milling Company used it as a staging area for harvested logs. The lumberjacks stacked the cut timber at McNamara Landing awaiting the spring run-off where, in high water, they'd float the trees downriver to the mill.

When the Anaconda Mill completed the section of the railroad to Bonner, the forty-acre area remained in the McNamara family as a small ranch. Gone were the days of the modest lumber community, stories of moonshine, shanties, and brothels.

It would be a snap if I trespassed through the McNamara's place to access the fishing hole. But everyone else would do the same, and it would fill the prized spot with partying college kids instead of trout. For now I'd continue the dangerous crossing, but I'd just have to pay better attention.

Max leaped off my lap to a nearby boulder, and I stayed on my perch. Even with the hard bonk on my head, I was so happy to be home. Los Angeles and Milltown existed as worlds apart as one could imagine, and they couldn't get me out of there fast enough. True to his word, Joseph offered to put Abby, Max and me up at some fancy hotel called the Bel-Air, but Abby had to work first thing this morning so they flew us home. We'd arrived shortly after midnight. I would have liked to have seen what a seven-hundred-dollar-a-night room looked like. The best part of the evening, as it turned out, was when we got home. Abby kissed me on the cheek and told me she was proud of me. Not sure I'd ever heard those words.

Joseph said they discussed the possibility of flying me back for another interview or that a crew would come to film me in my "natural habitat," as he called it. I hoped they would do neither. After all, *this* was my natural habitat, and I didn't want to bring anyone here. Joseph also suggested that he'd return and arrange a meeting with the mother and baby for follow-up, as they wanted the program to air soon.

Last night we drove past the lit-up Hollywood sign, but honestly, Abby and I left unimpressed. Joseph also pointed out another studio where they filmed *The Mandalorian*. He said that next time we came to L.A. he would take me there, but seeing how fake and disappointing the entire city seemed, I feared I would feel just as disappointed with that. In my heart I figured the filmmakers most likely made Mando's silver helmet of Beskar steel out of plastic, and I could hardly stand to face that fact.

I also imagined that visiting Los Angeles was probably as unsettling to me as Mando going to the planet Nevarro, where lava rivers burned with sulfur. The skyline of L.A. appeared similar—a city of unimaginable wealth, co-mingling with heartbreaking destitution. Perhaps once you lived there for a while you'd stop noticing it, but I'd never seen so many homeless people who wandered the streets and had built cities bigger than Milltown, full of tents and homemade shelters. The sad part was that in about six days I would join their ranks. I'd paid my rent on the trailer through the end of the month, but after that I did not know what I would do. Even if I found work on Monday, I wouldn't get a paycheck for at least a couple weeks. If Mrs. Jarvi took pity on me, she might let me pay it late, but however nicely she treated me as a neighbor and landlord, I'd heard she never tolerated delinquency.

Meeting Joseph and Oprah became the highlight of our visit. She was one of the most gracious and warmest people I'd ever met in my life. Before leaving home yesterday, I'd retrieved two small carvings off the table. I gave the three-inch carving of Mother Mary and baby Jesus to Oprah. I'm not sure why she cried, but she told me it was the nicest gift she'd ever received—not true, I'm certain, but she was so sincere that it made me feel good. I gave the other carving, a small lion, to Joseph since his hair reminded me of a lion's mane. Oprah asked if I knew anything about "Over-on-a-gal" carvings. She told me the master carvers there would be envious of my craftsmanship.

I didn't take the time today to look the city up, but on the plane ride home Joseph wrote the name down for me on a card and explained that Oberammergau, Germany, was a place famous for their Passion play and their wood carvings— some of which sold for thousands of dollars. My abilities impressed him, but I told him I just carved for relaxation.

I looked up toward the sun as it hid behind a small cloud. The salmon fly hatch neared its end, and the big trout were probably resting comfortably on the river bottom with full bellies. But I was happy to be back on such a beautiful, warm Montana summer day.

Joseph told me the remainder of the interview with Oprah went great. I can't even remember what I'd said. I just hoped it wasn't too stupid. Most of all, I remembered being embarrassed that Oprah asked if I had a significant other, and when I told her no, she announced to all the single ladies out there that I was available. She reassured me that girls would come knocking on my door.

Like most people, Mama and Pop and our large family fascinated Oprah. I told her that out of the eleven only five remained: three older sisters, me, and my youngest brother. All except me had moved away from Montana and the lingering painful memories. Oprah wondered out loud if the tragedies my family had endured made me so tough.

She wanted me to talk more about Pop, but I just couldn't, especially yesterday—the anniversary of when he died twenty-two years ago. It just didn't seem right to talk bad about the dead on that day. I already felt plenty guilty knowing Mama turned over in her grave for missing the remembrance of his death. For the first time, I'd be late placing flowers at the bottom of Strobel Cliff on the nineteenth of June, where we laid his ashes to rest.

On that day, the family had driven upriver to Whitaker Bridge and walked back the five and half miles to the cliff with his urn. There were seven of us siblings alive when Pop died. A younger brother died ten years later when he drowned in Milltown pond, trying to prove he could swim across it, and my older brother Larry died last year at a relatively young age from a heart attack. The two oldest girls took turns carrying my four-year-old brother, and Larry had demanded to carry the urn the entire way, even though the rest of us asked for a turn.

On the day the Strobel family marched to the cliff, Mama was sixty-eight and never complained once about the walk, but asked me to cross the river and place some flowers at the site every year afterward.

Max barked, waking me from my thoughts. I stood from my innertube perch, climbed onto the rocks, and pulled the float to shore. It was a day late, but I'd still pick some wildflowers and place them for Mama. I shook my head, hearing one of Pop's many sayings often spoken my way, "A day late and a dollar short." How correct he was today.

The day had warmed enough that if I wanted to dive into the river to find my lost keys, I'd still have plenty of time to dry off. I looked back at the river and decided to lay some flowers first. I'd estimated where I'd collided with the boat and made a mental note of the spot. The current would carry them downstream, but they were on a heavy lanyard and hopefully wouldn't have ended up in Milltown by now. The chances of finding them were slim, but Marty would want all the truck keys back and it held the key to my trailer as well. Hopefully, they sank to the bottom and got stuck between the rocks like a California fish lure.

"Okay, Maxi-boy. Let's go say hi to Pop."

The area around the creek had come alive with wildflowers: Indian paintbrush, lupine, and arrowleaf balsamroot—red, purple, and yellow hues.

I picked a nice bouquet that Mama would've loved, climbed up to the trail, and walked the twenty feet to the bottom of the cliff. Strobel Cliff started at the juncture of Gold Creek and the Blackfoot, with one cut just above the water where the Milwaukee had laid the tracks, now barren and full of debris from the cliff. As I examined the rocky crag, a sickening feeling hit my stomach, and I remembered that the filing fee for Pop's claim came due in a few weeks. The hundred-dollar-a-year fee kept the claim alive, but maybe this should be the year to finally give it up. It was time to stop believing in fairytales.

"Sorry, Pop." I could almost feel the slap at the back of my head.

A large rock tumbled from the face of the cliff, as if Pop's spirit had pushed it. I sidestepped to keep it from hitting me. The rock had a nice vein of quartz running its length and probably where the fracture had happened. I looked around to see if a mountain sheep had knocked it down, but saw nothing. Hopefully, something roamed up there that I couldn't see, as I didn't believe in fairytales or ghosts. All I knew was that right about now I could use the few thousand dollars spent over the years on this dumb cliff.

At the halfway point of the twenty-acre rock face, a recess in the cliff created a small alcove. Next to an enormous ponderosa stood the small wooden cross I'd carved, hidden by the knapweed that grew around it. I knelt onto my hands and knees and cleared the weeds and pine needles, then fanned the wildflowers on the ground in front of the cross. After twenty-two years, Pop's ashes were long gone—dust to dust, but I did what Mama instructed. I made the sign of the cross over myself and recited the Lord's prayer. "Our Father, who art in heaven…"

I understood that the father in the prayer meant God, but as I finished the prayer, I had to wonder where Pop's spirit roamed. Father Papadopoulos clearly taught that all who believe in Jesus were saved. I didn't know who to attribute the saying to, but I believed that "God had a special providence for fools and drunkards."

Looking up at the cliff, I knew Pop was certainly both. The biggest emotion I always fought on this day was not sadness, but anger. I guess Pop was as close as anyone for the outlet of my wrath surrounding the station of my life. Why I'd started at the bottom of the totem pole and remained stuck there I had no reasonable explanation, except that Pop and Mama had but hardly a penny to their name and what they'd had, Pop spent on booze and this stupid rock pile. Why he'd left the stupid claim to me and not to one of my older and wiser sisters was beyond me. It had turned into more of a burden than a blessing.

I sat back, adjusted my ball cap, and leaned against the wall. I took a large rock next to my leg and hefted it into the river. It splashed down with a loud *kur-thunk* and sank into the deep hole below the cliff. Profound grief filled my chest, rolled up my neck, and spilled out of my eyes. All those things Pop, my brothers, most of my teachers, and my own brain told me throbbed in my head. "You are worthless."

I picked up another rock and tossed it into the water and added, "More than."

Across the river were two families enjoying a Saturday picnic at Johnsrud Park. Those few days spent here as a family remained my only fond memories—until Pop finished a twelve-pack and frightened us with a drunken ride home. The family had one scrapbook with pictures of Pop and Jimmy camping, hunting, and fishing. "Once Jimmy died, there were no more pictures like that," Mama said.

I reached to my side and unbuckled the sheath of Pop's knife. Rudy Ruana himself gave Pop the Ruana knife for a pair of handsome six-by-six elk antlers, or so he told the story. I pulled out the five-inch steel blade, then inspected the elk horn handle. I'd always wondered if the horn came from the bull Pop killed. The metal stamped with an "M" meant that Rudy had handcrafted it. Rudy, thought to be one of the finest artisans in the world, hammered out his first blade from a Model-T leaf spring in the 1920s. Pop gave this knife to Jimmy on his sixteenth birthday, who gave it to Sam to take care of when he left for Vietnam. When the drunk driver killed Sam, the knife ended up with Larry, then to me when Larry died last year. I supposed that I'd pass it down to my youngest brother one of these days, but he lived in Seattle and had no interest in either hunting or fishing. Smelling the knife blade, it had a hint of what I remember Pop smelling like—earthy and woodsy. I wondered how many deer, elk, and fish the knife had cleaned. I always wished Pop would have given me a knife of my own, but I'm sure he couldn't have afforded one. Pop told me early on that once I got good enough at carving, he'd consider buying me a Ruana of my own. He never did.

On the plane ride home, Joseph told me he'd teared up when Oprah asked me about my dad. He'd confessed that he'd struggled with his father as well. "I wasn't exactly what he had in mind for a son," Joseph said sadly.

Abby was right that I had some things to talk about with a psychologist, and that started with my dad. For now, I'd force the emotions back down. I guess I was lucky to have the few splendid memories of him here at Johnsrud.

"Rest in peace, ol' man," I said, then stood up and slid my knife back into the leather sheath and snapped it closed. I patted Max on the head, who waited patiently for me.

I returned to where I estimated I'd collided with the boat and followed it down a good twenty or thirty feet to where I thought the current might take my keys. The spot lay at the edge of the deep hole below the cliff. If the keys ended up at the bottom there, I'd probably never find them. There was still a chance they'd caught on the lip of the drop-off. I looked at the afternoon sun. It would drop below the cliff in an hour, and if I was going to make the plunge, it was now or never.

I walked upriver thirty or forty yards and stripped down to my boxers. I figured the people at the park either couldn't see me or wouldn't care, thinking that I wore swim trunks. Max danced nervously on a rock beside me as I picked the place to dive in. This was not a river that you slowly entered, getting used to the cold. You simply had to take the plunge and hope your heart didn't stop.

If I dove upriver, the current would carry me through to where the keys may have settled. The crystal-clear river allowed me to open my eyes under water. I'd predicted that the keys would reflect the sun and why big lures worked so well in the hole. My splashing around would not do the hole much good for fishing for a while, but going now would give me a chance to dry off before the sun disappeared.

"You stay here, boy," I commanded Max.

I dove toward a spot about six feet or more in depth. As soon as I hit the water, I decided I'd made a foolish decision. The icy water squeezed the breath out of me and filled my arms and legs with cold lead. I tried swimming hard and fast to the bottom, but the current took me quickly past the lip of the hole. As I passed, something shiny glinted in the sun. I had underestimated the strength of the current and was nowhere close to making a clean grab before it forced me past and through the deep hole. Fortunately, with the bend of the river, the water pushed me to the rocky edge under the cliff and I climbed out quickly into the sun.

"Brrrr," I exhaled as Max met me on the rocks. Obviously, he'd watched and followed me the entire way.

I gingerly tiptoed over the rocks with frozen bare feet and headed back upriver. Now that I knew where the keys had landed, I'd dive more directly to the spot. I looked at the water and half decided it was a fool's game to play with the river. With only one or two more plunges to go before my body temperature dropped, I determined to not let it win. Even in the middle of the summer, hypothermia was possible.

I leaped off the rock and paddled hard to the spot, but came up short again. I got closer, but between the bubbles and the cold I now couldn't decide if the object was my key ring or not. It could just be a big lure or beer can that got stuck in the rocks.

I climbed out and walked back with Max barking at me, encouraging me to stop the nonsense. "One more try, and then I'll quit."

Since I now knew where to look, I could see glimpses of something shiny, but it was a good twenty feet underwater, enough that it made my ears hurt from the depth. I hopped three more boulders upriver. I would try a fresh approach of diving downriver at the same angle of the slope and hope that my momentum and the current would take me deeper. "Okay, Maxi-boy, wish me luck."

I dove straight. As soon as my body was underwater, I

swam hard toward the ledge. For once in my life, I'd chosen correctly. I made my grab for the object and when I took hold of it, my momentum stopped, and my feet and legs flipped past me. I hung on for dear life and for a moment stopped, suspended on the ledge. I sure the heck would not let go.

The object finally gave way.

I swam with one arm and kicked with my legs to the shore, grabbed on to a boulder to stop myself, and pulled myself to waist-deep water. The cold had disappeared, and I sat blinking my eyes, examining the fist-sized rock in my hand.

A gold nugget.

16

GOLD FEVER

I'd never driven as carefully as I drove home with the nugget resting on the passenger seat. My hands trembled and heart pounded, unsteady with nerves. Now, I practically wore a path on the kitchen linoleum where I paced and waited for Abby. I'd called her when I'd gotten cell signal and explained it was imperative that she come over as soon as possible. She'd asked if I was okay. I didn't know how to answer that, but for whatever reason, I withheld the explanation for the urgency. Disappointingly, she said she'd stop by after work.

When I'd climbed out of the river I tugged on my jeans, stuffed the heavy nugget into the front of my pants, waved goodbye to my lanyard of keys, jumped into the tube to paddle across, almost forgot Max by accident, retrieved him, made the crossing, grabbed my spare key, drove home, bolt-locked the door behind me, pulled the drapes closed, and paced. I had caught "gold fever," as Pop called it.

In rare moments of self-reflection after visiting his claim, and, of course, with Hamm's beer flowing through his system,

Pop would tell stories of people who discovered gold—the nugget named the Welcome Stranger weighed in at one hundred seventy-three pounds, the Welcome Nugget at one hundred fifty-two pounds, and the Hand of Faith at only a measly sixty pounds. There were others, but these were the most famous. Besides finding gold for himself, Pop always dreamed of going to the Golden Nugget Casino in Las Vegas to see the Hand of Faith Nugget firsthand. He had done neither, but that didn't stop him from his harsh warnings about characters who would steal treasure from you. "Gold makes people do strange things," he'd said with a distant look in his eyes.

Larry always whispered in my ear, "Yeah, like wasting money on a pile of rocks."

But Pop would say, "Gold's easy to find with a metal detector, and they would zero in on it instantly and rob you blind." I'd never been sure of who *they* were and why *they'd* sweep a dumpy old house in Milltown with a metal detector. But the story gave me visions of special government spy planes, flying low over houses, searching for gold.

Gold fever had infected Pop, and now I had it.

When a car pulled up to my trailer, I threw a towel over the nugget on the table. If the person carried a metal detector, I knew both my prize and me were done for.

I blew a sigh of relief when I recognized Abby's distinctive gait stride across my porch. I walked over and unlocked the door.

"Hey Andy, sorry it took me a while…" She stopped and looked at me. "You okay? You look like you've seen a ghost."

I nodded as I let her in. Max leaped into her arms and licked her neck.

"He's probably going after all the sweat on my neck from walking so many miles today," she said, and set him down.

She accompanied me to the table and sat down beside me. "You okay?" she asked again.

I shook my head, and she followed my gaze to the towel, which I lifted.

She leaned in to examine the lumpy, pockmarked stone. She furrowed her brow, shrugged, and bent closer. Then she blinked, looked at me, and back to the nugget.

"Holy cow, Andy, is that what I think it is?"

I shrugged, then grinned.

"It looks like a huge gold nugget." She reached for it but pulled back. "Can I touch it?"

I nodded.

She struggled to lift it with her one hand and dropped it on the table, causing some of my carvings to tip over. "Oh my God, Andy. It has to be gold. Where'd it come from?"

"I found it in the Blackfoot today," I finally said. "Right by my fishing hole, at the bottom of Strobel Cliff."

Speechless, we both sat and stared at the rock.

Max jumped onto Abby's lap and broke our trance.

"Have you weighed it? It's got to be close to twenty pounds."

I stood, retrieved the bathroom scale, and set it on the floor by the table.

I picked up the sizable, large-enough-to-be-weighed-on-its-own nugget and placed it on the scale.

Abby and I banged our heads together when we both leaned in to read the scale and laughed. I looked at the results again. "Twenty-two," I said, and moved the stone to check again. "Maybe twenty-two and a half."

Abby held her hand to her forehead. "I think I saw something at work today that gold was, like, at eighteen hundred."

I quickly did the math. "That's like forty thousand dollars!" An amount of money I couldn't fathom.

Abby laughed. "No Andy, eighteen hundred an *ounce!*"

Not able to make the calculations in my head, I used the calculator on my phone to convert the twenty-two-and-a-half pounds to ounces. I turned the screen to show her. "Three hundred sixty ounces." Then I multiplied it by eighteen hundred. I couldn't say the number out loud and showed her the phone again.

"Holy cow," Abby said again. I picked it up off the scale and handed it to her. She studied it one way and then another, flipping the lumpy, irregular nugget over and over, and then set it back on the table. "Looks like a lion's head, but with horns," she said, and we both examined the nugget as if it might come alive and devour us both.

"I thought it looked like a bear, but now that you mention it..." I studied it again.

"Pop always told me the old prospectors would name their finds."

"How about the Bear Nugget?" Abby said.

"I think I'll name it the Lion Nugget."

"How about the Lioness Nugget?" Abby smiled. "Where did you find it again? And how?"

"I crossed over to my fishing hole and did a dumb thing. I dropped my keys into the river, so I had to swim down to the bottom to see if I could find them."

"Not so dumb, I guess," Abby said, and patted the nugget.

"It was there in the rocks. When I first latched on to it, I thought it was just an old gold can of Miller beer. I couldn't believe my eyes when I got to shore. Still can't."

"I know there is both public and private land around Johnsrud...like the McNamara's place. You've told me your favorite fishing hole is somewhere around there, but I don't know exactly. You think you were on public land or private?"

"Does it matter?" I said with a sinking feeling in my gut.

Abby opened her eyes wide and nodded, like "Duh."

"How would I know?" I exhaled.

Abby grabbed her phone out of her back pocket. "There's a local company that produces detailed hunting maps called OnX Maps. We use it at the post office for figuring out boundaries."

She typed in some information while sweat broke out on my upper lip. Nothing other than "finders keepers" had crossed my mind.

"Okay," she said, and scooted her chair close to mine to share the screen. "Here is the area of Johnsrud. This is Highway 200," she said, and traced her finger along the yellow line. "Gray is private land, light green is Bureau of Land Management—BLM—and dark green is National Forest."

I used two fingers to zoom in and out of the area, amazed that OnX Maps showed the landowners for each tract of land. I followed the curves of the river, past the park and around to the Gold Creek confluence. The map clearly marked Gold Creek and the surrounding area in dark green—Lolo National Forest. A sliver of light green followed the Blackfoot and across the fishing hole. "BLM," I said, uncertain if that was good or bad.

When Abby crossed her arms, I knew it. My bad luck followed me.

She picked up the nugget like she was going to take it and give it to its rightful owner.

She handed it to me. "Congratulations, Andy Strobel. You're rich."

"Oh, my gosh. Are you serious? You're killing me. Then it's okay?" I said excitedly.

Abby smiled. "Yes, Andy, it's yours. Gold found on BLM and most National Forests belongs to the finder. Congratulations!"

"Are you sure?" I knew there had to be some sort of catch or way my usual bad luck would prevail.

"Yes, I'm positive. But now what are you going to do with it?"

I shrugged. "I have no idea. Do I just take it down to the bank or something?"

My question made Abby laugh. "Yeah, I'd like to be there when you do." But then turned serious. "I honestly don't know what you should do."

"I could call Marty—"

"Oh God, no!" she said before I got the sentence out. "Andy…" she scolded. "You need to be very careful with who you tell about this."

"What about Willie? He's good with money."

Abby grimaced and tilted her head from side to side. "I don't know, Andy. Willie is all about Willie." Then added, "Maybe."

I picked up my phone to look up his number, but Abby guided my hand back down to the table.

"You're a praying man, Andy—maybe we need some divine guidance."

I looked down at her hand that lingered on top of mine and then back at her face. She smiled with kind eyes.

"You're a good man, Andy. You deserve this. But you have to be so careful and decide who you can trust with this much money," she said, and squeezed my hand. "I don't think you should tell anyone about this tonight. Sleep on it. There are people out there who will rob you blind."

I so appreciated Abby's friendship and advice. I smiled at her, nodded, and withdrew my hand. I knew that she, too, had caught gold fever.

17

ONE BIG TURD

Removing the packing from my nose felt like getting smacked in the face again, complete with watery eyes and bleeding nose. Each pledget ripped nose hairs out with the dried blood. At first I thought I might have to have the doctor remove them, but I took a deep breath and yanked. It sounded like I'd torn out part of my frontal lobe. The bleeding coagulated quickly, but the sting lasted until I arrived at the church. My face looked like crap and my nose still pointed a bit to the left. *Close enough for government work*, I thought. "Might even improve my looks," as Marty had said.

I sat in the truck and watched the last of the parishioners file inside. I checked the time on my phone. Sunday Mass started in two minutes and I hoped to sneak into the rear pew. Once I'd pulled into the parking lot, I almost returned home to make sure I'd extinguished my prayer candle. I couldn't remember for sure if I'd blown it out, and it would be just my luck to burn the place down.

The candle burned all night while I slept on the couch,

afraid to take my eyes off the nugget in case it disappeared. Mama had taught me that lighting the votive prayer candle was a simple act of prayer, and God heard these humble pleas. I surely needed the divine guidance.

The day Mama died, her prayer candle still burned when the EMTs carried her body away. And when I had to extinguish it, an immense wave of guilt washed over me, like I'd just doused her essence. Of course, she wouldn't have agreed. In her mind, the glow and flame of the lit candle represented the presence and power of God—nothing to do with her. So honoring Mama and God, I'd lit a candle every morning since.

I still didn't know the right thing to do with the gold. I'd hoped that God would slip me some revelation during the night, but instead I waited for the creeps that Pop talked about coming and stealing it from me. Before walking out the door this morning, I had tried to stuff it into the front pocket of my jeans to keep it with me, but how it pulled at my pants, I looked ridiculous. It would have caused a memorable event at church if my trousers fell to the floor. I thought about burying the nugget, but changed my mind and decided the robbers wouldn't look under the grate of the barbecue grill. For good measure, I scraped off some black, greasy soot from the side to camouflage it.

Then I called Willie. There was no one else I knew who was more successful with money, and if anyone could figure out what to do with it, it was him. When I talked with Willie, I sounded like a babbling idiot from lack of sleep, especially not wanting to divulge my secret over the phone. He sounded like typical Willie—annoyed and irritated that I disturbed him at their lake place. He reassured me he'd taken care of my crapper mess, so I didn't need to bother them. But when I insisted it was a matter of extreme importance to see him, he relented and told me to come to their house tonight after they got home from the lake. I thanked God that he didn't tell me to come right over, so it would give me time to talk with Abby and see if she'd go with me. Right now, she seemed like the only person I could truly trust.

I got out of the truck and slammed the door behind me. I loved this truck and would be sad to see it go, still not believing my good fortune would last. As I walked toward the church doors, I realized I had lots to be thankful for, including my life.

My timing was poor. Father Papadopoulos stood with his two acolytes at the vestibule of the church, waiting for the processional hymn. When he saw me, a wide smile spread across his face.

"Here is the hero of the day!" he shouted, causing the parishioners to turn around.

"Come in, Andy. I am preaching on you this morning from John 15:13. 'Greater love hath no man than this, that a man lay down his life for his friends.'"

An applause erupted from somewhere in the nave and spread until the entire congregation stood and clapped.

"A standing ovation for you, Andy. How do you like that?"

I took a step backward, but Father P walked forward, draped his arm around my shoulders, and whispered in my ear, "Come, Andy. I know you despise this attention, but we need a glimmer of good news these days."

Abby drove me down Heaven's Gate road toward Willie and Carrie's house. I'd dug the Lioness out of the grill, wrapped it in a hand towel, and now cradled it securely on my lap. The sun set over Missoula in streaks of oranges and reds layered between fluffy clouds, with the lights of the city twinkling below.

"I think you'll be living like this soon," Abby said, and smiled at me.

I shook my head. "I'd be happy to pay off my truck, get enough to pay rent for the year ahead, and somehow reimburse Marty for the septic truck I cost him." Beyond that, I didn't think my life would change much. "I stopped by the truck stop for the Sunday Missoulian and scoured the help-wanted ads. So far, my eighth-grade education afforded me little in credentials. Tomorrow I'll probably apply at Taco Bell or McDonald's."

"Andy, you might not have formal schooling, but you're actually super smart."

I huffed out my nose at her compliment, glad I could breathe through it again.

Abby took a double take of my face. "Hey, now I know what's different. You took the packing out of your nose."

"Yeah, looks so much better, right?" I waved my hand over my face like the product models on *Let's Make a Deal*, to show it off.

"Well, I wouldn't go *that* far," Abby teased.

I looked down at my feet.

"I'm sorry, Andy, I…" she stammered, contrite.

"No, it's not that," I interrupted her. "I just can't seem to tell the truth about it. A young girl asked me about it this morning at church, and I didn't have the guts to tell her my face got banged up before the accident."

"Well, in both situations you were doing the right thing."

I shook my head. "Somehow getting my face smashed up in the accident sounds better than a bar fight. The only people who know the truth are Marty, you, and Father P."

"Your secret is safe with me," Abby said. "How was church this morning?"

"Terrible. Father P caught me sneaking in and escorted me to the front. His whole sermon was about me saving that mother and her baby. Abby, everyone is giving me too much credit for what I did. Nothing that anyone else wouldn't have done if they were in my situation."

"I'm not so sure, Andy."

"I think the entire congregation wanted to shake my hand. Even Mrs. Jarvi was nice to me, although she reminded me that her lawn still needs mowing."

That made Abby laugh. "Well, your stardom can only get you so far," she said, and pulled into the circular drive in front of Willie and Carrie's house. She looked out the side window. "Yikes, this is impressive."

"You've never been up here?" I asked.

"No, I'm sure my invitations for their fancy parties got lost in the mail."

"Aren't you the mailman?"

Abby slugged my arm. "Exactly. And it's mail carrier, now."

I rubbed where she'd hit me. She packed a punch.

"I don't think I've seen these two since high school, except for when they hit the social section in the Missoulian for one of Carrie's pet projects or Willie's business advertisements," Abby said. "We kind of run in different social circles." She smiled at me again as we got out of the car and walked up the sidewalk to the front door.

I reached to ring the doorbell, when Abby stopped the momentum of my arm. "You sure you want to do this?" she asked.

I must have stared at her in horror. I was already having the hardest time finding the courage to face Willie and Carrie.

"We could ring and run," she said. "Or, in my case, just ring and limp."

We were both laughing when Carrie opened the door. A white poodle yapped loud enough to hurt my ears. Carrie looked gorgeous and perturbed all in the same instant. Even with no makeup, her sun-kissed face radiated beauty, making my knees melt. "Andy!" she said. "What a star you are. I saw the article in the paper about you and even saw you on the news. Who would have thought?" She hugged me, lessening the sting of her insult. "Well, we're very proud of you," she said over the dog's racket.

"Wait until his interview with Oprah comes out," Abby said.

Carrie laughed like Abby teased, but then looked at her as an unwelcome visitor.

I followed Carrie's gaze to Abby's deformed arm and back to her face as she recognized her old classmate.

"Abby…hi," she said, stumbling over her words. "Wow, it's been a long time. You weren't at the ten-year high school reunion."

"No, I couldn't make it," Abby said, and blushed, making me wonder who fibbed now.

"Well, you missed a splendid party. Me and the girls did a cheer for the crowd. Everyone loved it."

"I'm sure," Abby said coldly.

Carrie gave Abby a hug and patted me on the arm. "Come in. Willie's watching baseball." She rolled her eyes. "He's in one of his moods for being disturbed," she whispered across the back of her hand.

Carrie reached down and scooped up the dog. "Duffy, it's just our friend, Andy," she said, and spanked it on the nose, then turned to place the dog in Willie's study and closed it inside behind French doors. It continued to bark and scratch at the wood. "I hate that stupid mutt," she said. "I don't know why Willie loves it so much," she muttered.

We followed Carrie through the marble foyer. Abby looked at me and mouthed, "Wow."

Heat filled my face as I thought the same thing, except about how Carrie's derriere wiggled in her yoga pants. I hoped Abby hadn't caught my stare.

Carrie already had an assortment of flavored teas and a plate of cookies set at the breakfast table where we had shared a glass of lemonade the other day. She invited us to sit. "Hey, Riley and Grayson, come here."

Both kids leaped up from the family room floor and walked over to stand by the table where we sat.

"You kids remember Andy, from the news? He saved that mother and child from the river. Wasn't that something?"

The boy, still looking much like Yoda, took a step back, and probably for the first time put the two faces of hero and crapper guy together. He shrugged his shoulders and ran back to join Willie on the couch to watch the game. The girl smiled and handed me a piece of paper.

"I made this for you," she said shyly.

I smiled at her and took the drawing from her hand. She had her blond hair twisted into a similar bun as her mother's and her eyes shined with the same brilliant blue. "Thank you," I said, and inspected the picture. I forced back tears. It showed the truck, nose first into the river and me holding the mother in one stick figure hand and the baby in the other. Not exactly accurate, but the most meaningful thing I'd received since the accident. "Wow, thanks," I said. "That means a lot to me."

"Willie, our guests are here," Carrie said over the noise of the TV.

He ignored her until a commercial came on, then

yawned, rubbed his son's bald head, and slowly made his way to the table. "Whew, a little sore today from all that waterski-ing," he said, and stretched his back. "Andy, now what trouble did you bring?" he snarked. He looked at Abby without recognition.

"Willie, you remember Abby? We went to school together."

"Uh…yeah, hi," he said, and shook her hand. Obviously, he didn't.

"So, what is this life-or-death problem you're having, Andy?" he asked, looking back at the TV.

I glanced at Abby, then to Carrie, unwrapped the surprise, and placed the Lioness down in the middle of the table with a clunk. When I sensed Willie and Carrie scoot back, I realized I should have cleaned off the black grease.

"Jeez, Andy, what did you bring us? Another turd from your collection?"

His declaration made Abby burst out in a loud guffaw and me into a sweat. Fortunately, Abby came to my rescue. "Carrie, could I get some paper towels?"

Carrie jumped up, retrieved a roll from the kitchen, and handed it to Abby. Abby carefully picked up the nugget and polished off the soot. The lumpy, creviced gold nugget came alive.

I waited for Willie to say something, but when I looked up his attention was on the baseball game until Carrie gasped and whispered, "Oh. My. God."

Willie turned and glowered at the stone, dumbfounded. He glanced from me to the lump and back to me. "Holy crap, Andy. Is that gold?"

18

INVESTMENT

Willie didn't wait for an invitation and plucked the nugget off the table, bouncing it up and down in his hand to judge the weight. He still seemed skeptical that someone like me fell into such good fortune. But when he jabbed his thumbnail into the metal and it gave way, he nodded. He put the rock to his nose and winced. "Why does it smell like pork ribs?"

"I didn't know where else to hide it, so I put it in the barbecue grill for safekeeping when I went to church this morning," I said.

He looked at Carrie and rolled his eyes, but then asked, "Have you weighed it or told anyone else about it?"

"Just Abby...and I weighed it at home on the bathroom scale. It's around twenty-two-and-a-half pounds."

Willie bounced it up and down again and did the math, which he'd always been good at. His eyebrows rose. He then broke out into a laugh and shook his head. "How in the world did a guy—" He didn't finish his sentence.

Carrie, who had flunked algebra, stared at Willie, trying

to make sense of it all.

Willie frowned at her in disgust. "Well over a half-million, depending on the purity."

"Dollars?" Carrie gasped.

Willie ignored her and turned to me, "Where did you find it?" he demanded.

Thankfully, Abby and I had talked about this and decided that this bit of information should stay elusive. "I found it in the Blackfoot."

Willie's eyes squinted. "At your old man's claim?"

I hadn't expected for him to know about that, but obviously the Milltown gossip mill was up and running.

"Uh...I..."

"No," Abby came to my rescue. "It was upriver," she added.

It wasn't a lie. It was just that it was only a few feet upriver.

"I was fishing yesterday and found it in the middle of the river." I worried my fiery face betrayed me.

"The place Andy discovered it is on BLM land. We looked up the laws, and it belongs to him," Abby said firmly.

"How far up the Blackfoot?" Willie asked, glowering.

"Far enough," Abby answered for me.

Willie seemed to let it go and handed the nugget to Carrie, who seemed surprised by the weight. She showed it to Riley and Grayson, who had re-joined us at the table. Willie paced on the hardwood floor and rubbed his chin.

The children inspected the odd-shaped nugget.

"You found this?" Grayson asked.

"How in the world did it get there?" Carrie asked.

"I looked that up last night," I said. "I guess since gold is soft, it can collect in a stream like bubblegum and meld together in cold fusion. That's why it's so lumpy."

"I think it looks like a dragon," Grayson said.

"No, it's a lion," Riley said. Both of them rested their chins on the table, looking at the nugget. "With horns," she added.

"We've named it the Lioness," Abby said, and laughed.

"What will you do with it?" Carrie asked.

"Invest it," Willie answered for me, and we all turned to look at him. "We must determine the value: the exact weight, purity, and current gold prices," he said, and crossed his arms. "Although with some of these larger nuggets, there may be some inherent value to collectors as a whole. I know a guy I can ask."

I looked down at the floor and Abby asked, "Andy, do you want to sell it?"

Before I answered, Willie said, "Well, it won't do him any good in the grill or buried in the backyard. If I remember correctly, you're required to pay taxes on it, whether you sell it or not. Whatever value it has today, you just bought yourself a 28% federal and 7% Montana state tax. If the value of the gold is, say, 500,000 dollars," he did the math in his head, "you now owe 175,000 dollars."

"Seriously?" Abby asked.

Willie nodded, raising his hands in surrender.

"Do I have to tell anyone?" I asked out loud. "Can't I just stick the money in the bank?"

Willie laughed at my suggestion. "Look, you can throw it back in the river, I guess." He crossed his arms again. "Or give it to me...to invest, that is." He smiled.

The numbers made my head spin. "How much would I have left after taxes?"

"Close to 325,000 dollars."

"Wow, that's a lot of money," I said.

"What would you do with the money?" Carrie asked.

"I have to pay off my truck by Friday and pay rent the next week."

"How much do you owe on the truck?" Abby asked.

"Marty carries the loan. I don't know for sure, but he sold it to me for eighteen thousand."

"That piece of shit!" Willie exclaimed. I wasn't sure if he meant my truck or Marty.

"I also want to help Marty with any expenses of the accident," I added.

"No, no, and hell no!" Willie yelled. "That's exactly what you don't want to do. Don't be a fool." Willie sighed and lowered his voice. "Once it's gone, it's gone, Andy. I can help you turn that money into more money. That's what I'd do. Otherwise, you might as well chuck it out the window," he said, his anger returning.

"What's your cut?" Abby asked him.

Willie gave her a sour look, but winked at me and said, "We can work that out, Andy. Like our ad says, 'We do better when you do better.'"

"But Marty's going to take my truck back if I don't pay him by Friday."

"I say let him," Willie huffed.

Carrie grabbed my wrist. "Andy, if you really want to keep your truck, and we can't sell the gold by Friday, I bet we could loan you the money until then," she said, and looked at Willie for confirmation.

I couldn't read the look that Willie shot back at Carrie, but he shrugged. "I imagine we can get money for the gold by then, even if it's just an advance."

Like Carrie's mind finally caught up to an earlier discussion, she turned to me. "Andy, did you really do an interview with Oprah?"

19

PRAYER CANDLE

One of the worst parts about living in a single-wide, there was nowhere to store things. While cleaning this morning, I simply shuffled the clutter around. I stood by the table, twisted side-to-side, and decided that my attempt to put the trailer in order was as good as it would get.

I'd stacked some of Mama's boxes against one wall, then piled the rest in the bedroom, along with my dirty clothes, an assortment of dog toys, and closed the door. That room still looked like a disaster zone, but at least no one would go in there. "I probably needed to hang a hazard sign on the door," I said to Max, who spun in circles, sensing we were about to have company.

Perhaps if the gold afforded me anything, I could buy one of those pre-built storage sheds and stuff half of my junk in that. Willie had offered to store the nugget in his safe, but I'd read the look on Abby's face and told him I'd keep it with me. Willie promised to call me sometime this morning after he talked with the gold man. I honestly didn't know what gold did to people, but the lump of metal had mesmerized Willie and Carrie and even their kids.

Lying in bed last night, I'd pondered the fact so much I finally searched Google for answers. As the seventy-ninth element on the periodic table, it's listed as a transition metal, surrounded by platinum and mercury to the right and left and silver and the highly radioactive element roentgenium on the top and bottom.

As an element, scientists notated gold as Au, which came from the Latin, aurum, meaning the glowing dawn, perhaps representing the sun. But the mystique and hoopla surrounding gold and the look in people's eyes when they see it remained a mystery to me. I guess the rising of sun brought hope and maybe what echoed in their hearts when people admired the reflective metal.

For now, potential thieves would have to brave dirty laundry and an unmade bed to get to the nugget of hope under my mattress. At least I'd slept in my bed last night, but the chunk made for a lumpy mattress.

I glanced around one last time and nodded. My carvings and tools still cluttered the kitchen table, but I had nowhere else to store them. "I guess that will have to do," I said to Max, and walked to the corner of the trailer to light Mama's prayer candle that stood on a table as a shrine to God and Mama. "Man, I need some peace to stop my head from spinning and my mind from racing," I told Max. It was all too much, the attention, the gold…and I was too inadequate—the over-arching emotion that defined my life. I did not know what to do with any of it. If I didn't feel that way on my own, everyone around me readily reminded me of it. I guess except Mama…and Abby.

I looked at the picture of Pop, Mama, and me and my surviving siblings, the one that hung over our kitchen table growing up, but now completed my home altar on the corner table. Mama loved this small lamp table. She'd run her finger over the grainy top and tell me that her grandpa made it. It wasn't anything fancy, but like so much of what Mama loved, it was simple and rough-cut. "Kind of like me," I said to Max, who wagged his tail in agreement.

Besides the candle, a carved crèche I gave to Mama twenty years ago adorned the tabletop. Instead of the usual hand-hewn stable, I'd fashioned a teepee from sticks and rawhide. I thought it an appropriate housing for a Montana Christmas. The gift made Mama cry when she opened it, something that filled me with pride. Somewhere along the way, Joseph's arm holding his staff got busted off. Probably when a few of us were roughhousing. But he faithfully watched over Mary and baby Jesus while the three wise men admired the scene from the other side of the table.

Mama's Bible completed the contents of the altar. Not that I thought I suffered from an obsessive-compulsive disorder, but I laid my palm on the Good Book—always starting my prayers by running my hand over the worn leather. Growing up, I'd run my finger over the grain when I sat on her lap as she read passages to us. I imagined my actions brought me closer to her.

I made the sign of the cross then opened the Diamond matches, took one out and struck it across the box. The match flared, and I lit the candle. It wasn't the typical glass container votive candle with a religious icon printed on the side, but one of Pop's old Jack Daniel's bottles with a candle stuck in the mouth. He normally drank beer, but on special occasions he brought home a bottle of whiskey. And this one, for as long as I could remember, sat in the middle of our dining room table as a candleholder. I had burnt so many candles the wax now obscured the label, cascading like a rainbow waterfall. In fact, the lumpy, irregular wax reminded me of my gold nugget.

I set the box of matches down, crossed myself again, and watched the flame flicker. "Mama, I know you're there with God. Would you mind asking Him what I should do?"

I heard a car pull up and wondered who arrived first. My trailer was about to hold more visitors than ever before. Last night, Joseph called and said that they were hoping to air the program sooner rather than later and hoped to get some footage of me meeting the mother and baby. Apparently the doctors planned on releasing them in the next few days, and Oprah's team wanted video of us all in the hospital. I was still at Willie and Carrie's house last night when Joseph called. Until that moment, I'm not sure Carrie believed Oprah had interviewed me. Surprisingly, Carrie asked if she could join us today for the taping. How could I refuse showing off a bit in front of her, especially since Joseph said that Oprah might join them? But Willie reminded us all to say nothing about the gold nugget.

I looked at the prayer candle. "Forgive me, Father."

A knock on the door brought me to my senses and made the perspiration run down the inside of my shirt from my armpits. I blew out the flame and used my fingertips to extinguish the glowing ember on the end of the wick, wishing things could just return to normal.

It was Abby who stood on the porch when I opened the door.

"I didn't think I could get anyone to cover my route today…but surprise!" she said.

"Hey, Abby." I stepped outside and gave her a hug. "Thank you so much for coming to help keep me sane. I don't know about all this. It makes me so nervous."

"I don't think I can help with the sane part, but I'm glad

to tag along. You'll do fine," she said, and slugged me on the arm. She then looked around. "I must have beaten the princess here. I thought she'd be knocking down your door first thing this morning."

Before I could answer, Carrie's brand-new black Lexus bounced over the tracks.

"It's probably been a while since she's been on this side of those," Abby said. Even though Carrie grew up with us, her father was a physician so she had grown up without want. Their home even had a garage and a pool. "I'm surprised she could still find Milltown," Abby murmured. "By the way, it was sure nice of you to buy her the new Lexus."

I looked at her. I never thought of Abby as a cynical type, but in a way I had to agree. Willie had explained last night that he'd convinced the insurance company that the white one was a total loss from the septic explosion, and they provided a full replacement.

She smiled and shrugged. "I'll be nice, I promise." She held up three fingers in the Boy Scout's honor salute.

Carrie pulled in beside Abby's Toyota, and we waved away the resulting dust cloud.

She looked stunning as she hopped out of her car. Her hair bounced over her shoulders in large ringlets. Carrie's face hardly ever showed a blemish, and today was no exception, as her skin glowed smooth and flawless, like a professional had applied her makeup. She wore form-fitting linen pants and a lacy blouse.

"I'm not late, am I?" she asked, looking around.

"Oh shoot, you just missed her," Abby teased.

"Oh, you're kidding me. She was here, for reals?"

I guess I'd have to add sarcasm to the list of blond jokes and idioms that flew over Carrie's head. I smirked at Abby and then said to Carrie, "No, Abby's just kidding. They should be here any minute."

Carrie bounded up the steps and surprised me with a warm embrace. She smelled delicious, like cotton candy.

The same Escalade that Joseph arrived in last time pulled onto the dirt road, and Carrie turned but kept a hold of my arm. Her breast pushed into my side, and I took a small step sideways to pull away. My head spun enough already.

The SUV stopped and all four doors opened. Joseph stepped from the driver's side, and from the passenger side emerged the celebrity—Oprah. Just like at the studio, the atmosphere seemed to expand with her presence. She raised her arms in praise of the clear blue morning. "Big Sky country," she announced. "It's beautiful!"

A man with a shoulder camera and another staff member exited from the back seats of the Escalade. I sensed both Carrie and Abby move closer when the cameraman started filming.

Oprah marched right up the steps and gave me a warm smile and hug. "Hi, Andy. Thank you for inviting us to your home." She backed up and looked at the trailer and surrounding area, nodding her head. She said something, but choked back the words and her eyes misted over.

I reintroduced Abby, but Oprah interrupted me and hugged her as well. "Hi, sweetie," Oprah said. "Good to see you again, Abby."

Joseph joined us, nodded, and looked at his watch. "The other part of the crew is at the hospital, perhaps we should get going?"

"Oprah and Joseph, this is Carrie Carver…my friend."

They shook hands, but the lack of an endearing hug seemed to disappoint Carrie when she crossed her arms over her chest and lowered her gaze.

"Andy, do you mind us filming you in your home and then possibly walking out the door? I know it feels a bit staged, but Hollywood magic will make you look great."

"Just like Chris Hemsworth," Abby snorted.

I blushed, but Oprah grabbed my arm and pulled me toward the trailer. "Besides, you promised to show me the rest of your carvings."

We filed through the door. I never realized just how small my single-wide was until we crammed six people inside.

"Wow, you really cleaned up the place," Abby said.

Embarrassment heated my face and more perspiration dripped down my sides. I hated for everyone to see how I lived.

Oprah went right to the table. "Ah, the craftsman's work-shop," she said, and bent over to look at the carvings. She seemed to study each one and then stood. "Amazing, just amazing."

"Here are a bunch more," Abby said as she pointed to the soffit above the cabinets.

Oprah followed her to examine them.

Joseph patted me on the back. "She really wanted to come see you today," he said.

"I'm so embarrassed by my place," I whispered back.

"Oh, she understands. She grew up with very little. It doesn't bother her in the least," he said into my ear. "You should read her book. Remind me to get you a copy."

I watched as Oprah shook her head.

"Andy, dear...I am just speechless, and that doesn't happen very often." She laughed.

"Please take whichever one you'd like," I said.

She walked up to me and searched me with her beautiful dark eyes. A wide smile crossed her face, and she said, "You are something special, Andy Strobel."

20

BABY ANDREW

Oprah wouldn't take another carving. She told me they were much too valuable, and she'd have to teach me about entrepreneurship. Not sure what she meant by that, but Joseph suggested I bring one to give to the mother. I decided that was a great idea and held the carving of the Mandalorian in my hand as the hospital elevator door closed. I nodded at Joseph, who seemed in an exceptionally good mood.

It seemed kind of dumb, but they filmed me playing video games and then walking out of the trailer. They made me go through the doorway five times and kept telling me to act naturally. I guess whatever I did was not natural. It delighted Joseph and Oprah when I sat at the table and pretended to work on a carving. The cameraman then photographed my collection.

Abby held Max the entire time—except for when they wanted to film Max licking my still swollen and bruised face. While Abby was uncharacteristically quiet, Carrie hadn't stopped talking. But I was glad she carried the bulk of the conversation until Joseph had to tell her to shush. She may have caused one or two of the retakes. Now both women were especially speechless, standing in the back of the elevator. I turned to smile at them, thankful to have their support.

The elevator dinged for the third floor. "The hospital agreed to let us use a conference room for the meeting," Joseph said. "And the crew's ready for us. We're simply going to have you walk in and shake the mother's hand and exchange a few words."

I hope I don't screw that up too badly.

Oprah must have read my anxiety and patted me on the back. "You'll do fine, Andy."

Joseph led us down the hallway.

"It's only been four days since the accident. With her broken arm and leg, are you sure she feels up to this?" I asked, imagining her like what I'd seen on TV medical dramas— with tubes sticking out of every orifice.

Oprah looked at some papers she carried in her hand. "Her name is Suzanne, but she goes by Sue. She's married and has the one child. The doctors fixed both her leg and her arm, and she has already started physical therapy. They put a titanium rod in her leg...the wonders of modern medicine," she said.

As we rounded the corner into a large conference room, my eyes went wonky from the bright lights and camera flashes. A nurse led me by the arm to a young woman sitting in a chair holding a baby. She had frizzy dishwater-blond hair and wore a hospital gown. Her face mirrored mine—black raccoon eyes and bruising that extended down her nose and a large gash on her upper lip. She looked as scared and uneasy from the attention as I felt. Her baby, wrapped in a blue blanket, squirmed and fussed from the growing commotion. She readjusted the bottle so the nipple went back into his mouth, looked up at me, and gave me a smile that revealed a missing front tooth.

Her eyes reflected sadness, but she let go of the bottle and reached for my hand.

As we held hands, cameras whirred.

"I'm Andy," I finally said, not knowing anything better to say.

Her crow's feet deepened as she smiled. "Thank you," she said, and then refocused on the baby's bottle.

"Is he doing okay?" I asked.

"Thanks to you." She looked back up and nodded. A tear ran from the corner of her eye and down her cheek. She supported the baby with her splinted arm wrapped in an elastic bandage.

"Are you okay? I'm sorry your arm and leg got busted."

She wiggled her fingers from around the splint and extended her leg at the knee. "The docs tell me they put everything back together."

I nodded and glanced back at Oprah and Joseph, who remained at the doorway, hoping they would indicate that we were finished.

"Sorry you got banged up as well," Sue said. I looked back at her. "I'm so sorry," she said with compassion.

Oh God, here it is again. The cameras rolled, and now I had to come clean.

I glanced at Abby, who stood behind Oprah, then back at Sue.

"This was not your fault," I told her, circling my face with a finger. "My face got banged up in a fight the night before the accident." The words took my breath away, and the weight of my confession muddled my mind with guilt and shame.

"Mine, too." Sue's admission came like a whisper. "Well, no one asked me about it, but it's the reason we had the accident." She looked around the room at the doctors and nurses gathered, and the temperature in the place seemed to rise ten degrees. "I don't know why I didn't tell y'all. I guess I was ashamed. The boy's father did this to me that morning and I ran from him. Used a small bat..." Her voice drifted off, and she opened her mouth to show the gap to emphasize the point.

It sucked the oxygen out of the room, and she studied me for support. I knelt on one knee in front of her. "It's not your fault," I said again.

"I should never have been speeding through that construction, but I was so afraid he followed me." Now her tears flowed freely. "I don't know what I'm going to do. That car contained everything I owned." She looked at the medical staff again. "I have no way of paying for all this." The declaration made her weep, and I worried the baby might bounce off of her lap.

I reflexively reached for the infant and Sue let me take him. I sat on the floor and cradled the little guy, not having held a baby in a long while. At one time, I was the only person who could get my baby brother to fall asleep.

The infant whimpered, so I moved him to my shoulder and rocked him back and forth. Remembering that I still clenched the carving in my hand, I held it out to Sue. She finished wiping her tears and took it. She looked at it inquisitively.

"I carved it and wanted you and the baby to have it."

A smile broke out across her face, and she nodded in understanding. "You a Mando fan?" she asked. "The protector of little ones."

Joy rose inside me, knowing she knew the subtle meaning behind the carving. "This is the Way." I repeated the creed of the Mandalorian and grinned.

It made her and any other fans of the show in the room laugh.

I cradled the baby in my arms and lightly stroked his cheek. "What's his name?" I asked.

Sue exhaled a long sigh. "His father called him Lance, but I don't like that name." Tears brimmed her eyes again. "I guess since we're going to get a fresh start, I can give him a proper name. I looked up the meaning of Andrew. It means strong…would you mind if I name him Andy?"

I stood with Oprah and Joseph outside the hospital. They were unusually quiet during the meeting and the walk outdoors. I figured the interview didn't go as they had hoped, as Oprah didn't say a word.

"I'm sorry if I ruined it all," I said finally.

Oprah and Joseph looked at each other, and I took that as an affirmative. But they both smiled, and Oprah reached out to hug me. "Oh sweetie, that was one of the most amazing things I've ever seen. You're a natural."

"What are they going to do to protect her from that monster?" Carrie spoke up from behind us, red-faced and shaken from the story.

Abby turned to her. "I stood next to the social worker, and she whispered into my ear they were so glad to know the full story," she said. "They all figured there was more going on, but couldn't get Sue to talk about it. Now they'll make sure she has whatever she needs."

Oprah, who still had her arm around my waist, said,

"We'll follow up with the hospital and see if my foundation can help in any way." She squeezed me hard. "So Andy, how does it feel to have a namesake?"

I shook my head. "I just hope the little guy has an easier go of life than me."

THE GRIZ

T he gold man went by the nickname, Griz, and once I met him I understood why. A beard and mustache hid most of the man's face, and his baritone voice matched his bear-like persona. He humphed like a grizzly as he inspected the Lioness—a name he approved of. The man had placed the nugget in a sonic cleaner and now held it, wearing white gloves to inspect every crevice with a jeweler's eyepiece. I squinted against the reflection off the gold from the sun coming in from the store windows.

I smiled at Carrie, who had offered to drive me to meet Willie and Griz. It disappointed Abby that she had to return to work after the visit to the hospital. She whispered in my ear, "Please be careful, Andy."

Riding in Carrie's Lexus felt like entering another reality, but she joked I had bought it for her and giving me a ride was the least she could do to help. Just being alone with her felt odd, but as usual she got fifty-thousand words in from my trailer to the business. I nodded occasionally, and that seemed to satisfy her. When we arrived at the downtown store, the fact that Carrie and I spent time alone didn't seem to have bothered Willie. He didn't even seem to notice. He wore an expensive-looking dark suit and colorful tie, and was laser-focused on the Lioness, as was the gold man.

I glanced around the cluttered store. Several shelves adorned the walls, filled with collectibles and pricey geodes and rocks. In the center of it all were bright lights directed on the glass display cases, sparkling with gold of all types: jewelry, coins, even a few small bars and nuggets. The store's security locked it all up as tight as Fort Knox. Griz was definitely the gold guy.

Griz humphed again, and I looked back at him. He picked a small rock out of one crevice with a dental tool, then set the nugget on a piece of blue velvet and let the loupe fall from his eye into his hand. He looked at me, nodded, and his eyes narrowed.

"Where did you find it?" he demanded.

"I bet he discovered it on his ol' man's claim," Willie answered for me.

The heat that rose in my face probably betrayed me, but I promised Abby I'd keep this a secret. "I found it in the... Blackfoot," I stuttered. "Abby and I checked...it's all legal, I promise."

Griz's eyes narrowed again, but he let it go.

"What do you want to do with it?" Griz asked, like I stood in the *Pawn Stars* store.

I deflected his question with another, "What do you think it's worth?"

This made a smile appear under all his facial hair. "Well hell, son, that's a fair question."

He hefted his weight out of the undersized desk chair that squawked as he rose. Holding the nugget with the velvet swatch, he limped to a scale on the back counter. "Not sure this thing goes up high enough," he murmured, and placed the nugget on the metal plate.

He shook his head and waved us over. He took a step back, and I peered at the digital readout with Willie over one shoulder and Carrie over the other.

"Twenty-three point nine three seven," Willie and I said together, then I added, "I weighed it on my bathroom scale. My scale must be a pound and a half light." I blushed.

"Isn't that around three hundred eighty ounces?" Willie asked.

Griz had picked up a calculator and corrected Willie, "Three hundred eighty-two point nine nine two ounces to be exact."

Willie whistled.

"But you got to remember that nuggets aren't pure gold," Griz added quickly.

"So what would you estimate its purity at?" Willie asked.

Griz crossed his arms, humphed, and stroked his beard.

I didn't know what to expect, but the man finally answered.

"I've been doing this a long time, folks. Never held a nugget quite like this." He raised his hands in surrender. "Maybe 94%."

"Holy crap!" Willie exclaimed.

Lost in the math, my head spun.

Thankfully, Carrie asked, "So, the value is?"

"Let's sit," Griz suggested, and brought the nugget and calculator with him.

He limped to his desk, and both he and the chair groaned as he sat. He held out his hand to the empty seat in front of him for me to sit. Willie stood behind me like a proud father, with his hands on my shoulders.

"You ready to have your life change?" Griz asked and

tapped the clear button on the calculator several times. Then he looked at a digital sign that hung on the back wall. The scrolling number seemed to please him. It jumped from 1830 to 1860 and back down to 1851. "Okay, let's use 1850." He hit the clear button multiple times again.

Willie squeezed my shoulders.

He spoke the numbers as he entered them, "Okay, 382.992 times 0.94 times 1850." He grabbed the calculator and held the number to his eyes and again shook his head.

Griz smiled and turned the calculator to face us.

Willie read off the number, "Wow...666,000."

Willie patted my shoulders, and Carrie squealed.

All I saw were the triple sixes—*666*, the number of the devil. Mama hated that number and anything else associated with the beast. It caused me to instantly break out in a sweat.

"But you have to understand, this is all just an educated guess. Could be more, could be less."

At least that made me feel a little better that the number appeared as a fluke. I sat and stared at the Lioness.

"So what do you think?" Griz broke my trance.

"I just don't know—"

"Son, you don't have to do anything you don't want to do," Griz said. I thought I read sincerity in his eyes. "Honestly, if it was me, I'd hold on to it for its inherent beauty."

"Andy kind of needs the money," Carrie said.

"Well, you and the rest of the world," Griz said kindly. "I'd be happy to sell it for you. A nugget this size should be kept whole. Eventually, a collector would buy it."

"Eventually?" I asked.

"These things can take time, but I could probably have it sold in six months if I can find the right buyer."

"And if you don't?" Willie asked for me.

"Maybe a year or more," Griz said.

"Willie said I have to pay taxes on it right away."

He tilted his head. "Legally, yes. For sure when you sell it." He smiled at me. "But I ain't telling anyone you have it."

"Andy needs some money this week," Carrie said. "Can you advance some to him?"

"What kind of money are we talking about?" Griz asked.

"I owe a bit over fifteen thousand. Thought it would be less by now, but I called Marty this morning. I guess it's the interest he's charging me," I said. "He wasn't too happy to hear from me either and reminded me he'd repo the truck on Friday."

"Scoundrel," Willie grumbled from behind me.

"I have other bills like rent, power…and my phone."

"I'm afraid I'm not in the banking business. I've learned over the years that doesn't work out for me." He blew out a long sigh and stroked his beard again. "The only other option I have is to buy the nugget from you outright. That's the only other thing I can do for you." He waved his arms for his final offer.

"I don't know—" I said.

"Look, I'm taking a chance even doing that much. I could underestimate the purity…by a lot," he added. "When I broker it as a nugget, my fee is 25%. I'd only take 10% off the value to buy it outright," he said, sounding now more like a salesman.

He reached for the calculator and hit the clear button a time or two, but did the calculations in his head. "Ten percent of 666,000 is 66,600, minus the original price is—"

"Right at 599,400 dollars," Willie finished the math, but then picked up the calculator from under Griz's hand and started pushing buttons.

"If you pay 27% federal and 8% state taxes, that leaves you with 389,610 dollars."

The numbers jumbled in my head. All I knew was that it involved more money than I would ever have in my lifetime —perhaps ten lifetimes.

"That's not as much as you'd hoped for, I'm sure, but let me invest it and then it will make you a bunch more," Willie said, and put his hand back on my shoulder.

I looked at the black-and-white-checkered tile floor and laughed at Willie's statement. Before finding this dumb rock, I hoped for a job at McDonald's. I looked up at Carrie and she put her hand on my other shoulder.

"You do what's right for you, Andy," she said.

I searched her eyes for clues. I had to trust someone.

Then I turned toward Griz and thrust out my hand. "Okay."

I understood when the bank teller's eyes bulged after I handed her the check. I hadn't seen such numbers as well. Over a half-million dollars—close to six hundred thousand. She called the bank president over when I reassured her the check was legit. Willie instructed me simply to tell them I sold some family gold today. "They don't need to know anything more," he'd said.

The president said they would cash it, but for security they had to report such huge deposits. Also, the funds would not be available until the check cleared, which, because it was from another Missoula bank, could be as early as tomorrow.

"You think I did the right thing?" I asked Carrie as she turned to park in front of my trailer.

"Yes," she said, smiling at me. "It wouldn't do you much use as a paperweight. Besides, Willie can help you. He's good with money."

We exited her SUV and stood by the porch.

"Willie wants me to meet with him and a tax attorney tomorrow, to set up an investment account. He wants the lawyer to advise us on taxes and any issues with the gold claim. I guess he knows where I found it."

Carrie smiled. "I think we all do," she said, and motioned to zip her lips and throw an imaginary key over her shoulder. Carrie looked at her phone. "I guess I better go pick up the brats." She leaned in and kissed me on the cheek. "I'm very proud of you, Andy. The rescue, the interview with Oprah, the meeting with Sue and baby Andy…the gold."

I looked at her in shock, but she smiled, turned, and got into the Lexus.

I waved as she backed out.

I touched my cheek where the pressure from her lips lingered. "Here I am, richer than Richie Rich, and all I can think about is that kiss," I said to no one.

CURSES

The Mandalorian paced back and forth past the lineup of
men and women. Sparks dripped from the walls and the
smell of molten steel burned my nostrils. The pounding and
grinding of mechanical gears and hammers rang in my ears, and
the taste of fear stuck in the back of my throat. I glanced to my
right and then the left. The group stood at attention but appeared
exhausted and dirty. Their clothes and emotions hung tattered
and dejected. I'm sure I looked the same. Glancing down at my
legs, my torn pants revealed wounds and scabs in various stages.
An open scrape from where the grade-school gym teacher tossed
me across the room oozed with infection and pain.

The inspection puzzled me. The expressionless aura of the
helmeted warrior examined each person. If he said anything, I
couldn't hear his words over the sounds of metal against metal.

I stared straight ahead. On the rugged table in front of the
lineup, bars of shiny Beskar steel were neatly stacked—an odd
harbinger to the chaos surrounding us.

Why was I here? I didn't belong. I never belonged. Yet
Mando searched. My knees went weak as he inspected the woman

next to me, then sidestepped and towered over me. I could see my reflection in the dark visor and Beskar steel helmet.

Without a nod or indication, he bypassed me and moved to the next person in line.

Just what I expected. Nobody ever picked me. I was never the one.

The mechanical hammering and thunderous hum of the surrounding machines crescendoed as Mando reached the end of the row. He stepped to the table and put his hand on the stack of valuable steel.

He raised his other hand, and the cacophony ceased instantly. Sweat dripped from my body. The temperature in the room was stifling. Perhaps this was it—a firing line. The Mandalorian would pull his blaster from his holster and annihilate us all.

Oh, my God. Is it me he's staring at? It was so hard to tell with the helmet shielding his gaze.

"Andrew!" his voice bellowed. "Come forward."

My feet wouldn't move.

"Come forward!" he demanded again.

One step forward, then another. I stood feet from Mando and my eyes stared at the armor covering his legs, then up his chest and to his helmet.

"I pick you," he intoned, his voice resounding in my quaking body.

He put his hand firmly on my shoulder as if he was tapping me out and placing a heavy mantle on my shoulders.

"You are the one."

I couldn't catch my breath.

"Andrew, you must do the right thing…no matter what."

I fought for air. My arms and legs seemed locked down and my body frozen.

Air. Finally. I gulped it down.

My brain jolted awake, and I shifted my body. My head

found its way out from under the covers. The room was pitch-black. I'd soaked my sheets with sweat.

I rolled onto my back and wiped the perspiration off my face. Max whimpered and then licked my neck.

A powerful dream, but I also knew it was a warning.

I had to do the right thing.

Father P pronounced a blessing over the parishioners, and I sat down on the pew.

My morning had started with a strong cup of coffee to clear my head from the dream. Since I didn't have to rush out to look for a job, I'd allowed myself the luxury of sleeping in. A call from the bank woke me at nine. I thought something had gone wrong when I recognized the voice of the president of the bank. I figured the check had bounced and the gold man had duped me. But it surprised me to learn that the check had cleared, and they had already placed the money in my account. He politely inquired if he could do anything personally for me and asked that I stop in soon to talk.

Jokingly, I almost asked if he'd bring me a coffee, but instead I just thanked him.

The president also apologized for his suspicion yesterday and told me he was sorry he didn't recognize me as the guy from the news. "It's just that we rarely see a check for that amount," he explained.

I told him not to worry about it, and that I didn't either.

I dreaded my meeting with Willie and the attorney at eleven-thirty. Pop trusted lawyers about as much as he trusted his bosses at the mill. "Both," he'd said, "are as welcome as an abscessed tooth."

Willie deemed it necessary, and I guess if the woman could help, I'd meet with them.

Until then, I killed time by going to morning mass. I hoped to have some time to talk with Father P afterwards. I leaned back on the cool wooden pew and closed my eyes, hoping the ladies passed me by.

Through my squinted eyes, I saw Mrs. Jarvi walk past me, then back up a few steps.

"Three times at church in a week, Andy. Good for you," she said. "Have you seen my lawn? We're going to need a hay wagon if you don't mow it soon." She furrowed her brow, and her voice grew stern.

"Mrs. Jarvi, I am so sorry. I'll get to it this afternoon. I promise."

That seemed to pacify her, and she added, "I know you will, dear. Thank you. You've had a lot on your mind. I've seen lots of visitors." She raised one eyebrow.

My face flushed. She'd always had acute radar regarding my comings and goings. *What if she saw Carrie kiss me?* I wasn't sure why it embarrassed me so. Maybe that was part of why I came to talk with Father P—Carrie was a married woman after all.

The priest escorted Mrs. Jarvi and the other women who regularly attended morning mass to the front door, and I heard it close behind them.

I sat with my eyes closed until the pew creaked under the weight of Father P.

"Good morning, Andy," he said in his strong Greek accent. "Good to see you again." He reached and patted my back. "But I'm not surprised. Mrs. Jarvi whispered to me you have enjoyed the company of some ladies." He rolled his eyes and swayed in the pew.

My stomach gurgled loudly, and heat flushed my neck.

"No worries, your secrets are safe with me," he bellowed. "Hey, Andy. Do you know what you get when you combine a priest with a lawyer? A father-in-law." His roar echoed off the rafters, and he slapped my back hard enough for me to cough out a laugh.

"Get it?" he laughed again. I got it, but maybe he didn't realize how close he'd hit the mark regarding my meeting later this morning.

"You okay?" his tone turned serious.

"I have to meet with a lawyer this morning."

"Uh-oh, now what?"

I looked at him, a little offended that he thought it was something bad.

"No…no, nothing like that. It's actually for kind of a good reason."

He raised his eyebrows in interest. I did not know where to start.

"I discovered a little gold," I whispered.

"At your father's claim?"

Jeesh, I guess everyone knew about that. I would not lie to the priest.

"Well, kind of. Below it, in the river. I found a nugget."

"Good for you, Andy, good for you! What are you going to do with it?"

"I sold it." I looked Father P in the eyes.

"Well, there is nothing wrong with that, Andy. Got yourself a little spending money, huh?"

"A little more than a little." I watched his eyes again, looking for gold fever.

"Good." He nodded.

I had to tell him to get the weight off my chest. "I sold it for just under six hundred thousand dollars, after the gold guy took his cut." I didn't want to tell him the 666 thing.

"You mean six thousand dollars?"

"No, really…six hundred thousand."

The big man leaned back and bobbed his head. "Oh my," he finally said.

"I'm required to pay a bunch of taxes, I guess. I meet with an attorney later this morning."

Father P folded his hands in prayer and closed his eyes. I wondered what he thought.

Finally, he opened his hands and smiled at me. "God has blessed you beyond measure, my son. It would be good for you to show your gratitude and tithe to the church."

I knew he was right, but I searched his eyes. Perhaps he had caught gold fever as well.

I drove down Highway 200 and decided since I was writing checks, I might as well stop at Butterfly Septic and write one to Marty. I couldn't wait to see his face, but I bet it wouldn't compare to the surprised look of Father P.

After confession, we discussed the tithe. Should I write it for 10% of the gross or net from the Lioness? Father P told me only I could decide that, and Mando's voice from my dream echoed in my ears. "Do the right thing."

My hand shook as I wrote the check for fifty-nine thousand nine hundred forty and xx dollars. I actually had to write two checks, voiding the first. Having never written such a large number and not knowing how to do it, I started by inscribing fifty thousand plus nine thousand plus nine hundred…before I ran out of room on the line. Father P helped me condense it to rewrite the correct amount.

I turned onto Riverside and then into Butterfly Septic. The building looked kind of pathetic to me suddenly. At least all the guys were out, and Marty would be alone to rib me.

The door to the shop squawked when I opened it, and I walked to the back to Marty's office.

"Well, Mother Mary of God and baby Jesus, look who the barn cat drug in. You have a whole lot of frickin' nerve to show your ugly face around here." His cigar bounced as he shot more curses at me. He must have already finished his pack of donuts, as the powdered sugar coated the front of his shirt. I let him spew.

"Number One is at the junkyard and damn if they didn't charge me two hundred dollars to take it. The frickin' scoundrels!" He slapped his hand on the desk. His face turned crimson. "Insurance only valued my truck at a measly four thousand dollars. You know what I can buy for that, shit-for-brains? A big fat ulcer, that's what." He thumped his fist on his chest and belched to emphasize the point.

Afraid the whole thing might give him a heart attack, I interrupted his rant by extending the folded check to him.

"What's this?" He glowered at me.

"You ain't suing me or some other knuckle-headed idea, now that you're a big shot on TV, are ya?"

I simply smiled and pushed it further toward him.

He warily took the check from my hand and unfolded it. I thought his cigar might drop as his mouth gaped open. He looked at me with suspicion and then thrust it back at me. "Yeah right, turd-face. You don't have that kind of money."

I took a step backward and held up my hands in surrender.

He laughed again and threw it hard toward the floor. It fluttered to the filthy linoleum, but he said, "Just seeing how far it will bounce."

I bent to pick it up and brushed off some dirt. It read

fifteen thousand five hundred and xx dollars, just like Father P had taught me.

"Paid in full," I finally said, and held it out to him.

He snatched the check back, like I might rescind my offer.

"Can I have the title?"

"You can have the frickin' title when I say you can have the frickin' title," he said in a sickening grade-schooler's voice. "When the check clears the bank," he added. "Where did you get this kind of money?" He scowled.

I wasn't about to tell him.

"If this thing is no good, I'm taking back my truck and a piece out of your hide."

LAWYER

I stood at the front door, looking up at the six-story building in downtown Missoula. As far as I could tell, the law firm of Borke, Finch, and Donahue owned the entire block except for the Subway and a bagel shop on each corner of the first floor. How in the world could they afford such an amazing structure? It was nicer than the Hollywood studio. I'd often driven by the fancy, copper-tinted window building in Number One and always thought it housed a bank or business that had bunches of money.

The script carved in the granite above the door, BFD, gave off an air of old money. I sighed. Being able to write checks to the church and Marty took some weight off my shoulders, but I hoped Willie wouldn't be too upset that I'd spent some of the money. He knew I needed to pay off the truck. I still didn't know what to do about wrecking Number One, and I felt bad for Marty. Losing a rig from the fleet would hurt Butterfly more than the sentimental value of losing the truck that started the entire business. Marty was definitely a curmudgeon, but it was my fault, after all, that the truck ended up in the river. Maybe for grins I should visit the Mack dealership just to see what it would cost to replace it. I honestly had no idea how much a septic truck cost.

I looked at Willie's text where he told me to go to the fourth floor and ask for Emma Rankin. He'd meet me there at 11:30. My stomach growled at the smell of fresh bread coming from the Subway, and I hoped this meeting was short so I could get lunch then fulfill my promise of mowing Mrs. Jarvi's lawn. I wanted to give her a check as well for my rent. I'd even thought of pre-paying some of it.

Pushing through the front doors, I went to the elevator bank stamped with the same monogram. I chuckled to myself. "Imagine being rich enough to own your own elevators," I mused.

Others filed in behind me and the doors closed. I glanced down at my faded jeans and worn t-shirt, and realized I was sorely underdressed compared to the other people in the elevator. The men wore suits and ties, and the women were in fancy business dresses or pant-suits. I just hoped my perspiration didn't make me stink. *I wish Abby was with me.* She was good at this sort of thing. I had spoken with her early this morning and told her my plans for the day. She made me promise to not sign anything with Willie. I invited her out for a nice dinner so we could talk about any contracts. It was the least I could do for all she'd done for me.

People exited the elevator on each floor until it arrived at the fourth. The doors opened to an extravagant, dark-paneled entry with an attractive young woman at an expansive desk. On the wall behind her hung a sign with the same lettering of the law firm—BFD—in script surrounded by an immense circle and back-lit with soft teal lighting. I swallowed down a smirk and wondered if anyone else noticed that BFD could stand for 'big frickin' deal'. Maybe they did and thought it to be true as well.

The young woman held up a finger as I approached the desk and murmured into a headset. I felt my face flush when she looked me up and down and probably assumed I was a transient off the street, something there seemed to be more and more of in downtown Missoula these days.

"May I help you?" she finally said to me.

"Uh…uh, I'm here to see a Ms. Rankin."

"Is she expecting you?" She frowned.

"Yes…I think so. I'm Andy Strobel."

A look of recognition crossed her face, and she nodded. "Yes, of course, Mr. Strobel. Let me escort you back."

I followed her shapely figure down the hallway. *Mr. Strobel…jeesh, I guess now I'm a BFD too,* I thought, and laughed to myself.

We turned the corner into a large office and interrupted Willie mid-sentence. He and the woman behind the desk laughed together, and I sensed they'd been talking about me. It made me mad, but I tried not to show it. It reminded me of grade school in Bonner when Willie made fun of me in front of his friends.

The middle-aged woman with cropped black hair stood from behind the desk and came around with her hand extended. "You must be Mr. Strobel."

We shook hands. "Yes. Andy," I said.

"Willie was just telling me you guys grew up together out in Milltown. Sounds like simpler times for sure," she said, and offered me the leather chair next to Willie.

"Hey, bro, I told Emma about the day we set off the fire alarm in eighth grade."

I looked at him, smiled, and gave an obligatory chuckle. He made it sound like we'd grown up best friends. We weren't, and I was confident that he didn't remember that I went home sick that day.

Emma sat behind the enormous mahogany desk. "I hear congratulations are in order on your find. That's fantastic." She opened a folder and fanned out some papers across the desktop. "Yesterday, after Willie called to set up this meeting, I researched your father's claim and confirmed that he left it to you."

I glanced at Willie, and he smiled. "Carrie told me."

"Well, it really wasn't on his claim," I said in defense. "Just below it," I admitted.

Emma must have read my discomfort. "That's okay, Andy. But if the gold came from the cliff, we need to solidify the claim." She handed me a near-photographic-quality bird's-eye image of the Blackfoot River, Gold Creek, and the Strobel Cliff. She had drawn Pop's twenty-acre claim with red boundaries. "Can you mark the approximate location where you found the nugget?" She gave me a red Sharpie.

The crisp image and the clear water of the Blackfoot revealed the fishing hole. It was amazing to see it from this viewpoint. I placed an X on the spot and handed it back to her.

She examined it and nodded. "You're sure?"

I smiled. "I know the river well."

"Do you think you understand the boundaries of your father's claim as accurately?"

I nodded my head and thought about how often Pop had proudly shown us the corners of the property. Even though we all knew we didn't own the land, it was the closest thing to it that any of us would ever have.

"You should go and clearly mark the corners, if they're not already established."

"Can you do that soon?" Willie added.

"Sure," I said.

Emma handed me another piece of paper with illustrations entitled: "Acceptable Examples of Conspicuous and Substantial Monument," which described how to denote the corners correctly.

"This is how you should mark your claim. We should think about getting an official survey as well," she said, then smiled. "I'm not sure how much you know about mining claims and the laws surrounding them. Your father only has a placer claim left since he never found a vein of gold to file for a lode claim. But just in case, I've finished the paperwork to do so. We have to pay the annual maintenance fee for the original claim on or before December thirtieth. We'll do that today when we file for the lode claim," she explained.

I nodded.

"The only complicating factor I can find is that there is usually a quarter-mile buffer zone around the location of a mining claim on either side of a stream while the watershed is studied for possible inclusion in the Wild and Scenic River System. I don't think that section of the Blackfoot is under consideration, but the sooner we file all the paperwork the better."

I swallowed hard.

"Don't tell anyone else about your find. Word is bound to get out anyway, but we don't want people scrambling around the rocks looking for gold."

"How much will all this cost?" I asked.

"My fee is three hundred dollars an hour, but it shouldn't be over three or four hours of work."

She smiled and rattled off a list of laws, forms, and permits. "Form 3830-2, Permit 43 CFR 3500, Regulation 43 CFR Parts 3834, 3835…"

I stopped listening. All I could think about was three

hundred dollars an hour. Since I made twelve-fifty at Butter-fly, I couldn't imagine. No wonder I sat in such fancy surroundings.

Mrs. Jarvi's husband had bought the push mower forty years ago, and it cut like it. And she was right—the grass had over-grown to the point of almost needing a scythe. The lawn encircled Mrs. Jarvi's home, then extended around my trailer and the other rental house on the corner. I had vowed to mow the entire area, and in turn she promised to not raise my rent like so many other landlords.

But on this hot June day, as the sun beat down and the grass hard to push through, I regretted my pledge. Honestly, I guess I'd probably mow it anyway out of courtesy to my ninety-two-year-old neighbor. The long grass required that I mow one short strip, bag the grass, and then go back over it another time or two to cut the stragglers down. Black garbage bags rapidly accumulated for the trash pickup, so now I'd have to listen to Mrs. Jarvi's complaints of the cost increase from the garbage company.

The only one that enjoyed the chore was Max. He found a neatly mowed spot and laid in the cool grass on his back, with all four legs drooped limply apart. His tongue dangled out the side of his mouth. If I didn't know better, I'd have thought the poor thing was dead.

However much I sweated, I'd rather do this than sit another minute in the haughty lawyer's office. Ms. Rankin was nice enough, but spoke in an unfamiliar language. She might as well have scrawled the paperwork in Greek with its 'whereas to, upon written request, moreover during the life-time,' and on and on for twelve pages. I'm not sure I understood any of it, and what was meant to instill trust made me that much more suspicious. Willie had other documents he needed me to sign and also to write a check to set up the investment account with Gray Financial Advisors. He seemed perturbed that I wanted to take them home and read them. To keep from making him mad, I never told him I'd already spent some of the money.

Mrs. Jarvi zig-zagged through the mowed rows, balancing a glass of ice water on a tray. Not sure why she didn't just hold the glass, but she liked to do things proper-like. I shut down the mower as she approached, and it sputtered off.

"You taking care with Mr. Jarvi's mower?" She scowled.

Little did she know, over the past year I'd replaced much of it at my own expense and it worked better now than when she assigned me to it. I just smiled, and she softened her tone.

"Andy, it's so hot out here today. I wish you would have started earlier in the morning."

She didn't know how much I agreed and picked up the glass of ice water off the tray. "Thank you, Mrs. Jarvi. Just what I needed," I said, and took three gulps.

"It's looking nice, Andy." Then, like she had a different agenda for tottering out, she looked at me and said, "I see some lady friends coming to visit you...when are you going to settle down?"

My upper body and face burned already, so I was sure I couldn't get more flushed, but I chuckled with embarrassment. All I could think of saying was, "I'd like to."

"Well, I'd move you into the big house," she said, and pointed to her other rental. "That couple is too...rambunctious," she said, then blushed, as if she kept an ear to her window at night.

She always called the other tenants "that couple," like she

didn't remember their names, but I'm sure they became heavy fodder for gossip with the Women's Club.

"I'd have to charge you a little extra, but I'd be fair," she added, and smiled.

"Speaking of rent," I said. "I've come into a little money and wanted to pre-pay my rent for the year." I reached into the back pocket of my jeans, produced the folded check, and handed it to her.

She unfolded the check for ten thousand eight hundred dollars and looked at it with suspicion. Just like Marty did.

"Oh my," she finally said, and squinted. "Andy Strobel, where did you get this kind of money?"

I knew she'd ask, so I'd thought up a story about getting back pay. But then she bluntly asked, "You're not selling drugs, are you?" My conscience made my head hurt, and I blurted out, "I found a gold nugget in the river the other day."

I tried reading her look. It seemed to be a mixture of reflection and understanding.

"Did your father's claim finally produce?"

If I could get my leg to bend around that way, I would have kicked myself in the rear. But she had said it in such a tone that contained no suspicion, malice, or shame. There was almost joy in her voice, like an underdog team winning a game. Maybe all these years, I'd been reading this wrong. Perhaps folks secretly rooted for the ol' man. If someone hit it big in the beat-down community, it gave other people hope.

"But please, Mrs. Jarvi, you can't tell *anyone*," I said too strongly for my liking. "My attorney and Willie would kill me." I regretted giving her even more gossip.

"Okay, dear," she said, and started walking to the house. Then turned. "The trash company is going to charge me an arm and a leg to haul away all those bags."

MACK

The Mack truck dwarfed the scrawny salesperson and me. The man appeared twice my age but was shorter and skinnier, which of course is not saying much. A cigarette hung from his mouth with a large ash cylinder ready to drop onto his shirt at any moment. Besides the chain smoking, he had a pleasant and jovial personality, and I was glad to meet with him before my dinner with Abby.

The man slapped the hood of the shiny gray diesel with well-deserved pride. "It's a beauty, don't you think?"

The 2021 Mack Granite tri-axle septic vacuum truck was a sight to see as it idled with a deep throb. Adorned with chrome accents in every place possible, it would be a shame to fill it with poop. The front grill and bumper reminded me of something out of the movie *Mad Max*, and people wouldn't be as apt to turn in front of it when they saw it headed their way. Besides, it had two air horns on the roof of the cab which, when blown, would give them a fright. It was further accented with a chrome exhaust pipe, enormous mirrors, extra exterior lighting, and silver vents on the sides of the cab that made it appear as if it was moving when standing still. Even the steps and tank were stainless. There was not one part of the truck that didn't reflect the sun.

The only accessory of a different color was a gold hood ornament. I stood on my tiptoes to get a better look at it.

"You know the history of the Mack symbol?" the man asked as he blew a large smoke ring and finally tapped the cigarette. We both watched the ashes fall to the ground.

I shrugged.

"Mack got their start during World War One," he said. "When the company shipped them to Europe, the soldiers all thought the front resembled the English bulldogs and named them such. After the war, the chief engineer had a medical issue sideline him and he sought something to keep his hands busy. He ended up carving a bulldog...and here it is," he said, and pointed to the emblem.

Now I understood why the dog appeared so blocky. I could have done a better job, but I loved the idea of one of my carvings gracing the front of such an exquisite truck.

"You said you were a septic guy, so you're going to appreciate this," he said, and waved me to the side of the rig.

He opened a stainless compartment behind the cab. "All your controls are in here. Super simple...but watch this." He depressed a lever and hydraulics tilted the entire tank toward the back until the front of the tank rose five feet from the bed.

"Holy cow!" I said. "No more climbing in and washing it out?"

"Exactly," he said. "You considering starting your own business? We have some pretty decent loan rates right now."

"No, I'm just looking. I wrecked my boss's."

A look of recognition crossed his face. "I was thinking you seemed familiar. You're that guy. I have a picture on my wall of that old truck with Marty's logo on the side, nose first into the Clark Fork. Funniest thing ever...well, I mean it's amazing you survived the fall."

I patted the front of the rig. "How much does something like this go for?"

"A mere two hundred twenty-five thousand." He gave a Groucho Marx eyebrow wiggle. "Actually, Marty's been in several times looking at it. He just doesn't have the finances to qualify for the loan."

I nodded.

"The owner is planning on sending it back to Mack, not sure we'll ever sell it here in Missoula. Bet he'd make you a deal," he said as a joke.

I'd reserved a window table at Missoula's best-rated restaurant overlooking a beautiful evening as the Clark Fork River rippled by. Sitting across from Abby, I didn't mean to embarrass her, but her cheeks glowed when I awkwardly told her she looked pretty tonight. I couldn't remember exactly how I'd said it. Something like, "You know how to fix yourself up." She really looked different. I'd never seen her with makeup on and her hair pulled into a bun. She wore a blue and pink summer dress with a string of small pearls.

"Well, I thought I would dress up for a night on the town." She smiled. If I'd blown the compliment, she covered for me.

The way she'd put on her eye makeup, I recognized her Asian heritage as well tonight. "Remind me sometime when we're at my place to show you the Oriental chest that Mama owned. Her father brought it back from Japan after the war. The chest is hand-carved, and my grandfather told her that the artisan may have taken his entire lifetime to carve it. It's truly something. Kind of inspires me to work on a bigger piece," I said.

"I don't remember seeing it," Abby said, and took a sip of water.

"It's in my bedroom..." I said, then choked on a bite of bread, realizing what I had just suggested.

"Oh, I see how you roll, Andy Strobel. Butter a girl up with a nice dinner and then invite her back to your bedroom."

She let the remark dangle long enough that I couldn't tell if she was teasing as I washed the bread and my unintentional suggestion down with a sip of water. Then she finally gave such a loud hoot, the people at the surrounding tables looked at us.

When I tried to apologize, it made her laugh that much harder.

"Oh, Andy. I hope you know I'm just kidding."

"Well, I..." I said, and then changed the subject. "You should have seen that truck today, Abby. It truly is something." I took another bite of bread. "I about passed out from the price."

"You really thinking of buying Marty a truck? He's not exactly one of my favorite people." She frowned.

"I don't know...I wrecked his. I guess I feel like I owe him."

"Just so you know, I don't think anyone would blame you if you walked away from him and Butterfly Septic."

"I know, but I have the money," I said, and smiled. "By the way, thanks again for your offer to look over the paperwork from Willie and the lawyer. I don't understand why they have to make it so dang complicated."

"I think it's how they make their money." She laughed. "I'll read them over tonight," she said, but her eyes filled with a sparkle. "Unless, that is…you want to show me that carved chest." She laughed hard enough to bring tears to her eyes that she wiped with her napkin.

I finally chuckled with her, then turned serious again. "I want to pay you for your time, too, Abby."

"No," she said without hesitation. A streak of disappointment crossed her face. "No, it's your money, Andy. I don't want any of it. This is nice enough what we're doing tonight. Please, no," she said again to make it clear.

I searched her eyes. If Abby had caught gold fever, it had passed.

She smiled at me and asked, "Andy, what do you want to do with the money?"

I stared out the restaurant window at the Clark Fork River. The setting sun cast hues of pink across the evening sky and reflected on the river. A lone angler stood in knee-deep water, frantically whipping his pole and dry-fly back and forth. Probably just got off the plane with all the newest Orvis gear. The man looked good, but the only thing I imagined he'd catch was himself.

Just as the thought floated through my mind, his backcast looped around and hit him square in the back of the head, implanting the hook in his hat.

Abby followed my gaze. "Looks like you need to give that guy some lessons."

I nodded.

"I don't know," I answered her original question. Sorrow swelled in my chest. "Seems like my entire life has been mostly a disappointment. Maybe the money will change things."

"Perhaps," she said. "For me, I'm working with my therapist on finding contentment from within. You know, learning how to enjoy the simple things in life."

"I guess I could use the money to see a counselor." I smiled.

"Well, it never hurts to heal those parts from the past," she said. "Besides, once Oprah's program airs, you're going to have women crawling all over you."

"Sounds kind of like scabies," I said, and snorted.

Abby looked out the window, and this time I followed her gaze as we sat in silence. She processed something internally, then turned back to me, smiled, and sighed.

"You okay?" I asked.

"Going inside is a lot of work. I'm working hard on a lonely part of me," she said, paused, then added, "I've gone out a couple times with guys, and they only seem interested in one thing." She made a funny face and tilted her head toward her lap. "Otherwise, I think men look at me with either pity or figure I have some sort of contagious disease. Like if they sleep with me their arm will shrivel and they'll develop a terrible limp."

"I'm so sorry, Abby." It made me mad that people could be so cruel. But I knew it all too well myself. "I think you're pretty swell."

"Oh, you're sweet, Andy Strobel. But when all those ladies come knocking, I'm going to have to teach you some better compliments," she said, and hit me on the forehead with a piece of bread.

We laughed just as the server wheeled over a cart with our seafood tower.

The closest thing to seafood I ate growing up were the occasional crawdads caught from the river or frozen fish sticks. "Wow," I said, and Abby echoed.

"Okay, folks. I hope you're hungry," the waiter said, and carefully transferred the three-story tower to the middle of our table. "On top are your steamed mussels and clams," he indicated with his hand. "Tier two is the succulent scallops and oyster Rockefeller on a half shell along with barbecue shrimp. And finishing off this decadence," he moved his hand to the bottom tray, "you have your lobsters and Dungeness crab."

"Oh my gosh, Andy, you really are trying to make me swoon."

Seeing Abby's eyes dance with delight as she examined the tower made my heart swell. I couldn't believe I was spending over two hundred dollars for a meal, but when Abby read the description of the dinner and said, "Can you imagine?" I knew I had to order it. And for the first time in my life, I could afford it.

The waiter lit the butter warmers in front of each of us and placed a few other small bowls of sauces around our plates. "Okay, enjoy," he said, and wheeled the cart away.

I examined the odd-looking food and grimaced. I had no idea how or where to start.

"Have you ever seen anything like this?" Abby asked.

I shook my head and smiled.

THE GIFT

Driving the new Mack truck, I couldn't be happier unless I'd won the Mega Million Lottery. I guess I kind of had in a way. Well, enough money I could write the shocked salesman a check for 198,000 dollars. He thought it was a joke when I pulled in this morning and told him I'd like to buy it.

It took a while to convince his sales manager, but I negotiated the price down and got the bank president on the phone, who reassured him I had the money in my account. I'd wished I had my camera ready to photograph the slack-jawed sales staff all lined up to watch me drive away.

I told the manager it was old family money, which I figured wasn't really a lie, for as all we knew the gold oozed out of Pop's claim. Still not knowing what to tell Marty, I just hoped I didn't give him a heart attack when I pulled in. I loved the feeling of generosity—this was the best I'd ever felt about myself.

I turned the new Mack toward the on-ramp of the interstate and smiled to myself. The dashboard looked like something from inside the Mandalorian's spaceship. The dealership had spent two hours going through all the buttons and capabilities of the modernized heavy-duty truck. The Mack shifted automatically and smoothly as I merged onto the freeway. I depressed the accelerator pedal, which the company termed the MackCellerator because of a two-position throttle, the first for 100% power and the second position for downshifting and passing. Without a manual clutch, the computer controlled the mDrive HD transmission and automatically sensed which of the fourteen gears maximized performance. No more tired shoulders from the manual shifting from one gear to another and the strong-arm steering of old Number One.

And to top it all off, it was a comfortable ride. The new two-toned, ultra-leather premium seats and leather-wrapped steering wheel ensured that. For good measure, I gave two long blows of the air horns, which I'm sure echoed around the Missoula Valley. I had arrived. I'd never flown this high or felt so happy.

The day had started with Abby waking me up with a phone call to thank me again for such a wonderful night. We both admitted we were still stuffed and couldn't believe we finished off the seafood tower of power. I told her that by the time I got home, I swore my gorged belly made me look pregnant. She said she'd have to diet for a month.

We'd laughed through the entire meal. Between a crab leg accidentally getting flung across the room, butter dripping down our chins, and the odd-looking mussels I'd refused to eat at first but became one of my favorites, it turned into a memorable night. I agreed with Abby that the primary purpose of seafood is as a delivery system for butter. We must have slurped up a whole stick each. Abby had struggled with her weak arm to pry open the crab and lobster, but I helped her, which just brought a more intimate sharing of the meal. In turn, she'd motion to me when the drip of butter from my chin grew large enough to fall…which it ended up doing multiple times, anyway—my shirt looked like a grease shotgun had riddled it by the end of dinner.

When the server offered to bring us the dessert menu, we chuckled with him. "Only if it comes with a stretcher," Abby had said.

Abby teased me a few more times about coming to see the Oriental chest in my bedroom, but I knew she just kidded me. I didn't think she or any other girl would really be interested in me like that. Not sure how it all works anyway, except for what I'd seen on the internet. It relieved me when we hugged and said goodnight, with Abby's promise to go through the lawyer's paperwork.

She'd told me this morning that she thought the lawyer's mumbo-jumbo made sense—writing it all for the benefit of further staking my gold claim and keeping me out of Dutch with the taxman or other government agencies. Abby had more concerns with Willie's paperwork and wanted to talk it out with me before I signed.

After spending so much money the last two days there was less money for Willie to manage, which was okay with me. With the debt to Marty and my truck paid off, and rent pre-paid for a year, the balance of 115,000 dollars and change still provided a ton of money for me. Almost five years of my salary, and if Willie could invest it and make more, maybe it could stretch for six years or longer, depending on what kind of job I found.

I pushed on the MackCellerator and the diesel shifted into its last gear and glided down the road. With an empty septic tank and the 505-horsepower engine, the truck had some get up and go. The Camelback suspension provided both a stable and smooth ride—a dream compared to the trouncing I'd taken in old Number One.

The Bonner exit rapidly approached, so I flicked on the blinker and exited. As if the mechanical marvel could read the road signs, it shifted to the lower gears as I let my foot off the accelerator. When I braked slightly, the engine throttled back, and I cruised easily around the cloverleaf.

I turned left onto Riverside just as a loud ringing startled me. I had forgotten that the salesman showed me how the truck hooked to the Bluetooth on my cell phone, but I hadn't expected a call. I pushed the answer button on the steering wheel.

"Hello?" I said tentatively, worried the check had bounced and I should immediately return the truck.

"Andy? Andy Strobel?" a woman asked.

"Yes, this is Andy."

"Oh hi, Andy. You sounded like you were in a jet plane or something. This is Sue…Suzanne…you know, from the accident."

"Hi Sue, I was just thinking about you and your baby this morning and wondering if you'd gone home yet." I felt bad that I said "home," as I knew she didn't have one to return to.

"They're discharging me this afternoon, and I'd hoped to see you again before we leave. Little Andy and I are going to live with my aunt in Washington State."

Hearing her say "little Andy" made me smile.

"I'm sorry…when they had that interview my head was still fuzzy, and I don't feel like I thanked you proper-like for saving me and little Andy."

"You're sweet, Sue. I'm just glad you both are doing well."

"I have something for you I'd like to give in person. Would you be able to come by?"

"Really, Sue, there's no need."

"Please."

"Okay, I'm dropping a truck off and I'll be there in about an hour. Does that work?"

"Yes…please," she pleaded again. "I'll see you soon."

I pushed the hang-up button just as I turned into Butterfly Septic. I didn't know why it was so important for me to give Marty this truck. I knew it was a thousand times more than what I owed him, but maybe that was the point. He was mean and nasty, but for one of the few times in my life I rose above all that. Giving this truck was more for me than for him, and I expected nothing in return.

I'd worked out all sorts of made-up stories, but all of them fell flat when I walked them past the real story. Not exactly a great liar, I decided I'd just plain tell the truth since I would sign all the paperwork for the lawyer this afternoon. Even at that, Marty might have a hard time believing me.

I crept along the dirt parking lot, not wanting to put one speck of dust on the truck. It should blind Marty as it glowed in the sun. Just for fun, I pulled in diagonally so when he opened the door to the shop the entire glory of the Mack would be in full view.

The diesel continued to run as I gave three short blasts from the air horn. I waited for a minute, and when Marty didn't appear, I gave three more.

He swung the door open in anger. His gaze started at the mighty front bumper, followed the lines of the cab, then backwards to the stainless-steel tank. His anger melted into confusion, especially when he followed the lines back and stared at me behind the driver's seat. The wheels in his head turned so fast, I worried they might go off kilter.

I killed the engine, enjoying the moment so much I didn't want it to pass too quickly. Marty's stare followed my every move as I pushed in the power brake button and a loud blast of air confirmed they locked in place. I took my time gathering my things. Then I climbed down the steps of the truck with the keys in my hand and came around to the front.

"What the hell is this?" Marty growled.

I held the keys out to him.

"Did those a-holes at the dealership put you up to this?"

"Well, that's where I bought it from…to replace the one I wrecked."

His brow creased into a deep scowl.

I pulled the bill of sale from my back pocket, unfolded it, and held both the document and the keys for him to take.

Acting like I either held out a venomous snake or that I was trying to pull a trick, Marty didn't move, but read the paper from a safe distance.

He looked at me, the bill of sale, then the truck and back at me.

I'd rendered him speechless, and it was worth every penny.

"Where'd you get this kind of money?"

"I found a gold nugget below my dad's claim."

"Well, I'll be a monkey's frickin' uncle. I wondered how you got the money for your truck." He looked back at the document and keys. "Why you doing this? What's it going to cost me?"

"I wrecked your truck…and here's the replacement. Nothin' more, nothin' less."

"I suppose you want your job back?"

It was my turn to look dumbfounded. I hadn't even thought about that, but maybe it was better than flipping burgers. Before he changed his mind, I smiled and nodded toward the Mack.

"Only if I get to drive the new Number One."

Before I'd left the shop for the hospital, Marty and I traded documents—the title for my truck and the Mack's bill of sale —and with a handshake I told him I'd return to work in a couple weeks. In turn, he promised not to let any of the other guys use the truck until I returned. I wanted to be new Number One's first. He also flung a few minor jabs and reminded me this changed nothing. He was still the boss. Although, at that moment, he treated me with more respect...at least what Marty could muster. He even sort of suggested he'd think about giving me a raise when he drove me to fetch my truck at the dealership.

As I stepped off the elevator on the third floor of the hospital, I looked at my phone. Sue had texted her room number: 312.

Walking down the hall I felt a little taller but understood the irony. Being a honey-dipper was an awful job, but also a necessary service that helped people. Since there were few things I was good at, I was glad to get my job back. For a moment, the voices in my mind telling me that I'm not enough were silenced.

I knew I could have started my own septic business with the new truck, but honestly, I saw all the work that it entailed and didn't want the headache.

I stood at Sue's door and knocked. When I heard, "come in," I pushed it open.

Sue sat in a chair with the baby cradled in her lap. It was kind of strange to see her cleaned up and in street clothes.

And like *my* face, hers would take some time to heal. The doctors still had her arm wrapped in a splint. The healing ability of the body is a remarkable thing, but I felt sad for the implications of her bruised face.

"Hey…is now a good time?" I asked.

"Andy. Hi! Yes, please come in. My aunt should be here any minute to pick me up. Thank you so much for coming back to see me."

"How are you feeling?" I asked as I stepped into the room.

"I'm getting stronger every day. I'm sorry, I would stand to hug you…but please sit." She nodded to the chair across from her and I sat.

"Andy…" She searched for words. "I can never repay you for what you've done for me and little Andy. I've done a lot of soul searching and have decided it's time for me to get my life in order…start fresh. Thank you."

She looked down at the baby who slept comfortably. "You mind holding him for me? I have something for you."

I helped to gently transfer the baby into my arms and sat back. Andy released a whimper, but as I tenderly bounced him he settled and closed his eyes again.

"You're a natural. Think you'll ever have kids?" Sue smiled.

I bobbed my head. "Probably best to find a spouse first."

She chuckled. "Yes, that is helpful." I watched as sorrow draped across her face. "Just choose wisely."

I nodded. "I'm sorry he did that to you."

"They tell me he's in jail, and very few know I'm going to Washington. Hopefully, I'll never see him again."

I looked down at little Andy, who was having a dream of sucking on a bottle, as his tiny lower lip quivered.

"Do you mind if I take his picture with you?" Sue asked. "I want him to know what a real man looks like." She picked up her phone from the table next to us with her uninjured hand and held it up to take a photo. I tilted Andy so she could see our faces together.

Sue put her phone back on the table and picked up a small jewel case. "I have something for you." She smiled brightly. "I'm so excited to give this to you."

She held out the three-by-four-inch black leather case, so I reached for it.

"But before you open it, I have to explain. I read the article in the newspaper and saw that you were a Boy Scout at one time."

"Well, I only went through Cub Scouts and then on to the first rank of Tenderfoot," I acknowledged. "My older brothers went further. I think by the time I came along, my dad's interest in scouting had waned."

"Well, I hope you know what this is," she said, and motioned for me to open it.

The jewel case hinged on one side. I cradled the baby in my arm and opened the case with two hands. I knew straight away what the contents signified. I grew up poring over my brothers' *Boy's Life* scouting magazine. Out of all the articles, pictures, cartoons, and advertisements of the seventy- or eighty-page publication, the one section I dearly loved was the depiction of a heroic act where the BSA awarded the Life-Saving medal to a Scout. If there was anything more I desired in life, it was to do something so heroic as to receive this coveted medal.

My hand shook as I held the award and inspected the bright red ribbon crowned by the gold bar that read Boy Scouts of America and suspended a red and gold medallion with the words: For Saving Life. The ribbon also included the two Crossed Palms, awarded only rarely when the person demonstrated unusual heroism at extreme risk to self. Oh yes, I knew what this was.

Tears flowed freely from my eyes and the lump in my throat blocked any words I wanted to say. I bent and kissed Andy on the forehead.

"I don't know what to say," I finally said.

"So you know what that is?"

"Yes, of course, the Honor Medal. Every Boy Scout knows...even ones who didn't get very far...we all dream..." My mind and words jumbled together. "How?"

"My uncle is a Boy Scout leader in Washington. He saw the video and said, 'If that doesn't qualify for this medal, I don't know what does.'" She smiled. "You mind holding up the award with little Andy so I can get your picture again?"

As Sue snapped pictures, there was a knock at the door.

"Oh good, maybe that's my aunt; I want you to meet her," she said. "Come in."

A young man in scrubs and a hospital badge wheeled in a computer on a stand.

"Hi, I'm Kevin from the billing department. I understand you're going home today, and I wanted to give you your final paperwork." He wheeled the stand around and typed on the computer's keyboard. "I see you have no insurance, so I'd like to set you up on a payment plan; but of course we will help you apply for charity care as well."

I searched the young man's eyes. He smiled pleasantly, even though he was the bearer of bad news. I decided there were worse jobs than being a honey-dipper. The hospital sent in this poor kid to be the bad guy. *Glad you survived, and now for the really grim news,* I thought.

Sue's cheeks flushed with color. "Can you tell me what the final bill is?"

The worker typed rapidly, studied the computer screen, and without hesitation said, "103,804 dollars. But this includes the emergency department, surgery, the anesthesiologist, and all the post-operative care," he said to justify this exorbitant number. The hospital administrators had taught him well.

I looked at Sue, who just shook her head. All the color in her cheeks drained. I realized medical care was expensive, but I also knew exactly what I had to do.

BROKE

I woke up the next morning feeling hungover, with my body aching and brain in a fog. Perhaps I suffered from a spending hangover.

After I said my goodbyes to Sue and little Andy, I walked down to the business office and proudly signed a check for one hundred three thousand eight hundred four dollars. The woman wrote across the front of the invoice: "Paid In Full."

Then I had dropped the signed paperwork off to the attorney and took care of her nine-hundred-dollar bill.

I hesitated to verify the damage to my checking balance, but I pulled my phone off the nightstand and typed in the log-in information for my bank account. The amount shown on the display made me sweat. If I didn't hate it so, I'd have to laugh. The account read $666.00. It was as if someone played a joke on me as the number of the beast followed me like a sticky booger—only the decimal point had moved three spaces. Willie was going to kill me. I had spent almost all the money except for the devil's sum.

But even with such a spending spree, the burden of

responsibility had lifted off my shoulders. I used my phone to search Amazon and found a new Mandalorian figure bobble head for Number One. This one had Mando holding Baby Yoda, a fitting replacement for the new truck and the past week. It cost twenty-nine dollars and meant my bank account would show a less disturbing number.

Max heard my stirring, came flying through the door, and in one bounce landed on my chest. His entire body wagged. In part, because he was happy to see me but mainly because I would feed him and let him out to pee. I dropped my phone, held his head with both hands, and scratched behind his ears. It made his body relax, and he yawned loudly and settled onto my chest.

"Well, how was that for my fifteen minutes of fame?"

He flopped to his back, indifferent to the past week, just wanting his belly scratched. "You're my role model." I laughed. "This is all we need, isn't it?"

A train air horn blasted, and the bed shook as the locomotive rumbled by. I knew I needed to call Willie and tell him of my deeds. He'd be pissed, but down to the very deepest part of me, I felt I'd done the right thing—for once in my life.

I signaled Max to get off the bed, tossed the covers aside, and stretched. The morning sun already warmed the inside of the single-wide. I rubbed my chest, walked out of the bedroom into the bright sunlight streaming through the windows, and adjusted the waistband of my pajamas. I opened the door to the trailer and Max bounded out, barking at three robins feasting on night crawlers from the freshly mowed lawn.

"What a beautiful day, Maxi-boy," I said, and stretched in the sun.

A meadowlark, with its distinctive melody, tweeted out his mating call. "If it was just that simple," I sighed.

Max quickly did his business, ran between my legs, leaped through the open door, and spun in circles for breakfast. I obliged him with half of a cup of Purina.

I walked to the corner of the living room, pulled out a match, and lit my prayer candle. Then made the sign of the cross and touched Mama's Bible. For whatever reason, I missed both Mama and Pop this morning, but I sensed a new strength within me. Not sure what it all meant—life continued as such a mystery. Rich one moment, poor the next. At least what I'd lost in finances, I'd gained in confidence.

"Pop and Mama, I hope you're proud of me."

I recited the Lord's prayer, crossed myself, and blew out the candle. Whatever meditation remained, I could continue it on the Blackfoot. I promised the attorney that I would mark the corners of the claim today. Abby offered to go with me, but I worried about her taking so much time off from work on my behalf. She reassured me she had oodles of paid vacation that she rarely took, and her boss would be glad she finally used some of it.

I pulled my phone out of my PJ bottoms to get the berating from Willie over with.

I dialed his number, and he answered after the first ring.

"Hey, bud. I was just picking up the phone to call you. Great minds think alike, right?"

"Sure. I, uh—"

"I heard from Emma today that you signed her paperwork and dropped it off to her yesterday," he interrupted. "We should do the same with the documents I gave you, but Emma also told me you're going up to mark the corners of your old man's claim."

"I wanted—"

"Hey, I told Carrie about that and thought it would be a

hoot to take her and the kids up with you. What time are you leaving?"

I sighed at the bull in my china shop. I had to identify the property boundaries and needed to tell him, but I could do all this face-to-face.

I'd explained to Willie that McNamara's place blocked the simple way to the claim, and we'd either have to cross the river or take the long way around. Neither was great for their kids, Riley and Grayson, as floating across by innertube brought dangers; if we hiked it, they might not make the eleven-mile round-trip journey.

Willie had surprised me when he borrowed a friend's rubber raft. But now, sitting in it on the river, we looked like odd shipmates as we loaded the boat with a picnic lunch, a couple shovels, and a brand-new metal detector that Willie had purchased.

"Why don't you let me paddle across?" I said to Willie, who took the pilot's seat.

"We're just going to there." He pointed to the other side. "I'm a little better equipped," he said, and flexed his biceps.

"It's only that the currents and boulders can be tricky in this area, where Gold Creek pours in and the river rounds the bend."

"I've got it," Willie said.

"It wouldn't be a bad idea for us all to wear life vests," I said to Willie, who peeled off his shirt, revealing his muscular chest.

I looked at Abby, who had dressed comfortably in jeans, a blue tank top, and ball cap. She scratched Max behind his ears, who sat nervously on her lap. She seemed indifferent to the handsome Willie Gray.

"Oh, we'll be fine," Willie scolded.

"Yes, said the Captain to Gilligan," Carrie said under her breath, and smirked.

I struggled not to let Carrie's description of me as Gilligan sting and tried taking in the scenery on the Blackfoot and look beyond Carrie, who sported a black bikini top and her ever-present tight yoga pants. She argued with Grayson about putting on a life vest.

"I'd head in that direction, toward that big ponderosa. The current will hit us pretty fast halfway across, and Gold Creek will want to drive us backward into the main stream. That's when you'll really have to put your back into the oars or else we'll hit the corner spinning and take on some real rapids."

"I got it, I said." Willie's temper flared. "Just push us off, already."

I smiled and nodded to Abby and Carrie. "Hang on to the rope," I said, and gripped the large nylon rope strung along the inside of the raft. "If by chance we tip, stay with the boat."

Willie murmured something I couldn't hear clearly as I shoved us toward the current and jumped into the raft.

I knew we were in trouble with Willie's first few pulls of the oars, and a fact that most people don't appreciate about a wild river—things happen fast. Maybe he'd never rowed a boat before and didn't know what he was doing. With his right arm stronger than his left, he spun us in a circle so that when we hit the middle of the river we faced backward. He tried to push the boat across instead of pull it.

The rubber raft hit the confluence of Gold Creek and spun us like a top. Carrie screamed, I yelled instructions, and

Willie swore. At that point we were on a Disney ride, one that had no safety controls.

Then I saw it coming, but there was absolutely nothing I could do. The current flung the raft up against a large boulder in the river, nearly folding the boat in half for a split second.

Thank God everyone heeded my warning and held onto the rope, otherwise we would have all ended up in the ice-cold water.

When the raft spun around the other side of the rock it sprang open and, like a trampoline, launched Willie off his perch into the river.

Before the raft hit the next boulder, I made a lucky grab for Willie's arm and hoisted him into the boat, jumped onto the pilot's chair, stopped our spin, and miraculously landed us on the other side.

Willie, dripping wet, jumped up in victory, "That was awesome! I told you I'd get us across."

I looked at Abby, then at Carrie, who both answered with eye rolls.

"Yeah, way to go, Gilligan," Carrie added, but I don't think Willie knew she directed the insult toward him.

The river had mercifully landed us in a calm spot between two large boulders. Max leaped out of Abby's arms and stood sentry on top of one and barked to prompt us out of the raft and away from danger.

"How are we going to get back across?" Carrie asked.

"If Willie will let me, I'll guide us around the corner, through the rapids and to the other side, where there's another boat launch before the bridge."

"Otherwise, we'll end up back at Milltown," Abby added.

Willie shrugged and ignored our comments as he picked up the shovels and metal detector and hopped out of the boat.

I jumped out next and secured the raft to a huge rock, helped Carrie, Abby, and the kids safely to shore, then retrieved the cooler full of drinks and picnic food.

The afternoon sun had warmed the rocks, and I took a deep breath of the fresh piney air. But the chatter of the kids and the clatter of Willie throwing down the shovels interrupted the solitude. I already regretted bringing them. Not so much, I suppose, Carrie and the kids, but definitely Willie.

Carrie stretched toward the sun. "Wow, Andy, I can see why you love it here."

Abby caught me looking and smiled. I looked away, embarrassed, after admiring Carrie's assets. I pointed to a doe and her twin fawns flashing their white tails as they ran up Gold Creek.

Carrie spread a Pendleton blanket on a flat spot amongst the wildflowers.

Max chased a screaming Grayson around a tree as he fled from a large horse fly. At least Max seemed happy to have the company.

"Yeah, thanks for bringing us here," Abby added. "It's beautiful, and so peaceful."

Willie cursed as he cut his finger on a staple holding the metal detector's box together.

"Well, it was," I mumbled. I still hadn't told Willie about spending all the money from the Lioness, but I felt better about it at this point. I'd found the words to start, but Carrie interrupted my thoughts again.

"You said Lewis and Clark took this trail?" she said, and pointed to the pathway above the waterline.

"Well, Lewis and nine of his men did. The old rail bed of the Big Blackfoot Railway fully covers the trail now, but further up you can actually see the evidence of the Native

American travois tracks. 'The Road to the Buffalo' is what they called it."

"Wow, lots of history here. You can almost feel it," Abby said.

"So where's your father's claim?" Carrie asked.

"It starts here at Gold Creek." I indicated the corner where the creek dumped into the Blackfoot. "Follows the creek up about two hundred yards, then extends along the entire cliff, almost to McNamara's place." I pointed down-river, along the large amphitheater of rock and trees.

"That seems like a lot of real estate," Carrie said.

"It's twenty acres…about the size of fifteen football fields put together in a large rectangle that entails this entire corner where the river has carved into the cliff. You can see where the water sculpted shelves over the years."

"It's like a beautiful tiered garden of ponderosa pines," Abby added. "Looks like you'd need rappelling ropes to explore some of it."

I laughed. "Pop got a rattlesnake bite and a broken leg, doing just that."

"Rattlesnake?" Carrie asked nervously. "Riley and Grayson, please come sit down on the blanket and eat."

"And you said your family scattered your dad's ashes here?" Abby asked.

"Hey, let's get this expedition going," Willie demanded, interrupting my answer.

I sighed. *I'm sorry, Pop, that we're disturbing your peace.*

ACT THREE

INTERLUDE 2

Glory, Gold, and Girls

Again, there was a day when the sons of God came to present themselves before the Lord, and Satan also came among them to present himself before the Lord.

The Lord said to Satan, "Where have you come from?"

Then Satan answered the Lord and said, "From roaming about on the earth and walking around on it."

"Have you considered my servant, Andy?" God asked. "For there is no one like him on the earth, a blameless and upright man fearing God and turning away from evil. Even though you incited Me against him to ruin him without cause, he still holds fast to his integrity."

Satan answered the Lord and said, "Skin for skin! Yes, all that a man has he will give for his life. Andy has been faithful and true against the glory and gold of man, but now put forth Your hand and put Eve in his path and he will forget you."

So the Lord said to Satan, "Behold, he is in your power; only continue to spare his life."

Then Satan answered the Lord. "He was protected from harm during the accident." Then Satan went out from the presence of the Lord and smote Andy with lust.

STROBEL CLIFF

Fifteen thousand years ago, the Strobel Cliff amazingly survived the emptying of Lake Missoula, not to mention constant erosion and the passage of time. Like what I imagined the Rock of Gibraltar, one pillar of Hercules, did for the exit of the Mediterranean Sea to the Atlantic Ocean, our cliff did for the mighty Blackfoot River; forcing the water to turn an acute ninety degrees. The carved Paleozoic rock layers of green, red, and gray argillite provided a beautiful mosaic pattern to the interspaced tiers of cliffs that gave way to tufts of hundred-year-old ponderosa pines that lined each plateau.

Pop's claim, shaped as a curved rectangle—a rainbow almost—followed the bend of the river. From the river's edge to the top of the cliff it arched around like a natural, but very steep, amphitheater. After a picnic of fried chicken, a few assorted salads and Cokes, the women and the kids and I had worked on the corners of the property. Willie couldn't be bothered with either and was busy searching the area with the metal detector.

According to Montana State law, we must mark the

corners with a three-by-three-inch wooden fencepost, a two-inch metal post, or a mound of rocks. The latter seemed less ecologically intrusive than the posts, but the state required the pile to be over three feet high.

We started with the easiest corner, near to where we'd picnicked. With tons of river rock, Abby, Carrie and her kids, and I built the rock pyramid quickly. The second, two hundred yards up Gold Creek, came together just as easily. The hike around the mountain proved to be a challenge, something that Riley and Grayson surprisingly accomplished with minor complaints. I worried more about Abby's ability with her weak leg but, like a trouper, she did great. Thankfully, once we hiked to the top of the mighty wall, the relatively flat top provided a peaceful walk around to the other side of the claim. Grayson's tendency to want to peer over the edge made us all nervous, but when we scared up a small herd of Bighorn sheep that ran further into the woods, he clung closer to Carrie.

Our inability to find enough rocks for the corner made the third pyramid difficult, but using Grayson as a measuring stick, I think we met the three-foot requirement.

We had picked our way down the side closest to McNamara's place with the help of a line of ponderosa pines. I carried Riley, and we all helped each other down the steep bank, then worked on the fourth and final corner pile.

"I'm not sure I wore the best outfit for manual labor," Carrie said, and laughed, dusting off her bare stomach and yoga pants. "I certainly could have used some gloves." She peeled off a fake fingernail, flicked it to the ground, shrugged, and slung a shovel over her shoulder.

"Mommy, I'm tired," Riley whined.

"I know, sweetie; we're almost finished," Carrie said, and looked at me. "Are we?" She wiped the back of her hand across her forehead, pushing back a strand of hair that had fallen out of her bun, leaving a smudge of dirt on her face.

I swallowed down a chuckle at her appearance, never seeing Carrie Carver so disheveled before. Even as a manual laborer, she glowed. Trying not to stare, I looked at the map the attorney had given me and nodded in satisfaction. "That should do it." I smiled, folded the picture, and put it in my pocket. "Thank you so much for your help. You guys ready to head back?"

I led the group back using the other shovel as a walking stick.

"That was actually pretty fun," Abby said, and slapped her ball cap across her leg as we walked along the trail beside the river. "What a magnificent place."

"I think we went to Johnsrud in high school to drink beer and make out," Carrie whispered to Abby and me, and pointed across the river to the park.

Abby smiled at me, apparently thinking what I was: we didn't exactly share the same fond memories of our youth with Carrie.

"Abby, I don't remember you in high school," Carrie said, adding to the insult.

"Yes, I was there."

"Well, you were probably in all the smart classes," Carrie said. "Andy, what about you?"

"I never went," I said. "My dad died when I was in eighth grade and I went right to work."

"It was nice of him to leave you this," she said, pointing to the cliff above us.

I scoffed. "I don't own the land, Carrie," I said in frustration, but softened my tone, "just the mineral rights. Dad searched for gold all his life here. I think the nugget I found was just a fluke and has nothing to do with his claim."

We watched Willie scramble further up one of the two scree rockslides that formed a large 'V' in the center of the amphitheater cliff wall and walk along one tier with the metal detector thrust out in front of him. He knocked down a large rock that tumbled down the cliff's face and splashed into the Blackfoot. Strobel Cliff may have survived the test of time, but I hoped it would survive Willie, and vice versa. If he injured himself up there, we'd have to call search and rescue to get him down.

From past visits I knew exploring the cliff was not for the faint of heart, even where Willie stood, halfway up the three-hundred-foot cliff. "It makes your butt pucker," like Pop would say. All the tiers, a few feet to twenty feet wide, sloped acutely toward the river, so you always felt like you were one step away from tumbling over the edge. When my brothers and I would explore the cliff with Pop, he'd make us hold on to the pine trees as we leap-frogged from one to another. It made me sweat just thinking about going back up there.

"Please be careful, you fool!" Carrie yelled.

Willie either didn't hear or care and gave no response. I'm sure he hadn't realized how big twenty acres was compared to the six-inch disc of the metal detector. I didn't have a clue about how to calculate the odds of us finding more gold, but as much as Pop had searched and scoured the area I thought it pretty unlikely. Through millions of years, the Lioness could have just as easily washed down Gold Creek from the Rattlesnake Wilderness and melded together ounce by ounce.

"Your dad must have been proud of you to leave this to you," Carrie said, knowing nothing about my relationship with Pop.

"Yeah, nothing like a great wall of rock to make you feel special," I murmured. Abby patted me softly on the back, knowing there was a ton of pain there from not getting what I needed from Pop. I wondered if it was true of every father and son—boys just needed to know they were all right in the sight of their fathers? "I'm afraid I really didn't know my dad very well."

Carrie either ignored or didn't understand what I felt inside, but nodded and eyeballed Willie. "Hey, Jacques Cousteau, come on down. The kids are tired and hungry!"

I looked at Abby and smiled. At least she got the name of the explorer correct. She just didn't know he explored the oceans. I also thought it was probably an insult to Mr. Cousteau.

This time we got a wave from Willie, and we all started down the trail again.

"Andy, you said that your family scattered your father's ashes here?" Abby asked.

"Right up there," I pointed to the large ponderosa pine protected by an alcove in the rock at the apex of the two rockslides.

We walked to it just as Willie came sliding down the rock scree, holding the metal detector out to the side and looking like he was skiing down a chute.

"Cowabunga!" he yelled.

As I watched him surf down the rocks, I had to admit his physical prowess stirred jealousy. But when he hit the bottom of the slide, his momentum carried him forward. His feet couldn't catch up and he ended sprawled out in the dirt.

He popped up with one hop and held the detector over his head in victory. "Saved it!" he yelled. But a large patch of road rash formed on his chest.

"Willie, you fool, you could have killed yourself," Carrie scolded.

He brushed at the gravel embedded in the skin of his

chest and grimaced. "Just a little flesh wound," he said, and smiled.

"Find anything?" Abby asked.

"Not a bleep on the stupid machine." He held up the metal detector again. "Hope this thing even works."

"Not a bleeping thing, huh?" Carrie added, and they laughed together. "Andy was just about to show us where his father's final resting place is."

I pointed to the spot near where Willie stood, worried he was about to trample on Pop's cross. "It's right where you're standing," I said, hoping he'd move.

He leaped forward like he was resting on a rattlesnake den and finally noticed the cross.

"Sorry," he said sheepishly. "Nice of your ol' man to leave you this claim, but I sure wish we'd find some more gold. At least you have the money from the Lioness. We should get that working for you."

I looked down at my feet.

Beyond the ripple of the water and a few joyous sounds from the park across the way, we fell into an awkward silence.

"You still don't trust me?" Willie finally asked.

I looked at Abby, then back at the ground. I'd already told her. "It's just that I've spent some of it."

"That's okay, Andy. I know we had to tuck a sizeable chunk away for taxes and you paid off your truck. Big deal. What, you settled your rent?"

My forehead burned like I was on fire. Or even worse, back in grade school, facing Willie thumping me on the chest, quizzing me about something dumb. But this was serious.

"Well...I...uh..." I said, not being able to find the right words. "I've spent all of it," I blurted out.

Willie huffed and then laughed. "Yeah nice try, dumbo. Trying to get me back for all the times I razzed you in school."

That made me mad, and I answered more strongly. "I spent every last dime of it…well, all but about six hundred dollars of it." I tried to straighten my spine.

This time even Carrie laughed with Willie, "What do *you* have to spend money on, anyway?" Carrie teased. But when they both looked at Abby and saw the seriousness of her face, the color drained from both of theirs.

Willie's knuckles turned white around the metal detector. "No!" he screamed. "You *cannot* be serious…or that stupid," he added with rage.

"Andy, please tell us you really didn't spend all the money," Carrie implored. "What did you buy?"

"I replaced Marty's truck I wrecked, and I paid off the woman's hospital bill from the accident. Oh, and I tithed to the church."

Willie put his hand to his forehead and paced in tight circles. "No, no, NO!" he said, his voice rising.

"I'm sorry," I said, even though I wasn't.

"You're an idiot…" he said, and added some words I couldn't catch. His face was now so red I worried for the man. In a tantrum, he sent the metal detector flying toward Pop's grave. It missed the cross by a fraction of an inch but hit the pine tree, bouncing and rolling toward the back of the alcove.

"Jeez, Andy, you really are a dumb…"

Willie was about to unleash one of his famous tirades, but he stopped as the metal detector sent off a large whine.

"Look what you made me do! The metal detector is busted and now I can't even return it."

I walked over to retrieve it, mostly to see if I could turn off the annoyingly sharp wail. I picked it up and took two steps toward Willie. When I did, the unit quieted. I paced back and forth a step and it went from shrill to silent.

"Hey, let me see that thing." Willie grabbed it from my hands.

Turning the disc side down, he stepped toward the source and it beeped louder.

Willie and Carrie grew more excited, and even Abby looked at me with arched brows. I shook my head toward them all. "Pop used to sit here after a long day of exploring and drink…and drink. There's a whole pile of Hamm's beer cans around here that he buried. Congratulations, I think you found it."

My comment did not deter Willie. "Give me one of those shovels," he demanded of Carrie and began digging at the point of greatest intensity of the detector.

It only took one shovelful before he turned up rusted beer cans.

"Sorry, Willie. But I told you so."

The more he shoveled, the more densely packed crushed cans appeared.

"Wow, you've really struck it rich," Abby teased.

Willie ignored her and continued to dig. Now they came out easier and easier as he dug a foot deeper until only a few more cans appeared.

He threw down the shovel and grabbed the detector. It beeped as he swept it over the cans, but no one was more surprised than me when he held the metal detector over the empty hole, and it continued to sing.

MYSTERY

S trobel Cliff shielded the hot afternoon sun as we sat in the alcove near where we had scattered Pop's ashes. Two Monarch butterflies fluttered and twisted in some elegant mating ritual. Willie dug the pit under the beer cans down another foot for safe measure and widened it by three feet.

"I guess that's it," he announced, leaped out of the hole, and threw the shovel down onto the ground. Just for good measure, he picked up the metal detector and pushed it down into the crater, then scanned around the edges. The only sound it made was near the stack of rusted Hamm's beer cans.

"Nothing else?" Carrie asked.

"Yeah, just these three measly nuggets!" Abby exclaimed, and laughed.

Willie turned to the three large chunks of gold piled on a stump that the rest of us stared at. We fell silent, as if the gold emitted a power and energy all its own—mesmerizing us.

Finally, Willie broke the spell. "I say we split them three ways. That makes sense, as all of us had a hand in finding them. They're all about the same size, so that's fair," he said, making his case. "Andy should get the biggest one, of course," he said, like he was being ultra-generous.

We'd judged each nugget to be heavier than the Lioness, with the largest resembling the shape of a ghost.

"You would have never found these without me," Willie said, still making his argument.

Gold fever returned to Willie, but at least it had displaced his anger with me.

"Andy...do you think your dad knew about these?" Carrie asked, nodding toward the nuggets.

I looked at Carrie and smiled. *Ah, here was the real question that even naïve Carrie had the smarts to ask before anyone else,* I thought. It was the genuine mystery. The gold was a foot or more below where Pop had buried his beer cans, even offset by half a foot to the side. Nothing indicated that Pop put them there. They weren't wrapped in anything. There was no note or sign that human hands had touched them. But there they hid in the dirt, clumped together like Pop had plopped them into the hole and covered it up. Sure, there were plenty of times that Pop came to the claim by himself, but we always figured it was to get away from us kids. Wouldn't he have come home in glee when he found even one of them? God knows our family could have used the money.

Nothing made sense and I could only say, "I have no idea."

"I bet that old man of yours just had the same bad luck that you have," Willie snorted. "Can you imagine sitting here drinking beer and this gold was right under his nose the entire time?"

I tried to ignore Willie's slam against me or Pop, but after all, by definition, Strobel meant *unkempt or scruffy-hair,* and I guess that could loosely translate to us being losers. But if Pop had found this gold, he would have told his boss at the mill to go take a flying leap first thing.

Willie walked to the stump and picked up the two smaller nuggets, weighed them in his hands, and extended one to Abby. "They seem about the same, but you can have this one."

Abby didn't budge. She looked at Willie, then at me and smiled. Then back to Willie.

"You know who the most despicable of the low-life criminals were in the Old West?" she asked.

Willie's brow furrowed.

"Claim jumpers." She smirked at him. "And the gold claim laws of 1872 still apply. I know, I read them myself," she said. "You happen to read all the paperwork your fancy attorney gave to Andy? Any gold found on his claim—and this *is* his claim—is Andy's."

"Well, we must finish the official survey to—"

"Oh Willie, this is all Andy's," Carrie interrupted him. "And maybe if you're nice, he'll let you invest it for him."

Willie shrugged and looked at me with a sheepish grin. Then pursed his lips and nodded. "You're right. You're also the luckiest devil I've ever known," he said, and tousled my hair. "How does it feel to be rich? And I'm not letting you go spend it on a bunch of nonsense," he said like an endearing big brother.

I hated being patronized or called a devil and started to tell Willie to go take his own flying leap. "I, uh—"

"I wasn't even going to tell you this, 'cuz I didn't want you to feel bad. Griz called me the day after you sold him the Lioness. Any guesses how much he sold it for?" He didn't wait for my answer. "One point two mil…as in million."

I shrugged. For me, it was water under the bridge.

"Now *that's* a shrewd businessman."

"More like a crook," Abby said, her face turning red.

"Sometimes you can't tell the difference," Carrie said, and laughed.

"Well, we won't let him do that to you again. Judging by the size and weight of these babies, I bet you have three or four million in gold here. That is, if you let me help you."

29

HEADSTONE

Dark rain clouds hung over the Missoula cemetery as I stared at the weathered and chipped family headstone and remembered the stories Mama recounted every time we visited. "When your father purchased the marker sixty years ago, we had to go without ground beef for three months."

I made the sign of the cross as Mama's words echoed in my brain. I'd soon be wealthier than I could've ever imagined. Probably three or four times more than after I sold the Lioness, if Willie was correct and could find a buyer for the three new gold nuggets. But my mind and spirit couldn't wrap around the possibility that Pop found them and concealed the treasure. *Why would he do that?* Now that I'm thinking about it, Pop left specific instructions for us to scatter his remains in that exact spot—near where the three were buried.

That question prompted me to visit the cemetery today. Even though we'd spread Pop's ashes by the big ponderosa, we still carved his name in the modest grave marker along with Mama, Jimmy, Fred, Sam, Ernie, Frank, and Larry.

Pop originally bought the small granite headstone when Fred died at one, never thinking he would memorialize five more sons on it. Pop had hand-carved Fred, Jimmy, Sam, and Ernie's names into the stone. Mama had me chisel Pop and Larry's names after they died, but I had a real stone mason place Mama's name across the top; something that cost me a bundle. The military entombed Jimmy's ashes in the Wall of Honor at the veterans' cemetery, but Mama always wanted the family together...at least the names. I guessed it was her attempt at having that family picture after all, grim as it may be.

We'd opened and closed this ground too many times, I decided. Now, looking at the headstone, I surmised it wasn't healthy to be a Strobel boy.

We had gone without so much and so often, that if he knew and withheld the wealth, it made anger boil in my belly. Would he really be so cruel? And worst of all, did Mama know?

At least now I could replace the grave marker with a proper monument to the Strobel clan, however dysfunctional. Hardly an inch remained for another name—not that I was looking forward to having my name added one day.

The Strobel marker was barely one step up from a pauper's grave. I glanced at the surrounding markers and monuments. Some fancier ones had granite vases to place bouquets, and others were large enough to plant real flowers. *Mama would like that. Pansies perhaps.*

I knelt and pulled handfuls of long grass that the groundskeepers missed next to the headstone. With the number of times we had disturbed the soil, the marker tilted at an awkward ten-degree angle—something I wished I could correct. Somehow it made it look that much more pitiful.

"Mama, please tell me you didn't know about the gold."

I put my elbow on my knee, rested my chin in my hand and sighed, knowing I wouldn't get an answer. I might never know. But I'm not sure I liked the alternative any better—that Pop had worked and toiled on the claim, hoping against hope, and came within a foot of striking it rich. The irony and sadness of it was too much for me to bear. That somehow, in his pitiful life, he was inches away from changing the course of our family's fate.

That would be such a cruel stroke of fate from the universe…or from God. *Then I'd have to be mad at You, God.* I could never do that, for Mama's wrath would fall on me from her side of the grave. No, I just couldn't go there, even though that possibility was more likely.

"Mama, help me understand this."

The low rumble of thunder echoed around the Missoula Valley. I looked up to the threatening sky and decided I didn't want to be caught in a lightning storm that would secure my name on the headstone.

"Miss you, Mama," I said, stood and turned.

Raindrops landed on my head as I walked back to my truck. I might never get the answers I longed for. *I guess I'll just have to be happy becoming a millionaire.*

A flash of lightning and boom of thunder came almost simultaneously, and I quickly jumped into the truck. Just as I slammed the truck's door closed, my cell phone rang, and I dug it out of my pocket. The caller ID showed it was Carrie.

In my thirty-four years, I'd never gotten a phone call from her. In the past I'd call her to let her know I was headed up to clean out their septic tank, but she invariably called Marty if she needed something from me. I wondered where she got my number and figured Willie gave it to her.

"Hi…Carrie," I said nervously.

"Andy, hi. This is Carrie."

I chuckled inside, having already greeted her.

"Andy, our adventure yesterday was a blast. Thank you for taking me and the kids along. They can't stop talking about it. Finding the gold was unbelievable, but I have to admit that I'm sore today despite my workouts. I guess different muscles—"

She continued telling me how sore her butt muscles were, and I'm afraid it short-circuited my brain back to the memory of her buns in her hot pink bikini the day of the septic accident. When she started in on stories of her kids, I knew it might be some time before I got a word in edgewise, and with an occasional "Uh-huh" I hoped she'd think I was listening.

After we had found the three nuggets, Willie allowed me to get us safely back to the other side while he held them on his lap. Then there was the question of what to do with them, which started a fairly heated discussion.

Willie wanted to take them and put them in their safe, while Abby insisted they remain with me. I leaned toward Abby's thinking, until Carrie became the peacemaker. She assured me that with the vault bolted to the floor it was absolutely the most secure place for them for now. She even told me the combination to the safe, which made Willie mad. Then she invited me to stay at their house with a cot set up in front of it if I wanted. When she told me that the safe was in their bedroom, I got all flustered and said that putting the nuggets in the safe was good enough.

I saved Carrie the embarrassment of not being able to control herself with me in the same bedroom. That thought made me laugh.

"Andy, are you still there?" Carrie asked.

"Oh sorry, Carrie. I got distracted for a moment." I grimaced and hoped she hadn't just told me bad news.

"Did you hear me say that we saw the ad on TV for Oprah's show?"

"Uh, yeah…no, what?"

"The show you're on, Andy. It airs this next weekend, on the Fourth of July. A week from tomorrow. Isn't that exciting?"

My heart pounded in my chest, and perspiration leaked from every pore. I hadn't answered or returned Joseph's phone calls from yesterday, but now I knew what he was so excited to tell me. Except for meeting Oprah, I was sorry I'd done the interview and decided I'd made a terrible celebrity. Max wouldn't have to go on double duty against all the girls that Oprah told me would be knocking on my door.

"Uh—"

"Andy, would you please let me throw a party for you that day?"

"I don't—"

"Oh please, Andy? I will make it super small. You'll see, it'll be fun. I want to introduce you to a few of my friends. After all, you're a new millionaire so you have to meet some other people."

She probably had Marty and Abby in mind with that comment, but if Carrie was going to torture me with a party, I sure as heck wouldn't do it without Abby. And if I invited Abby, I had to invite Marty, or I'd never hear the end of it.

"Well, can I invite Abby and Marty?" I said, not believing I might agree to her suggestion. I figured I could stand Carrie's friends for a few hours if it meant I'd get some extra time with her.

There was a long pause, and I looked at the phone to make sure I hadn't lost the connection. When I heard her sigh, I knew she wasn't happy about my choice of guests. "Uh,

Abby…sure," she muttered. "But are you sure you want to ask Marty?"

"Yes," I said strongly. "*If* we have a party, Marty will harass me for years to come if I don't invite him." I put the emphasis on *if*, so she got my message loud and clear.

"Okay, okay…you're the star."

30

EXTRAORDINARY

T he sulfuric stench of the volcanic air on Planet Nevarro burned my nostrils. Warfare rumble shook the area, causing dust to settle from the ceiling of the abandoned building. The Mandalorian should have been here by now. What delayed him from such an important transaction? The bars of Beskar steel, the most sought-after alloy in the galaxy, tugged at my shoulders from the backpack straps. Marked with the Galactic Empire crest and its inherent ability to withstand direct blaster fire or to repel a light saber strike, its value overshadowed the danger of carrying it. Everyone desired it. The Mandalorian told me I could trust these people, but only as much as I can trust anyone around Beskar.

The inescapable heat radiating from the planet's core and the rotten-egg smell nauseated me. Or was it the disfigured face of the man sitting at the table in front of me? Perhaps the results of a fire or the slash of a light saber.

"The Beskar belongs back in the hands of a Mandalorian!" he shouted over the industrial grind of machinery.

"Yes…but I thought he would be here by now," I stammered.

"He?" he growled.

"The Mandalorian, of course," I said, trembling.

"He's not here," he replied, and added, "Obviously." His frown intensified. "What did he tell you?"

"Uh…to do the right thing. Is this the right thing?"

"What do you think?" The man gave no sign one way or the other.

An ear-ringing explosion from outside startled me.

It didn't seem to faze the man, but he said, "Decide now. There is not much time."

"Okay," I said, and unslung the bag from my shoulder. I spilled the alloy bars out on the table in front of the man.

The amount of Beskar seemed to push him back into his chair, and his eyes widened. But when he looked at me, his eyes filled with disgust. "Where did someone like you get this much Beskar?"

"My…f…father," I stuttered again.

The man laughed, then slammed his fist down on the table. "Nothing good has come from—"

Another explosion rocked the building, sending more debris falling from the ceiling. Unfazed still, he stared at me. "You don't know what you're doing, do you?"

That was as true a statement as there ever could be. I didn't have to answer. He already knew.

"Why does it always have to be someone like you?" he asked with disdain.

I noticed he slid his hand under the table. He withdrew a laser blaster, pointed it at my chest, and sneered.

My body and mind moved involuntarily. I somersaulted to one side, feeling the heat of the laser blast scald my deltoid.

An explosion tore the door to the room off the hinges and flashes of lasers bounced around the chamber. The men guarding the deformed man dove for cover and fired back as stormtroopers poured into the room.

I spied an exhaust vent to my right. It was my only escape, and I took it with laser blasts bouncing around me.

Falling. Down further I dropped.

Blackness.

Tumbling.

I expected to hit an exhaust fan at any moment and get torn to bits, but I kept falling.

Laser blasts lit the chute. They'd followed me.

Whoomp!

I woke with such a start my hand hit my nose, causing my eyes to water as I shot up to sitting in my bed—panting, like I had just finished a marathon.

I pinched my nose to make sure I hadn't knocked it out of place, wiped the sweat from my forehead, and looked at Max. His body wagged uncontrollably, but his concerned eyes reflected my nightmare.

I reassured him with a pat on the head. "Yeah, that was another bad one." Each dream was different, but the theme was always the same. Someone or something was chasing me.

Neither Max nor I seemed to have gotten used to the unsettling dreams I'd had all week. Carrie said she wanted to throw the Fourth of July party with me as the guest of honor only five days ago. Now, the celebration was only three days away, and I hoped that once it was over the night terrors would stop.

My psyche rebelled against the expected social interactions and the spotlight that would shine on me. Once I heard Willie had sold the gold, I thought that it truly was time to go see a shrink. Abby kept talking about the different parts that make up our personality and how many of these parts get stuck in the past. The problem was, this part that I'd come to know as my "inner critic" wielded a vivid imagination and constantly reminded me I was not good enough.

Abby reassured me that there are no bad parts, and also how each of these parts had roles to play. All trying to actually protect a younger part of me called an exile, but also how sometimes they created more damaging messages to do so.

"Hey, Andy, are you in there?" A loud knock pounded at the door and woke me completely from my nightmare. It sounded like Willie, but with urgency in his voice.

I coaxed Max off the bed and slid a t-shirt that hung on the corner of the bedpost over my head and adjusted my pajama bottoms. My hair was a mess and I'm sure I had terrible morning breath, but there was no way to hide the fact that he'd roused me out of bed.

I slipped my feet into my slippers by the door and opened it.

"Jeez, Andy, I've been standing here pounding on your door. You deaf or something?" Willie looked me up and down and chuckled. "Well, I guess when you're Milltown's newest millionaire, you can sleep in however late you want."

"What time is it?" I yawned.

He looked at his Rolex. "It's quarter to ten, you knuckle-head. You tie one on last night?"

I wanted to explain that I hadn't slept well for days and had fallen into a trap of staying up late playing my video game then sleeping half the day away, but he wasn't listening and bumped past me into the single-wide.

He looked around the cramped quarters with disgust, trying to find a decent place to sit, and finally decided on one of the folding chairs at the table. "Well, you won't have to deal with this crappy trailer much longer." He pushed my carving tools to the center of the table and put a stack of papers in their place.

"You want a cup of coffee?" I asked and shuffled past him into the kitchen and started the coffeemaker.

"Uh, sure," he said tentatively.

I glanced at Willie. No wonder he got whatever he wanted. He had celebrity good looks. The dark business suit and bright blue silk tie made him appear like he'd just stepped out of the pages of *GQ*, a banker's office, or from the latest Matthew McConaughey movie set. He brushed his golden hair back with one hand. The one anomaly with his appearance that made me laugh inside was that he didn't wear socks with his patent leather shoes—reminding everyone he was one step away from darting to the lake.

I probably lingered too long on his feet, and he shot me a look. "Well…aren't you going to ask me?"

"Ask you what?"

"How rich you are, you lucky son-of-a-gun." He didn't wait for my response. "Three point two mil. Congratulations, my friend!" He held his fist out for a bump.

I obliged him and went back to pour two cups of coffee. Then sat down on the other folding chair across from him.

I sipped from my cup.

"Aren't you going to say anything, Andy?"

"Wasn't that what you were hoping for?" I asked. Willie had called me two days earlier with the news that he'd found a buyer.

"Yes, of course…but now it's real. I sold the gold this morning." He seemed exasperated and mumbled something under his breath. "I brought all the paperwork. The bill of sale and, of course, my paperwork so we can get this money working for you. No more trucks or goodwill offerings nonsense. I'm not leaving here until it's safely tucked away." He rapped his knuckle on the top of the papers he'd spread out. "And—"

A wide smile crossed his face, and by the way his pupils dilated, I knew there was more good news.

"The guy who's buying your gold wants to talk with you at the party this weekend. He has a proposal for you. The investor bets there's more gold on your father's claim, and either wishes to buy you out completely or partner with you to excavate it. He thinks it would be a good idea to purchase McNamara's place for access."

"Is McNamara's for sale?"

He smiled coyly. "My dear Andy. Everything is for sale if you've got money."

"And the claim?"

"We're talking real money, Andy. He'd want it surveyed, of course, but I think I could get you over a hundred million for it. And I would only charge a 10% finder's fee for my services."

After Willie left, I took a shower and drank a second cup of coffee, but my head still spun. I felt like one of those movies, where the lead character wakes up in someone else's body or is transported to another reality. My new existence seemed that much more unlikely, and I didn't know what to do.

All I knew was that I had dodged Joseph's calls all week, but now I had to talk with him. The segment aired in three days, and maybe my new truth should be a showstopper. I was no longer the poor hick from the wrong side of the tracks who did a good thing. Somehow I felt like a fraud.

I took a deep breath and dialed his number. He picked up on the first ring.

"Andy, thank God. I've been so worried about you! Are you okay? Please tell me you're okay!"

"Hey, Joseph." I didn't know where to start.

"Andy?" He sounded concerned.

I decided to tell it straight up. "Joseph, I'm rich."

There was silence, and I wasn't sure he heard me or understood what I had said.

He cleared his voice. "Andy, did you just say you're rich? Like wealthy?"

"Yes, like millionaire rich. Like Richie-Rich rich."

Joseph laughed. "Andy, I've seen how you live—" He sucked back his words.

"I've ruined it for you, Joseph. And for Oprah." I didn't know why, but an involuntary tear ran down my cheek. I hated disappointing them after they treated me so nicely. The inner critic part in me cried out loudly, *"You disappoint everyone!"*

There was an uncomfortably long pause on the phone, confirming the voice in my head.

"It was you, wasn't it?" Joseph finally said.

I didn't know what he was talking about.

"Oprah and I pondered and pondered who would have beat her to the punch. I called the hospital on behalf of Oprah's foundation to see how we could help Sue and her baby, and they told me that some anonymous donor had paid her bill in full. It was you, wasn't it?"

I cleared my throat. *Now I'm in trouble.*

"You know what's crazy? I knew in my heart it was you. I didn't know how, but I knew it had to be you. That was over a hundred thousand dollars. How did you do that?"

I still didn't know where to start. "My dad," I stammered. "Pop held on to a dream of finding gold on a claim he'd put in for years ago. I'd always thought it was a fool's errand. But, he may have found gold there all along." The words nearly choked me as they came out. "I don't know, Joseph. This has turned my world upside down and I don't know what to do." Another tear rolled down my cheek. "The day after Abby and I were in Los Angeles, I found a large gold nugget near Pop's claim, and since that time we discovered three more."

"Amazing."

"But don't you think we should call off the show?" I asked and swallowed. "I'm kind of no longer ordinary."

That statement made Joseph laugh again. "No Andy, you're right, you are anything but ordinary. I think you're extraordinary." Joseph's voice cracked. "I couldn't think of a better person for something like this to happen to…but now you must tell me the rest of this remarkable story."

I blew on the small carving to remove some shavings as I sat at my dining table.

Joseph had made me start from the beginning and bombarded me with questions to learn every detail. I heard him type as we talked, and when I had finished he made me chuckle when he said he could see this story made into a movie someday. In turn, I made him laugh when I joked about Brad Pitt playing my character.

I looked again at the number on my phone. 133.333333…and on to infinity with the threes. After getting off the call with Joseph, I'd made the calculations. At twenty-four thousand dollars a year, that's how many years it would take me to make 3.2 million dollars, but the infinity part was more like it. If there was more gold, or Willie's investor really wanted to buy out the claim…*well, that amount of wealth didn't even compute in my brain.*

"What in the world am I going to do now?" I patted Max on the head, who was curled up in my lap.

I did the math. New trucks cost around sixty-five thou-sand dollars—I could almost buy fifty of them—a new one for every week of the year—with, of course, taking two weeks off to rest. I laughed.

Would I stay in my little single-wide? *I kind of like it here. Actually, I like my old truck for that matter.*

And Marty…what was I going to tell him?

The money wasn't even in my bank account yet, and it seemed like a burden somehow. How in the world does a person spend that kind of money? I could already feel a signif-icant part of my brain worrying about it. *Would there be enough to last my entire life? How would I protect it?* It made my heart feel like it shriveled inside.

I picked up a sharp pick and worked around the eyes on my carving. Baby Yoda was not one of my more complex carvings, but the key was to capture the innocent expression and emotion of the little guy with his eyes and long ears.

On the show, Baby Yoda wore a burlap bag. Trying to carve the texture into the wood was difficult, but I thought it had turned out well. I gave it another puff of air.

I examined it, and then with my best attempt at a Yoda impersonation I said, "When you look at the dark side, careful you must be. For the dark side looks back."

Max lifted his head and cocked it to one side.

I spun the carving by the base in front of his face.

"Judge me by my size, do you?"

JULY FOURTH

From a distance, I could see the white circus tent set up on Willie and Carrie's property. With two-and-a-half hours of daylight left, the Missoula Valley was awash in green. And just like the residents, every tree basked in the July warmth. The evening hadn't even cooled down yet, so Abby and I drove with the windows open. The last remaining ranches around Missoula spread the sweet fragrance of fresh-cut hay, and I inhaled deeply.

Abby had picked me up from home so we would arrive shortly after seven. Carrie told us she had a barbecue dinner catered. "The airing of the Oprah interview is at eight, and there will be plenty of celebration, then we'll shoot off fireworks once it gets dark," Carrie had said.

I looked across the vista as we drove up snob-knob and around a 100-acre cattle ranch to get to their house. "What do you think that's about?" I asked.

"The tent?" Abby glanced over across the plateau. "I don't know. Maybe Willie is selling fireworks." She laughed.

Abby was correct that most of the large-scale firework

stands had moved into big tents instead of the small mom and pop trailer stands I grew up with. Pop never let us shoot off many fireworks. "Might as well take your dollar bills and light them on fire," he'd say. But whatever money my siblings and I could scrape together, we'd buy a handful of firecrackers and a fountain or two. The hardship that every kid growing up in Montana endures is the wait for it to get dark enough to shoot them off. Even though the sun set around nine-thirty, the light lingered in the sky until ten-thirty or eleven and the delay was agonizing.

I shrugged, then glanced back at Abby. The entire drive I'd tried to say something nice to her, but didn't want it to come out sounding stupid like when we'd gone out for dinner. She really looked pretty, having done something different with her eye make-up that accentuated her Asian features. She also had braided her hair in a circle around her head like a crown, with loose strands of hair framing her face. With soft pink lipstick I thought she resembled a Chinese princess, but didn't know how to say it.

Heat rose in my neck with embarrassment, but I said, "You look pretty tonight, Abby."

Her face blushed crimson, and I thought I'd messed up again. She smiled and then glanced at me out of the corner of her eye. "Thank you, Andy." Her lips seemed to force back a smile or a giggle. She looked at me. "Really, thank you for noticing. Do you like my hair? It's called a Bohemian braid. One of my favorite actresses sometimes wears it like this."

I did like it, although I also wanted to tell her I liked her pale icy-blue blouse that made her beautiful skin glow, but decided I'd better stop while I was ahead. If I tried dealing out too many compliments I'd head into troubled waters, so I changed the subject. "I talked with Joseph today. He's super excited about the airing tonight." I stuck my tongue out like I might be sick. "I'll just be glad when it's over and done with."

"I've been a little nervous for the party myself. Mixing with all the *hoity-toity* people. I guess it's nice of them to invite us poor folk." She laughed.

I looked out the side window and grimaced.

"I'm sorry, Andy. I didn't mean to—"

"You didn't," I interrupted. Abby misread the nerve she struck, and I tried to find the words to express how I felt. Abby and I had talked all week about my new wealth. She didn't even seem to care about it, but expressed her concern of how heavily it seemed to weigh on me. And we'd laughed together when she'd told me I could now act like the *hoitiest of the toittiest*. "I feel like a different person, and I'm not sure I like it. As if someone else has taken over my life or I've woken up in someone else's reality." I tried to describe what I felt inside. "I don't know, I just can't explain it."

"It's okay, Andy. It might take some time to adjust to your new normal. People like you for who you are, not what you have."

I looked out over the city as Abby drove up to Heaven's Gate, the road leading down to Carrie and Willie's.

"I don't think they do."

Abby glanced at me for understanding.

"I don't think they like me for who I am. And now Carrie Carver is throwing me a party and wanting me to meet her friends? It's like the gold has changed everything, and I'm not sure it's right."

"You don't have to change one thing in your life if you don't want to," she said, glancing over at me. "It's your choice."

I ignored what Abby said as I focused on Willie and

Carrie's property that drew close. Rows of cars had parked in their field next to the house. "Oh no," I said.

Abby looked over at me, grimaced, and nodded her head in understanding. "Just a small party," she repeated Carrie's words. "She told me to get you here no earlier than seven."

I slumped down in my seat. "This is terrible."

A horn blared and interrupted my thoughts of asking Abby to turn around, and I looked in the side mirror to see Marty's white Ford tailgating us. His thick arm waved out the window, and he honked wildly to where I thought he might ram Abby's car if he wasn't careful.

"Well, at least one person is going to enjoy the party," I said, and shook my head. "Might as well get this over with."

Abby drove under the Shady Acres archway and a guy standing alongside the road signaled for us to stop. Abby pulled up beside him, and the young man in black pants and white shirt ducked down to talk with us. "You Andy?" he asked.

I nodded.

"Ms. Carver wanted me to tell you to pull all the way up in the circular drive as the guest of honor."

Abby followed the boy's instructions, and we drove to the front of the house. My stomach flip-flopped when I saw the hundred or more people gathered on the lawn. Carrie, in a gold lamé shirt, white slacks and sparkly gold high heels, came clipping down the walkway to the car.

Abby looked at me and, with fake enthusiasm, said, "Surprise."

In the side mirror, I saw Marty jump out of his truck and move his heavy frame toward us as well. I knew he couldn't help but want to be part of the center of attention. He opened my door and pulled me out by my arm.

Like Vanna White, Carrie stopped in front of the car and

raised her arms in victory. "Surprise!" The other guests echoed this and then started in a round of "For He's a Jolly Good Fellow."

Carrie then gave me a tight embrace, put her arm through mine, and escorted me to the crowd.

I glanced back at Abby and rolled my eyes as Marty slung his arm over my shoulder from the other side, not to miss one moment in the limelight.

As the song ended, and probably just as Carrie had scripted it, Willie strolled from the wrap-around porch and down the sidewalk to meet us halfway. He held out his hand for me to shake.

I shook it. Then he lifted it high in the air and said, "The man of the hour is here, let's get this party started!"

Abby and I stood at the back of the tent after the last few people had finished congratulating me. I'd survived the past two hours. Carrie and Willie had set up a large projection screen in the tent and I endured the hour-long showing of "Ordinary People, Extraordinary Events." Carrie's friends had patted me on the back and told me I'd done a great job in the interview, but even I knew I looked like a fish out of water and that I stumbled over the few words I spoke.

I glanced at Abby as she watched Marty working the crowd, handing out Butterfly Septic business cards. We had to laugh. Carrie and Willie's friends studied the big man wearing a T-shirt imprinted with "Official Bikini Inspector" in bright pink lettering with curiosity, especially since his shirt didn't quite cover his entire beer belly. But I also recognized the look of disdain when the people would glance at the card. A mortician probably receives the same reaction when he hands out

his business card. Poop and death, two certainties in life, but
no one wanted to think or talk about them.

The thump of helicopter blades grew louder and interrupted my thoughts, and I saw Willie making his way
toward us.

"He's here!" he shouted. "He made it!"

Willie told me the investor would be at the party, and I
overheard people talking about the man with reverence—
making it sound like he had more money and influence than
God. I kept waiting for Willie to introduce us, but the chaos
had made me forget until now.

"The guy who has made you rich…and possibly even
richer," Willie told me, scowling at my look of confusion.
"Anil Gupta. He just called and wants us to meet him out at
the helicopter."

Willie grabbed me by the arm and led me out of the tent,
but I pulled away from him and reached my hand out for
Abby.

"That's okay. You two go and talk business," Abby said.

"No," I said firmly. "I need your wisdom."

She reluctantly took my hand, even though Willie scoffed
and gave me a look of disapproval.

Once outside the tent, I watched the helicopter hover
overhead—swirling dirt, dried grass, and anything not nailed
down into a dust devil. The pilot swooped the chopper down
for a smooth landing in a flat area of their ten acres behind
the pool.

Willie directed us and motioned to keep our heads down
as we approached the aircraft.

The helicopter door popped open and an older man in a
business suit hopped out and waved us over. He shook
Willie's hand, then mine. "You must be Andy!" he shouted

over the roar of the engines. "I'm Anil Gupta." He shook Abby's hand as well. "You two mind going for a ride?"

I looked at Abby and shrugged. She returned an enthusiastic nod. Mr. Gupta helped Abby into the helicopter. Willie stepped onto the landing skid to enter, but the man waved him off and said. "Sorry, Willie. I want to talk with Andy alone."

Willie's entire demeanor changed, and his shoulders drooped. Mr. Gupta motioned for me to jump up into the aircraft and closed the door behind us. I nodded to the pilot, and he pointed to the headsets. Mr. Gupta hopped into the front passenger seat and placed his headset on his head as well. His voice came through the earpieces clearly.

"Okay, Andy and Abby, can you hear me okay? I thought this might be more convenient for us to talk without all the distractions. Besides," he looked at his watch, "the city fireworks will go off soon and we can give you a bird's-eye view."

The vibrations of the aircraft swelled as we lifted off. I looked down at Willie, who looked like a disappointed child on Christmas morning. I don't think I'd seen anyone tell Willie no. I, on the other hand, felt like this amazing adventure eclipsed every Christmas and every happy memory prior to this experience. As the distance between us and the ground increased, amazingly I didn't even feel afraid.

"Have you ever ridden in a helicopter before?"

Both Abby and I shook our heads. Abby's smile reflected mine.

The lights of Missoula twinkled as our altitude increased. Then streaks of light broke the stillness of the night, erupting in huge fire balls of red, blue, and gold sparkles.

"Ah, we got up here just in time," Mr. Gupta said through the headset. "God bless America."

The man was saying something more, but time and reality took a pause as the sky lit up with brilliant colors.

I looked down and Abby was holding my hand.

I'm not sure how business meetings normally go, but our time with Mr. Gupta was nothing like how I thought one should. We really just chatted, and even though Willie told me that Anil Gupta was one of the richest men in the world, he was easy to talk with. I told him I'd be happy to take him out to the claim tomorrow.

I hadn't seen Willie since we landed and hoped that the party would wind down soon. Feeling exhausted, I didn't have one more word to say to anyone. After slipping into the house to use the bathroom, I heard Marty's voice booming around the marble entryway as I walked down the hallway.

"Where is my little buddy?" His boisterous, slurred words made me cringe. "Andy, Andy, Andy! I saw you come in here!" he yelled.

I opened a door to my right, snuck in, and quickly shut it behind me. The room was dark, but with the familiar smell of gasoline, lawnmower, and yard supplies. I'd escaped into Willie and Carrie's garage. I leaned my forehead against the wall and hoped that Marty wouldn't look behind closed doors. As he stumbled by, cursing loudly, I held my breath.

My shoulders relaxed, and I sighed. The spotlight exhausted me. Although, I had to admit the attention I received from Carrie was confusing and pleasant all at the same time. She'd cozied up to me several times, introducing me to her friends and holding my arm like sweethearts, as she reminded everyone that we'd known each other since grade school. She always forgot to introduce Abby with the same affection.

I turned with my back to the door and slid to the floor. Here I was, around more people than ever before, feeling lonelier than at any other time in my life. Somehow, I didn't feel like I'd struck it rich.

A weird memory popped into my mind as I sat in the darkness. Instead of attending high school as a freshman, I bagged groceries at the local store. Most of my paychecks went to help Mama, but she'd okayed the purchase of a record player. My sisters and brothers all gave me a hard time for the first album I bought, but there was something about the girl on the front that made me swoon—Olivia Newton-John who graced the cover may be the reason I had such a crush on Carrie. Even at that age I knew God created us to love and be loved, but it sure hadn't worked out for me.

About to venture out so I could quickly find Abby and we could sneak home, I froze when I heard a noise in the garage. I held my breath again. Then there was a giggle and voices. *Oh no, I'm not alone out here.*

I slid back up the door to stand when one of the car doors opened and the interior lights came on, illuminating the garage.

Willie staggered from the backseat, holding a wine bottle, then stood and took a swig. He then offered his hand to a young lady with short black hair.

I turned to make my escape when she saw me and giggled.

Willie belched loudly and stared at me. "What are you looking at, dumb-ass?"

MIDAS TOUCH

I'd hardly slept a wink last night between the excitement of the upcoming helicopter ride with Anil to the claim and the weight of the secret I held about Willie. I wanted to believe the best in Willie, but down deep I knew he was up to no good with that young brunette. He'd brushed past me in the garage with the girl in tow, mumbling about getting something out of the car. I didn't even tell Abby what I'd seen, as Mama taught me not to gossip, but it made me sick to my stomach for Carrie. When Mr. Gupta told me that I would be the only one to accompany he and his pilot out to the claim, it made me happy as I didn't want to face Willie.

The burden of his secret and zooming over Missoula at five-thousand feet in the helicopter brought queasiness to my stomach. Flying between Mount Sentinel and Mount Jumbo, then directly through the Hellgate Canyon was exhilarating—just what I imagined the Mandalorian must feel when flying with his jetpack. I think Mama would agree that Hell's Gate didn't look so ominous at this altitude. Amazingly, in minutes, we zipped over Riverside and then Milltown. My trailer looked tiny from this vantage point.

I glanced back at Anil, smiled, and gave him a thumbs up. He rested comfortably in the back seat, as if out for a Sunday drive, and nodded. He'd generously offered me the front seat next to the pilot. When we started off this morning, he laughed and said there were two rules today. First, I couldn't touch the controls of the helicopter and second, I had to call him Anil.

Originally from India, Anil fascinated me. His dark eyes and skin, warm smile, kind eyes and easy-going personality made the man, who Willie told me was in his late seventies, look much younger despite his bald head with gray hair around the sides. With a thin and wiry build, I was uncertain I could beat him in an arm-wrestling match. Beyond that, Willie said the man was wealthier than my brain could fathom.

The pilot banked the aircraft left, turning up the Black-foot Canyon, where the river glistened below. The drive that would've taken half an hour to make in my truck took only minutes, and soon we hovered over the big bend of the Black-foot River and Pop's claim. Through the headset, I explained and pointed to McNamara's place, then across the river toward Johnsrud Park—describing how the claim flowed around the curve of the river and ended at Gold Creek. From this vantage point, Pop's claim really looked like a natural amphitheater.

Anil and the pilot discussed potential landing sites on the flat plateau above the claim and picked an area with the fewest trees. The pilot then looked at me and said, "I called the ranger station this morning and gained permission to land on the National Forest property." Then he swooped the aircraft skillfully to the landing spot and shut down the engines.

I followed Anil's lead of unbuckling my seatbelt, removing the headset, opening my door, and hopping out.

We walked to the edge of Strobel Cliff and took in the panoramic view of the area.

"Wow, this is beautiful," Anil said with his slight British accent. He inhaled a deep breath of the clear mountain air.

"See where Gold Creek flows into the Blackfoot right before the big bend? That's where I found the first nugget—where the river turns to that deep emerald green is one of the best fishing holes in the world." I looked at Anil to make sure he was following me. "We found the other nuggets buried at the bottom of the cliff in that alcove in the rocks. My father's claim extends to Gold Creek." I pointed to the left. "And to McNamara's place." I turned and pointed to the right. "You can see why the claim is hard to get to—you either have to hike in from the other side or cross the river…or take a helicopter." I smiled.

Anil crossed his arms over his chest and then rubbed his chin with one hand.

"I can't tell you if there's any more gold in these rocks or not," I said.

Unusually quiet, Anil gathered his thoughts and finally said, "Oh, there is gold here all right. I can feel it."

I looked at him and thought that he was kidding, but he looked out over the area with all seriousness, then pointed to a big rock on the edge of the cliff where we could sit. I followed him, sat on the boulder, and pulled a water bottle from my backpack for him.

"Thank you." He unscrewed the cap, toasted me, and took a swig. I did the same with mine. "What a spectacular day. You did not want to bring your girlfriend?"

Heat rose up my back, thinking of Carrie. *He knows she's married. She only appears in my life in fantasy form.* I didn't know what to say, except it refueled my anger at Willie.

"Abby seems very nice." He looked at me. I hoped I didn't look like a deer caught in headlights. "Uh." I chuckled nervously. "Oh, Abby is just a good friend. She's not my girlfriend."

"Is it because of her disability?" he asked bluntly.

"Oh, gosh no. I don't think of her as disabled. She's probably more capable than most people I know. It's just that we've been friends forever and I...uh...I don't know." I felt flustered and wanted to change the subject. "Did you buy the Lioness as well?"

"So that's what you call it." He smiled. "Yes, it's a very intriguing piece."

"What will you do with all of them?"

"The Lioness, as you call her, I will keep for myself. I will sell the others as bullion. Even though I am an American, my home country of India has a ferocious appetite for gold. Indian households possess the largest amount of the precious metal in the world."

I thought about that as I inspected the sky. The day was warming, but not hot, and there were enough fluffy white clouds drifting by to make the sky interesting.

"Do you come here often?" Anil asked.

"As often as I can. Especially in the summer."

"Yes, I can see why."

"Most of my fondest childhood memories are here, the few that I have. Picnicking with my family, swimming in the river...it's where my dad taught me how to fly fish."

"Ah, the simple things in life. And I bet it was all free." I watched his eyes and thought I registered sadness. "Were you close with your father?" He looked back at me.

I took a swig of my water, trying to decide how best to answer that. I shook my head.

"Ah, that complicated relationship between a father and son." He sighed. "My father was a cobbler in India. We grew up very poor. Although quite successful in my life, I still don't know if my father would approve of me," he said with sadness.

I almost had to laugh. Here I sat, one of the lowliest men next to one of the wealthiest men in the world, and he, like me, cared about what his father thought of him.

"How wealthy are you?" I asked.

He choked on a sip of water and looked at me.

"I'm afraid, son, you should not ask those kinds of questions. It is like asking a rancher how many cows he runs or a farmer how many acres he owns."

I blushed from his reprimand, but he continued.

"But since you are bold enough to inquire, I will tell you. *People Magazine* tells me I have a net worth of forty-three billion dollars. Of course, that fluctuates by millions and even tens of millions daily." He grinned at me.

"What is it like to have that much money?"

"You ask hard questions." He laughed again. "Honestly, it affords me great possibilities—I can go wherever I want, buy whatever I want. And of course, it can be very convenient for getting places." He nodded at the helicopter. "It comes with a considerable amount of responsibility. But mostly, it makes me feel lonely, because people treat you differently because of your wealth. Money changes everything, for better or worse… don't you sense that already?"

He looked at me for acknowledgement. He'd spoken what I felt on the inside. I had just thought there was something wrong with me.

"Gold…money will change this beautiful corner of the

world as well." He spread his arms over Strobel Cliff, then pointed downriver to McNamara's place. "We will need to buy that property so we can access the claim."

"Access?"

"For the heavy-duty equipment to mine the gold."

I grimaced at the thought and wanted to know more, but he asked me, "Do you ever wonder why gold?"

I looked at him inquisitively.

"Did you know scientists think that all the gold found on Earth comes from meteorite bombardment over 200 million years ago during the formation of the planet? The Incas referred to gold as the 'tears of the sun.' They were not too far off. The craziest part I've read is that as the earth formed, molten iron sank to the core and took the vast majority of the planet's precious metals with it. Some researchers estimate that there is enough gold in the core to cover the entire surface of the earth with a twelve-foot layer."

He took a drink from the water bottle and continued.

"Chemically, gold is uninteresting and barely reacts with other elements. Yet, out of all the 118 elements in the periodic table, why have we placed such a value on it? And, oddly enough, it has been that way for as long as we know. I have seen Egyptian jewelry in museums originating from 5,000 years before Christ."

"Wow," I said. "I didn't realize that."

"I own gold coins from around 550 BC stamped with the image of King Croesus of Lydia. Which is modern day Turkey," he added. "His wealth came from the sands of the Pactolus River, where the legends say that King Midas washed his hands to rid himself of the 'Midas Touch.' Do you know that story?"

I thought I did. "Is that where everything he touched turned to gold?"

"Yes, but this will be your homework. Please read the whole story. We must be very careful that your wealth doesn't destroy your life, like it does with so many families. Just look at all the failed lives after people win the lottery."

We sat in silence. I contemplated all he'd said, and wondered if Pop knew any of this. My entire life I thought all he cared about was beer and the mill. But now I wished he was around to help me decide what to do.

Anil patted me on the knee. "I could make you a very rich man indeed."

LIPSTICK

T he small block of wood sat motionless on my kitchen table, begging for me to carve it. But like a blank canvas, it hadn't revealed itself to me. The only image I saw in my head was that of a dollar sign, and I didn't want to whittle that somehow. It was too, I don't know, impure.

I glanced over to the corner where my prayer candle burned. God was just as silent this morning. The flame flickered with life, but no answers came to me. The boxes full of Mama's belongings stacked along the wall might contain answers, but I hadn't had the motivation to go through them. Maybe doing so meant too much of a finality of her death.

I bent closer and inspected the fine grain of the four-inch cube of cherry wood. I'd saved it ever since the guy at the lumber store gave it to me. "A scrap end-cut piece the customer had no use for," he'd said.

I'd wanted to do something special with it and knew this morning was the time, I just didn't know what to carve.

Yesterday, Anil gave me plenty to think about and today all my thoughts jumbled in my mind. He'd asked me to repeat the story of finding the three nuggets clumped together no less than four times. Perhaps it stumped him as much as me. But he said, "Because of the location and how they were buried simultaneously, my only conclusion is that your father put them there. Was he saving them for later? Was he somehow protecting your family from the hazards and hardship of wealth?" he wondered out loud. "I've been around many gold discoveries and they don't happen like that."

Of one thing Anil was certain: the Strobel Cliff contained gold. It had the correct rock formation, plenty of quartz and, of course, we'd already found gold. He suggested the possibility that my father had discovered the nuggets in the surrounding area. I told Anil that Pop never explored or even seemed interested in any of the adjacent land, so it satisfied him that the nuggets came from the claim.

My phone vibrated on the table next to the block.

"Oh good," I told Max, who lay curled in my lap. "It's the lawyer lady."

"Hello?" I answered.

"Hi Andy, Emma Rankin here. I got your message yesterday and wanted to call you right back, but I was in court all day. First, congratulations on finding more gold. I think that's wonderful. Second, I went to work first thing this morning expanding your claim. I extended it as far as possible in all directions. Of course, McNamara's place blocks us from going any farther south, but we could enlarge it around the corner of the Blackfoot and north until it bumps up against the Rattlesnake Wilderness. All in all, the claim includes approximately another hundred acres."

"Thank you. When will you finish the paperwork?"

"It's done and filed, Andy," she said, and added, "I know someone in that department."

"Great. Thank you."

"Andy, this was a brilliant thing to do. I'm sorry I didn't recommend it before. I just thought the first nugget might be a fluke."

"That's okay, Emma. I didn't think about it until yesterday myself."

I disconnected the call, put the phone back on the table, and sighed. "Brilliant. She called me brilliant." I laughed, scratching Max under his chin, making him yawn, bored with my self-adulation.

It was actually Anil who'd recommended it. We'd walked along the top of the cliff to each boundary. At one end he said, "You know, a smart man would extend his claim," he said, and winked.

It relieved me to hear from Emma this morning that no one had beaten me to it. It made me trust the man that much more.

Anil also talked openly about my options. Even without me telling him about my income and resources, he seemed to comprehend my situation. If I wanted, I could do nothing and live comfortably. He called it "Milltown rich." Without using a calculator, he told me what he expected Willie to average with his investments, how much I could spend each month, considering my expected life span, and what I might leave to my beneficiaries. Anil had a remarkable ability to juggle numbers in his head. After calculating how much I'd have to pay in taxes, he said, "You could live comfortably, yet modestly, for the rest of your life."

I told him it surprised me that the money didn't go further, and he laughed. "That's exactly where lottery winners have their downfall. They think this vast sum of money is so massive there is no way on earth they could spend it all. They buy a nice new house and cars and use it like there's an unlimited amount. Then it's suddenly all gone, and they're just as miserable, if not more, than they were before. There is an illusion that wealth brings contentment and happiness," he said, "but it produces neither."

The second and third option involved mining the claim—either I sell it to him, or we work together as partners.

Right then and there, he offered me one hundred twenty million dollars to buy the claim outright. "Then you would be 'Los Angeles wealthy.'" He chuckled. For the amount of gold he thought the mine would produce, he told me that if we partnered, and I took on half the risk, it might mean more money even still. He laughed when I nodded to the helicopter and said, "You mean 'helicopter rich?'"

When we shook hands back at the airport, I told him I'd think about all this. He reassured me, "This is totally your decision, son. Just as it was for your father."

Two thoughts continued to pop up in my mind: Anil told me that wealth would change everything…both me, and the little corner of my world along the Blackfoot River. The other thought was when he'd asked about Abby being my girlfriend. *Had I truly never considered her like that because of her disability?* If I was totally honest with myself, I hoped I looked past that issue and saw a kind woman, but as my mind drilled down to memories of early grade school, perhaps there was a part of me that was afraid of her deformities. Kind of scary to a misinformed kid—an unknown that struck some underlying fear. Now it seemed so irrational, but as a child without understanding, fearing the person's hardship somehow.

But the gold and wealth notwithstanding, my heart cried out to be loved.

I picked up the wood block and instantly saw it. What I would carve into this beautiful block of cherry was a heart. I'd been looking for something way more complex, but I now saw it. A three-dimensional heart rising out of the base. When carving, the artist can smooth the image or leave it jagged and crude, like the bulldog on the Mack truck. The heart I created had to be imperfect, rough, like my life somehow.

I used my pencil to sketch the shape on the block and could see the 3-D heart come to life. I wanted to carve the base so it looked like it cradled the heart as it emerged, as if the heart rose from the ashes. But how to make it look like it was rising and not sinking? I wasn't sure yet. Such a metaphor of my life right now. *Am I winning or losing?*

I picked up my knife and turned the block over and over in my hand. The first cut always made me sweat. Especially in this fine block of wood. You could always take more off, but you can't ever put it back.

The grain of the cherry nicely resisted the knife's edge as a shaving peeled back and landed on the table. I'd told Anil that I tithed 10% of the value of the Lioness to the church, which he seemed glad for, but suggested that there were many other wonderful charities if I did the same with the other three nuggets. He thought that over three hundred thousand was a lot of money to go to a small-town church. But I believed the church would help lots of people in the community that were down on their luck.

He also suggested that I buy myself *one* thing. "Get that urge out of the way," he said. "Whether it's a new truck or travel trailer or vacation. Just treat yourself to that one thing and then be satisfied with investing the rest."

I forgot to ask him about his thoughts on Willie, as I noticed some indifference to him. Anil said Willie would do fine with the small amount that I have to invest for now, but if we became partners, or he bought out my claim, he wanted to see my wealth go to a real money guy. I probably got stuck on the thought that Anil saw my 3.2 million as peanuts.

Before I could whittle another cut, someone pounded an

urgent knock. Max startled awake and bounded toward the door with loud yapping. Being so deep in my thoughts, and Max so sound asleep, we'd missed a car pulling up and footsteps on the deck.

I put down the block and knife when there was a second knock and a voice calling my name. I picked up Max and opened the door.

Carrie stood on the other side of the threshold. Mascara ran down her cheeks. Her eyes were puffy and red. She dissolved into tears when she saw me.

"Carrie, what's wrong?"

She covered her face with her hands. "Willie and I had a huge fight yesterday," she sobbed. "Willie packed his bags and moved out this morning."

Looking to the right and left, and thankfully not seeing Mrs. Jarvi, I ushered Carrie inside.

"I'm so sorry, Carrie. What happened?"

"He ran off with another woman," she sobbed. "In his rage, he said you knew." Her aqua-blue eyes glowed as she looked at me. "Is that true, Andy?"

The images of Willie helping that brunette out of the car flashed in my mind and I swallowed hard.

"I didn't know…"

"You must know something," she demanded.

I moved an empty pizza box off the couch and invited her to sit. As I sat down next to her, I noticed that even though Carrie appeared disheveled, with smeared makeup and messy hair, she'd put on a pair of skinny jeans and red pumps that matched her blouse and lipstick.

"The night of the party, I slipped into the garage, trying to escape Marty." I looked into her eyes. "When I was in there, Willie got out of his car…" I swallowed again, "with a girl."

"Why didn't you say something to me?"

I glanced at her and knew she was mad, but it really wasn't directed at me. I wanted to tell her I didn't see what happened between them, and it wasn't my place to rat on him, and lots of other excuses, but that's not what she searched for. "I'm really sorry, Carrie."

She dissolved into tears and leaned forward, and I caught her in my arms. Every nerve in my body sizzled with conflict and desire. Her body felt warm against mine and her head snuggled into the crook of my neck. Strands of blond hair that escaped her bun tickled my nose. Her hair smelled like everything my fantasies had imagined.

My body wanted to linger against hers but my mind reminded me, even though married to a louse, she was still married. I pulled back and held her by her shoulders. "I'm so sorry, Carrie. What are you going to do?"

She wiped at the tears and makeup running down her cheeks. "I don't think it's my choice. He told me he's been unhappy for a long time. He said he has finally found someone who loves him the way he deserves," she said, causing her sobs to return. "That jerk said they're moving into the lake place and I can keep the house for however long I can afford it." Her bottom lip quivered. "I'm going to lose my house, Andy."

She tumbled into my arms again and I held her as her body quaked.

"Twelve years of marriage down the toilet," she sobbed. "That skank is taking all that away."

I wanted to ask her if he had told her who the other woman was but, internal conflict and all, I held her close.

"Carrie, I'll help you in any way I can," I said.

She pulled away, wiped her tears and flashed me her dazzling smile. "Oh Andy, you are so kind. You really would do that?"

She caught me totally off guard when she leaned in and kissed me on the cheek, catching a corner of my mouth.

My brain misfired, and I thought I was going to kiss her again on the lips when Max gave a single bark.

"Hey, Andy, got your mail…whoa!"

I looked up to see Abby in her uniform, standing at the open door, holding a stack of mail.

Her eyes were wide open in shock and pain.

"I'll just set it here for you," she said, then let the mail drop from her hand, turned, and limped across the deck.

I shot off the couch and ran after her.

"Abby, wait!"

I caught up to her, and she tried to push past me.

"Abby, wait," I said again, and held her arm. She looked down at my hand like she did at the college boy's the night of the bar brawl.

I quickly let go. "Abby, it's not anything like what you just saw."

She looked at me, pursed her lips, then reached up and wiped lipstick off my cheek.

"I know exactly what I saw."

TEMPTATION

My head spun like a top. Yesterday, Abby had marched off my porch to deliver the mail at the next house after she witnessed Carrie kissing me. I ran after her, only to be halted by the universal hand signal to STOP. Then Abby said, "Andy, I'm on the job right now and we can talk later." She walked away.

Last night turned out to be no more helpful to my friend-ship with her. I went to her home, hoping to reconnect. But she wouldn't let me in, both literally and figuratively. I'd never seen her like this, and it was all my fault. I felt terrible.

After finally convincing her to at least come out onto her porch and talk to me, through tears she admitted she'd enjoyed my companionship for the past few weeks. And no, that didn't mean at all that we were dating or that I should feel bad about being pursued by other women. She told me I did not owe her an explanation, or anything for that matter.

I tried and tried to convince her that Carrie was not pursuing me, and that I was merely trying to comfort her. I just couldn't read the wry smile Abby gave me when I talked about it.

The second part of the conversation hit me the hardest when Abby said: "Look Andy, Carrie is a beautiful woman. Heck, if I was a man I wouldn't be able to help myself either." Then a waterfall of tears released when Abby continued, "Romance doesn't come easy to people with disabilities. You have to find someone who can look past it. I can't do anything about this useless arm." She slapped her deformed hand hard enough to worry me. "Or this gimpy leg." She slugged her hip. "I'm not mad at you, Andy. Just kind of pissed off about everything, I guess. Sometimes life seems *so* unfair. Why are there the Carries of the world then the rest of us who limp through life?"

Near the end of her tears, we hugged and promised to remain friends. "I need you, Abby. You're a great friend. You're the only person I trust to help me make these decisions."

I'm not sure she appreciated hearing those words. They seemed to bring her more pain. When I told her about Anil's offer, I couldn't imagine what she meant when she shook her head, kissed me on the cheek, said goodbye, and told me I would know what to do.

Waking up this morning, I still didn't know what to do. Part of the problem was that I had no idea what to do with a couple million dollars, never mind a hundred million or more. It was as foreign a concept to me as living on Mars. Worst of all, I had hurt Abby. I enjoyed the attention that Carrie gave me, but it filled me with guilt and remorse.

And now I'd just agreed to meet Carrie this afternoon to look at a condo that her friend had up for sale that overlooked the Clark Fork River. Honestly, I couldn't care less about moving, but how could I turn down an offer to spend time with her, even with the alarm bells going off in my head?

I'd hardly slept a wink until sometime this morning when I fell into a deep sleep with unsettling dreams, waking up drenched in sweat and late for my meeting with Carrie.

Max gave me a weird look as I reached for the doorknob. I had not taken time to light Mama's prayer candle for the first time since she'd died.

"I'll do it when I get home," I said to Max, and jogged to my truck.

———

I thought about Anil's suggestion to purchase one thing. I'm just not sure it included a condo on the river for $370,000. The kitchen alone had more square footage than my entire trailer.

"Isn't it fabulous?" Carrie said, opening the black refrigerator door.

I watched her bend over to open the bottom drawer of the fridge and saw the lacy edge of red panties under her short yellow sundress. I quickly averted my gaze to the pearly white granite countertop with gold flecks.

She stood back up and turned to me. "Don't you think?"

"Uh...yeah," I said, watching her out of my peripheral vision. Looking at the front of her was not much more helpful since the sundress, suspended on tiny straps, revealed a generous view of her cleavage.

"Wait until you see this," she said, and walked to the full panel windows overlooking the river and opened a floor-to-ceiling sliding glass door. The sweet smell of cottonwood drifted in along with the gentle river sounds of ripples and singing birds. She stepped out onto the deck and motioned for me to follow.

Her sundress fluttered in the breeze, and she didn't bother holding it down. I didn't know why I was sweating so much.

I joined her at the railing. The morning sun warmed my face, and I took a deep breath.

"This will be the best room of your house," she said, like I'd already bought the place.

A group of young people floating by on innertubes tied together as one mass waved. One girl in a bikini yelled, "Nice place!"

I smiled and waved back.

Carrie shot me a wily smile and patted me on the arm. "I told you you'd like it."

I leaned on the railing and had to admit it was nice. The apartment itself did little for me with its fancy countertops, black appliances, and white cabinets in the kitchen which opened into an expansive living room complete with a fake fireplace and giant TV. *Okay, I guess that part is good.* I could imagine playing video games on it. But the deck really was something else. It had a large built-in grill on one side and comfy looking recliners facing the river.

I had this funny image of Max sitting on one of the *chaise longues* with sunglasses and a straw hat, watching the world go by. It made me laugh.

Carrie looked at me and tilted her head.

"I just had this hilarious vision of little Maxi-boy in the lap of luxury."

"Max?"

"You know, my dog," I said, a little annoyed that she didn't remember.

"There is a great dog park right over there for your mutt." She pointed to the left.

We stood in silence, watching two bluebirds chase each other through the willows along the bank of the river.

"Well, that's a good sign, don't you think?" Carrie asked.

I didn't know what to say. She hadn't said one word about Willie and seemed to live on a planet of oblivion.

I couldn't stand it another minute and said, "You okay?"

My question seemed to penetrate the perky façade, and sadness crossed her face. She exhaled.

"I don't know, Andy. Just when I thought I had my life figured out." She shook her head, and a tear rolled down her cheek. "Willie and I have been together for a long time and it hasn't always been easy. Don't get me wrong, I love him, but he's not the easiest guy to live with. I guess I knew this was coming." She looked at me, her blue eyes making my knees go weak. "This is not the first time that he's been unfaithful." She grimaced. "You blame them? You know what a stud he is."

I knew my facial expression reflected the shock in my mind—maybe from the news of his known infidelities, but mostly due to her acceptance of them.

"I'd thought about leaving him but didn't know what to do with the kids and the house…" Her voice trailed off. She wiped a tear from her cheek. "I guess he made that decision for me. So much for the perfect life."

I wanted to put my arm around her, but thought it would just complicate things.

"Well, *c'est la vie*, as my mother would say," Carrie said. "If you don't talk about it, it didn't happen." She waved it off. "My father was unfaithful to my mother. Wouldn't you know I'd marry someone who would do the exact same thing?" She shook her head and grimaced.

I felt my emotions falling into a deep sadness for her, but her smile returned. "Sorry, Andy, I didn't mean to turn so sour." She leaned in and lay her head on my arm and then kissed it. "You're sweet to listen to me. I don't have many people I can talk to. Even my so-called friends would totally judge me."

We watched another group of floaters drift by.

"So, what do you think?" she asked, and lifted her head off my arm.

My head swirled with confusion.

"About the apartment," she finally said.

"Well...it's nice, but I don't know. Anil said I need to be careful about doing a lot of spending right now. I suppose if I take his offer for the claim, I can do whatever I want."

"Are you thinking of not doing a deal with him?" She took a small step backward.

"I, uh...I don't know. They would destroy Strobel Cliff. I mean, the mine would totally change that entire area."

"Yes, but Andy..." She seemed to get a bit exasperated. "You would have more money than you'd ever know what to do with. It's just a dirty ol' rock pile, after all."

I shot her a look, and she softened her tone.

"What I meant to say is that I'm sure there are laws on how they could impact the river and the land. I bet they're required to make it look okay in the end. You may never get an opportunity like this again."

CLAIM JUMPER

The clouds and cooler temperature crafted a perfect day for a hike. The weatherman warned of a shower or two today, but I had put my rain jacket in my daypack and neither Max nor I were afraid of getting wet. Already four miles in, my head had cleared and my shoulders relaxed.

I'd parked the truck at the trailhead near Whitaker Bridge. I worried the five and a half-mile hike would be too much for Max, but when I looked down at him, he trotted beside me with his head held high and tail stuck straight out, on alert for the next chipmunk or other varmint to chase. The adventure had brought out his wild canine side. Sawdust and dirt covered his muzzle from digging for a squirrel, but he seemed happier than a wolf on a hunt. *He'll sleep good tonight,* I thought.

I had decided that making the hike into the claim today might be a better way to wipe the cobwebs out of my head. Not sleeping well didn't help, but there was too much for my poor brain to think through.

At least I didn't have another kiss from Carrie to feel

guilty about. Besides being flirty, we'd behaved ourselves and actually had an enjoyable time together—talking and reminiscing about grade school. She had to leave to pick up one of her kids, but asked if I would come over for dinner tomorrow night so we could continue our pleasant conversation. I saw little wrong with that.

Abby continued to dodge my attempts to reconnect with her. I invited her to join me today, but she had to work. And besides, she wasn't sure her leg could make the eleven miles. I thought about reminding her that she probably walked that far every day on her route, but knew she used both as an excuse to not see me.

I talked to Anil last night and told him I needed more time to decide. He'd called from his helicopter over New York City on his way to a meeting, which made me picture him as Bruce Wayne. Thankfully, Batman told me to take as much time as I required.

Marty, on the other hand, was far grumpier when I let him know I wanted to delay coming back to work. I had promised to start today, but when we'd found the other gold nuggets that whole timeline had changed for me, and now I had no idea what to do about my job with Butterfly Septic. He mentioned to me he'd sent one of the guys out with Number One today, and I thought that was fair. I wasn't sure, with all the money I had, that I'd ever go back as a honey-dipper. He told me, "You're getting too big for your own britches," and slammed the phone down. Honestly, I think he's mad that this good fortune happened to me and not him.

Last night I began the daunting task of sorting through Mama's boxes of possessions. Out of all the things rattling around in my brain, the most disconcerting was whether she and Pop knew about the gold. Not that I found anything that answered my question, but just going through her belongings brought terrible grief to my heart. I took for granted that Mama would always be present and now, in the great mystery of life, death had silenced her. No more of her chicken and dumplings or chocolate cake she fixed for my birthday. Even at ninety, for my last birthday with her, she put together the recipes from memory.

The one thing that became crystal clear going through her items was that material possessions meant little to her. Of course there were plenty of small trinkets and a few pieces of jewelry, most of which I never saw her wear. But the things she seemed to hold most dear were anything my siblings or me made or any memorabilia from our family time together.

I recalled that she was a great collector of rocks, and now I wished I'd written down what each one represented to her. She'd tell us: "I found this one when we took you kids through Yellowstone. This heart-shaped one I found the day I married your father. I picked up these when your brothers and sisters were born." There were also a number of stones from Johnsrud Park.

She'd even remembered to collect one the day I was born, even though Sam and Ernie were killed. But if I recalled which rock that was, I'd throw it into the Blackfoot.

In her belongings, there was one thing that forced me to wonder if she knew about the gold. It was a small shadowbox with a framed cross-stitch she had done. Her initials were at the bottom, so I knew she'd made it. It read: "*Lay not up for yourselves treasures upon earth, where moth and rust doth corrupt, and where thieves break through and steal. But lay up for yourselves treasures in heaven, where neither moth nor rust doth corrupt, and where thieves do not break through nor steal. For where your treasure is, there will your heart be also. MS—* Mary Strobel."

Mama displayed it proudly in their bedroom. I'd never

held it in my hands until last night, and when I placed the frame back in the box, it rattled. As I took it out for closer inspection, it shocked me to see a quarter-sized gold nugget loose in the frame.

A shrill alarm from a squirrel called out from a tree beside the trail, breaking me from my reverie. Max paused, saw it, and dove into the forest with full enthusiasm. The squirrel taunted him from a log he'd scampered to and loudly voiced his displeasure at being disturbed. Then the squirrel jumped from branch to branch and ran into the trees with Max on its tail.

"Max!" I called to him.

The forest turned quiet for a split second before I heard Max yelp. I took two quick steps toward the trees, when Max shot out at full speed and leaped into my arms. A few steps behind him ran an enormous black bear. It skidded to a halt at the tree line when it saw me holding Max. The bear rose to full height on its hind legs and pinned its ears back.

It huffed at me once, twice, then dropped onto all fours, turned, and ran back into the forest, chomping its jaws loudly, warning me not to follow.

I stood stunned and shaken. It had happened in a matter of seconds, and there was nothing I could've done about it. If the bear had charged, I'd barely have had time to cover my face.

"Holy cow, Max. That was a close one."

He whimpered, then licked my neck.

"Yeah, thanks for bringing him to me." I scrunched his muzzle.

He stretched toward the forest and growled.

"Oh, you're real tough in my arms, aren't you? We better move along. That darn bear may not give us a second chance."

I carried him and continued down the path. This was

indeed the wild side of the Blackfoot and probably a fraction of how it was when the Indian tribes and Lewis walked this trail. *What a sight that must have been.*

I could hear the ripple of Gold Creek around the corner and knew we were close to the claim. As we broke out from the trees, Strobel Cliff opened up like a grand amphitheater. But as I moved closer, I noticed someone up on a ledge of the cliff, so I quickened my pace.

Even from this distance, I realized right away the figure was Willie. Who else dressed in stretchy shorts with a bare chest and waved around a metal detector? No one but Willie —the claim jumper.

It took a few minutes to cover the quarter mile until I stood below Willie and waited for him to see me. The man was oblivious. I thought about tossing a rock up high enough to get his attention.

It proved to be unnecessary as he tripped and stumbled to his knees, thankfully not tumbling off the edge. Willie saw me when he picked himself up and waved, hesitated, then shrugged, and started his descent.

He came down much more carefully than the last time he skied down and fell to an abrupt halt on his face.

"Hey, bud. What are you doing here?"

I huffed. "Uh…what are *you* doing here?"

"I just needed some space, so I thought…I'd come help you out," he added quickly.

"You find anything?" I asked suspiciously and examined his shorts. The only lump I saw was God given.

He looked up at the cliff. "Hell no," he said, and glanced back at me. "I don't know what Anil sees in this pile of rock. I haven't heard a beep—you need to take his offer and run."

I crossed my arms and looked away. I didn't like Willie taking liberties with my claim, or telling me what I should do, and I sure as heck didn't appreciate what I'd seen and heard on the Fourth of July.

"You still sore at me from the other night?"

Steam seemed to fill my head. I had taken on some of Carrie's offense. I'd never had the nerve to stand up to Willie in my entire life, but I said, "What you were doing with that girl was wrong."

I half expected Willie to deck me until he took a small step backward, sighed, and looked down at the gravel.

We stood in silence as the Blackfoot rippled by, then he wiped the sweat from his brow and said, "Whew, I gotta sit for a minute."

I pointed to Pop's alcove in the rock where we'd found the nuggets. We walked over and sat with our backs resting against the large ponderosa.

Willie picked up a stone and tossed it into the river. "Maybe you've already learned that Carrie and I split up."

"I actually heard you left her," I said boldly.

He bobbed his head and looked at me. I thought he might fly into a rage, but our relationship had obviously changed. I knew a secret that no one else did, and besides that, I was now one of his clients.

"Look, I know it looks terrible…I look terrible. But no one knows what it's been like to be married to the queen."

I glowered at him, and he looked away.

"Everyone thinks of Carrie as this sweet, caring person. But man, they have no idea how vicious and conniving she can be. She judges and talks bad about all her friends. You don't even want to hear how she mocks Abby." He threw another rock toward the river. "Besides, you don't understand what it's like living with such a beauty. Everywhere we go, and I mean *everywhere*, men and women ogle and flirt with her. I feel like I always have my guard up because she's so naïve. I'm like, 'That guy just wants to get in your pants,' and she's like, 'Oh Willie, quit being so jealous. He's just being nice.'" He shook his head. "You should see how all the guys look at her. I think she loves it and eggs 'em on. She wiggles her tail and gets whatever she demands. She really knows how to work it to her advantage. And believe me, there's so much more."

I had a hard time feeling sorry for Willie, but everything he was saying was true. And what was worse, I'd been looking at her in all the same ways.

"When we got married, we had a red-hot love affair, but I'm telling you, once the kids were born, she wanted nothing to do with me. Us guys have our needs. Isn't that right?"

I didn't take the bait and said, "She's still your wife. If you're moving on, you need to take the proper steps."

Willie's face turned bright crimson and he said, "What would you know…" but didn't finish the sentence.

He tossed another rock into the water.

"Look, I'm sorry, Andy. I need to keep my business and personal life separate. But I promise I'll do the right thing with Carrie. I've already asked the attorney to draw up divorce papers. She'll get what she needs, just not all that she wants."

I sighed. I'd said my piece, and besides, my own conscience wasn't exactly clean. Maybe now I didn't feel so bad about my desire for her or for accepting her invitation to dinner.

"Let's me and you stay buds and make a gob of money." He held out his hand to shake. "How about it, pal?"

36

KALE

As I walked up the steps to Carrie's front porch, I couldn't help but feel sorry for Willie after our talk yesterday. All that he'd built for his family had crumbled. Even with a successful business and beautiful home, his personal life had crashed and burned. From the outside looking in, he had it all. I guess you never know what people are truly going through. I told myself that I'd accepted Carrie's dinner invitation as a helpful friend. But in the dark recesses of my mind I knew better, and I was no different than the scoundrels that Willie fumed about.

As I stopped at the front door, my cologne cloud caught up with me and I realized I'd overdone it. I'd swung by the truck stop near my house and purchased a small bottle of Brut. Never wearing cologne before, I didn't know how much to apply, but clearly I'd put on too much. I turned to run back to the truck to find a rag to wipe it off when the front door swung open.

"Hi Andy," Carrie said solemnly, a mostly empty wineglass in her hand. Her eyes were red and swollen. She wiped her nose with a tissue.

"Hey, Carrie. Um...you want me to come back another time?"

"No, no, Andy...come in." She opened the door fully. "I'm having a tough day, but I could use a friend right now."

I stepped over the threshold, and she patted my arm.

"Don't you smell good," she said, smiling for the first time.

"Uh, yeah, sorry...I didn't—"

Carrie pinched my sleeve. "New shirt?"

I nodded, hoping she didn't notice that my jeans were new as well and that I'd remembered to remove all the tags.

"It looks good on you," she said. "Movin' on up in the world." She patted my arm again and escorted me inside.

As we walked into the kitchen, it surprised me to see her in bare feet, holey jeans, and a red flannel shirt that she'd tied at the waist. Despite the emotional turmoil, she looked great.

She stopped at the kitchen island where she'd spread some papers out. I recognized the letterhead of Borke, Finch, and Donahue.

"Want to see how to destroy a life in one fell swoop?" She picked up the bottle of wine near the documents, filling both her glass and the empty one beside it. She handed me the glass of red wine and clinked hers against mine.

Not wanting to hurt her feelings by refusing the drink, I took a sip, hoping I didn't make an unpleasant face from the taste. I looked around for Grayson and Riley, but the house was quiet except for some soft music coming from ceiling speakers.

"Yeah, Willie has the kids at the lake," she told me, reading my mind. "Just great, huh? He probably has them out on the boat with that woman." Her bottom lip quivered and tears fell from her eyes.

I reached out for her, and she dissolved into me. I held her close, trying not to spill my wine.

"I haven't told anyone—not even my family," she sobbed.

I let her grieve, thinking she must have terrible friends and surprised that her family may be in the dark as to their struggles. *And I thought* my *family was dysfunctional.*

She pulled away and took a long drink. From the amount remaining in the bottle, this was not her first glass. "Wait until I sic my attorney on him. He won't know what hit him." She toasted me again. "Well, to hell with Willie!" she crowed, waving off the paperwork. "Let's go and enjoy the evening out by the pool." She turned and led me to the back patio. "I hope you don't mind that I didn't feel like cooking, so I had the Good Food Store deliver some dinner."

On the table near the pool, Carrie had two place settings, a few containers filled with a variety of salads, and another bottle of wine.

"You mind opening this? I think we have plenty of reasons to get drunk tonight, don't you?" She handed me the bottle and a strange-looking gadget I'd never seen before. It looked like a small rocket ship—a smooth cylinder with wings at the bottom.

My gaze went from the bottle to the device, and back to the bottle. Carrie giggled.

"You've never used one of those before, have you?"

She placed the bottle back on the table and put the cylinder over the top of it. She pushed a button, and after it whirled, she lifted it off with the cork hanging out of the bottom. "See, easy-peasy."

Carrie poured more into each of our glasses, even though I'd barely touched mine. She held hers to block her face. "I have so much to teach you, Andy Strobel." She peeked around her glass and smiled.

We sat in the shade, but heat rose up my neck. I looked away.

Despite my embarrassment, it truly was a beautiful evening. During the Fourth of July party I hadn't come out to the pool area, but wished I'd found this spot of peace. Strands of white lights twinkled like fireflies in the surrounding maple trees, enhancing the golden hours of sunlight. A soft breeze wafted down from the mountains, bringing cool, crisp air. An automatic pool sweeper drifted silently around the pool, and tiny bubbles floated to the top of the adjacent hot tub.

"Here, try this," Carrie said, and handed me a small container of dark leafy salad that, upon closer inspection, contained chunks of apple, dried cranberries, and some nuts.

As I scooped it onto my plate I must have looked at it suspiciously, as Carrie asked, "You're not allergic to pecans, are you?"

I shrugged. "I don't think so."

"This kale salad is absolutely my favorite meal," she said, and put a small helping on her plate. Then she pointed to the other containers. "This one is a regular garden salad, and this one is chicken curry."

I picked up the chicken curry and put a scoop on my plate. At least it had some meat. I now realized how Carrie kept such a trim figure.

Carrie took a large swallow of wine. "You better drink up if you're going to keep up with me."

I obliged her by taking a gulp of the wine. It tasted terrible. I didn't know why people drank it.

Neither of us had touched our meal, and I wondered if I should offer a blessing.

"You want me to say grace?" I asked.

Carrie choked on her wine and laughed. "You don't believe in that nonsense, do you?"

"Well, I...Mama did," I stuttered.

"Aren't you glad you're rising out of the mire of your family?" she said bluntly. "My God, Andy. No more living in a trailer. No more dumpy town. Now you can make something of yourself."

I looked at her in shock, not sure how to respond. She smiled at me like everything she said was true and encouraging. But even though I grumbled in my heart about my family more than anyone, they were still my family. I didn't know how to answer.

"What did Mr. Gupta offer you?" she asked.

I tried another sip of wine to wash down her statements about my family and move on. Then I replied, "He wants to acquire my claim or partner with me to mine it."

"Did he make you a solid proposal?"

I almost told her about the figure but pulled back. "Yes... a crazy amount."

"Andy, if I were you, I'd take the money and run. You want to be rich, don't you? Look at all it can buy you." She held out her hands toward the house and pool. "Who knew that pile of rock was worth anything, anyway? What a way to redeem all the hardship your family has endured."

My mind swirled in defense of Pop, the land, and the fact that she had all the trappings life could offer, but they had indeed become traps.

I felt like I was looking at a Hollywood set where everything looks authentic from one side, but on the other side, it's actually just a propped-up facade. If you looked beyond the glitz and glamour of it all, you'd discover an empty film set with rats eating the leftover garbage. At least my life was genuine, and you could clearly see the rats.

"I'm worried what the mining will do to the land and river…and my fishing hole," I told her, finally finding my words.

"Oh, Andy. There are plenty of places to fish, but there's just this one chance to make good with your life. Who cares about that silly old pile of rocks? And about the river—they'd probably just have to line it with that black plastic sheeting or something like that, and your fish would move on."

I wasn't sure if it was the wine or the salad, or the terrible thought of my heaven on earth spot looking like a construction zone that made me feel nauseated.

And it made me mad. Here I was finally with Carrie Carver, the dream girl of my life, and I felt like running away. *I don't belong here.* This was Willie's wife and Willie's life.

The blood drained out of my face, and I was sure Carrie noticed. She leaned back in her chair and sighed. "Well, let's not talk about those things right now. Let's just enjoy this beautiful evening." She picked up her wineglass and took a drink. She fumbled with the top button of her flannel shirt and unbuttoned it. "I know…we should take a dip in the hot tub. When it gets dark and cools down, that is." She smiled and fanned her chest.

I tried not looking at the cleavage she'd just revealed. "I didn't know I was supposed to bring my swimsuit," I said, feeling the heat as well.

"Oh we don't need suits, silly." She slid a foot onto my knee.

I looked at her bright red toenails on the foot she placed on my knee. *Even her feet are perfect.* I blushed at her forwardness and didn't know what to say or do, so I just looked away.

On the road across the field of the nearby ranch, a line of cars sped up the hill. Blue and red lights flashed on the lead car. It seemed strange, but as they passed the last row of houses and continued up to the top and took the corner, I thought it highly unusual. There was one other ranch at the end of the road, and I worried that an accident had occurred.

Carrie followed my eyes and watched the five black SUVs bounce along the dirt road and turn down Heaven's Gate. Her foot dropped off my knee and she sat up.

We sat frozen in place, half expecting that they'd soon realize they had taken the wrong road and do a U-turn at the archway to the property.

When they continued, Carrie stood and whispered, "Oh my."

She ran into the house. I followed her through the kitchen and out the front entry, where we waited on the porch for the caravan to pull to a stop in the circular drive.

The doors of each SUV swung open. Men and women in black military uniforms stepped out.

A tall man and a short but stout woman dressed in business suits marched with authority from the lead car to the steps in front of us.

They looked at me suspiciously and then past us through the open front door.

"Are you Carrie Gray?" the woman demanded.

"Well, yes, but I go by Carrie Carver…my maiden name," Carrie said nervously. "What is this about? Are my kids okay?"

"Is your husband home?" the man said, glowering at me.

"N-n-no," Carrie stuttered. "Is everything okay?" she asked again.

"And you are?" the man demanded of me.

I thought I might either wet my pants or forget my name, but I managed to say, "Andy…Andy Strobel. And you are?"

"I'm Agent Sandoval and this is Agent Gaertner," the woman said. "FBI."

37

FBI

The moonless night increased the fear and intensity of the raid. If the FBI agents meant to intimidate Carrie and me by putting us in separate rooms, I thought the firearms they readily displayed on their hips worked better. The man, Agent Gaertner, interrogated Carrie in the breakfast nook and the woman with no humor, Agent Sandoval, asked me questions in the formal dining room off the entry.

Agent Sandoval seemed annoyed that the men in black military uniforms and bulletproof vests marked with FBI in large yellow letters kept distracting me as they carried out Willie's computer and the contents of his desk and cabinets in cardboard boxes. I told her everything I knew and wondered if she was listening because she asked the same questions over and over. I couldn't help but feel like I was in trouble even though I explained I had found a gold nugget, spent all that money, and then we discovered three more that Willie sold for 3.2 million dollars that I'd agreed to let him invest. When I mentioned the amount, she nodded and wrote something in her notebook. Otherwise, I'd pointed out that Carrie, Willie, and I went to school together in Bonner. Willie was the smart and popular one.

With some of her questions, she seemed to know the answer before she even asked. Like who we sold the gold to, and how much they had paid. I think she knew about Sue and the accident as well.

"And you told me you last saw Mr. Gray at your claim yesterday?" she asked, recording my answer in the notebook.

I nodded.

"Are you and Mrs. Gray in a relationship?" she demanded, emphasizing the *Mrs.*

"Oh, no…no," I stammered. "We're just old friends." I said the words, but they sounded like a lie in someone else's voice.

She stared at me, urging more information.

What was I supposed to tell her? *That I'd swooned over Carrie since testosterone first circulated in my veins and had a huge crush on her ever since I could remember.*

I sweated like an inmate on death row. I worried she'd produce a lie detector test at any moment, and I'd have to confess my long, unrequited love for Carrie and what a schmuck I'd been for coveting another man's wife.

Agent Sandoval flipped through her notebook, closed it, and glowered at me. "You have any other statements you want to make?" she asked in a husky voice.

"I'm sorry?" I said, more as a question.

She examined me from head-to-toe, then watched agents carrying more boxes from the upstairs and out the front door, and finally back to me. "Mr. Strobel, do you have something to apologize for?"

I wiped sweat off the side of my face with the back of my hand and tears welled in my eyes. It was like at that moment everything in my life collided: all the times I'd screwed up, all the times I'd ruined everything, all the times I was too stupid, all the times I wasn't good enough, all the times I fell short.

"For being an ignoramus, I guess." I repeated the word that my brothers and kids at school called me.

She stared at me, showing no emotion, and waited for any other information I wanted to share.

I shrugged.

She nodded and finally said, "Okay." Then she tipped her head toward the kitchen for me to follow her.

Carrie sat with Agent Gaertner at the breakfast table. She had a blanket draped over her shoulders and what appeared like an entire box of used Kleenex crumpled around her. Agent Gaertner looked up and nodded to Agent Sandoval. Carrie stared at the tabletop and wouldn't look at me.

Agent Sandoval offered me a chair and then sat between Carrie and me.

I still didn't know what this entire mess was about and figured the handcuffs would soon come out and the agents would escort us to their car. Perhaps I'd illegally found and sold the gold.

"You're telling me you know nothing about your husband's business or finances?" Agent Gaertner asked Carrie.

"He's my soon-to-be-ex-husband now," she told them, flicking the divorce papers in front of her, "and yes, I have nothing to do with his business. I bought the groceries and paid for the kids and personal stuff out of the allowance he gave me."

"And that was?" he asked

"Three thousand a month," Carrie said.

I watched her eyes. She had sobered up completely and acted angry. At whom? It'd just be a guess, but three thousand a month seemed like a lot of money for groceries, but perhaps not enough to live with someone like Willie.

"And you had no clue about the financial trouble he was in?" he asked.

She pursed her lips and shook her head slowly, then wiped a tear from her eye.

Agent Gaertner turned to me. "Did you?"

It felt like someone punched me in the gut and I'm sure it showed on my face. *What are you talking about? Look at this house, the cars, the boat, the place at the lake.* I finally croaked out, "No."

Detective Sandoval's phone rang, making me jump.

She answered it and stood. "Hello?"

She took three steps toward the kitchen, listening to the information and quickly said, "Okay," and hung up the call.

She turned and nodded to her partner.

"Where are my kids?" Carrie demanded and sat up, showing the first signs of life since the agents arrived.

"They have just arrested Mr. Gray and are bringing your children home from the lake," Agent Sandoval said. She looked at her watch. "They should be here in about an hour."

"Arrested?" The words slipped out involuntarily. "Carrie, what is going on?"

She just shook her head, still not looking at me.

"He's taken all our money," she said, and kicked the table.

Agent Gaertner cleared his throat.

I stared at her and felt her anger build.

"He's taken all of *your* money, too, Andy Strobel...you're as dumb as that stupid pile of rocks you own."

38

THE CHEST

With all the distractions, I worried I'd lop off a finger as I carved this early morning, but I didn't know what else to do to keep my mind from ruminating on all the disasters. And if somehow this heart I fashioned represented my own, I might as well stomp on it or crush it with a hammer since that's how I felt. Just when I thought my existence couldn't get any shittier, the crapper truck of my life exploded.

Max sensed my sadness and had spent all night on my chest and glued to my side this morning. He now rested on my lap but laid his head on my stomach, looking up at me with worried eyes. Tears always came easy for me, something I guess I've been ashamed of, but last night grief hit me in such waves that I thought I might drown in them.

With the FBI raid on Willie and Carrie's house, any morsel of affection that had grown in Carrie for me evaporated. And with a flip of a switch I was, once again in her eyes, dumb-ass Andy. Rejection, the foundation of my life, poured into me like sewage. When I'd asked her if she wanted me to hang around until her kids got home, she actually laughed at the suggestion. I slunk into my single-wide with my tail tucked between my legs, Carrie having squashed whatever confidence I had gained the past week like a pumpkin.

I didn't know what a Ponzi scheme entailed so, because I couldn't sleep, I read all about it online. But this is exactly what the FBI agent described, and I lay at the bottom of the pyramid. My 3.2 million dollars allowed Willie to pay off his clients ahead of me, robbing Peter to pay Paul, *except I am Peter.*

And depending on how you looked at it, Willie was both unfortunate and a genius with money. But one thing was for certain, he was an immoral crook. He had made millions for some of his clients, but he also had to leverage his home, the place at the lake and everything else of value, so now they would lose it all. Willie and Carrie were beyond broke, and I guess that made him terrible with money.

Another thing that made me toss and turn for hours was, just like the gold and Pop, I really didn't know if Carrie knew what Willie was doing. I finally found a tiny piece of consolation when I realized the FBI didn't arrest her last night. But she got the same warning that they gave me. "Don't plan on leaving town anytime soon." Maybe in the back of their minds they thought I was involved at a deeper level somehow. *But didn't they see I'm just the stupid idiot who always ruins everything?*

Agent Sandoval told me they'd had Willie on their radar for some time and when 3.2 million dollars landed in his bank account then transferred to an account in the Grand Caymans, they made their move.

The one act of kindness the agent showed me was when I was walking out the front door of Carrie's house. I turned to her and asked, "You think I'll ever see any of my money again?"

She put her hand on my shoulder and shook her head. "Unlikely," she said. "But don't give up hope."

It was probably something Mama would have said. Pop would have kicked my butt and told me what a loser I was.

I blew on the carving to remove the dust. I did not know at this point if my heart was sinking into the mire or rising from the ashes, but it felt more like the former.

I wiped a remaining tear from my eye and looked out the window. Daylight peeked out from the east, but gray clouds blocked the sun and raindrops sprinkled on the roof of my single-wide. At least I had my truck paid off and my rent prepaid for the year.

I sipped at my latte that I had made first thing this morning. The day after I was with Anil at the claim, I had taken his advice and decided on one splurge…a fancy coffee maker. I spent a thousand dollars on the Breville Barista Espresso machine from Bed Bath & Beyond with my new credit card.

I glanced at the stainless-steel appliance on the counter in my kitchen and wondered if the store would take it back, even though I'd already used it. It barely fit on the counter space anyway, but the simple pleasure of making a latte or mocha was about the only joy I'd felt this last week. Perhaps I could keep it and slowly pay off the credit card once I got back to work.

I had decided that I would tell Anil that I didn't want the Strobel Cliff mined and risk destroying the area. When I called him late last night, he told me he was about to call and tell me he'd been thinking of that little corner of paradise in Montana and thought we shouldn't disturb it. "Some things are worth more than gold," he'd said. And when I told him what had transpired with the FBI, he said nothing for a long time. I could hear him breathing on the other end and waited.

The disgust in his voice was clear when he finally said, "Money can be such a powerful force—for good or evil." He paused. "I'm sorry, Andy; I looked forward to seeing how you would use yours. I think you would've chosen wisely, but I'm afraid this confirms my thoughts about the claim. I must formally withdraw my offer; I cannot afford to be swept up in something like this."

Max perked up his head as headlights flashed in my windows. He glanced at me and sat up, afraid to leave my side. As the car engine shut off, I wondered if the FBI wanted to question me further. It seemed awful early for them to come around.

I set Max on the floor and walked to open the door.

I creaked it open to reveal a smiling Abby. "I thought you could use a friend," she said, and held up a newspaper in her hand.

I reached for her and hugged her tight. "Abby, I'm so sorry. I am such an idiot."

She kissed me on the cheek. "It's okay, Andy. It's all going to be okay."

Not only had Abby picked up the Missoulian, but she'd also brought a box of donuts. "Health food," she'd said, and laughed. Unfortunately, she had to go to work, but promised to come back tonight and bring dinner. Terribly nice of her despite how much I had hurt her.

I made another mocha, sat at the kitchen table and bit into a chocolate-covered donut. *Just what the doctor ordered.* I stared at the front of the newspaper that read: "FALLEN

STAR." With the sub headline: "Grizzly Alum Arrested in Ponzi Scheme."

The article said it all. Willie, a once-beloved star quarterback for the University of Montana, was now in jail. The reporter must have had inside information, as they laid out most of the story, including quotes by Agents Sandoval and Gaertner. Fortunately, the paper didn't mention my name, nor did they say if the scheme involved Carrie.

No wonder he was so desperate to find more gold at my claim. His lies and deceit had finally caught up to him.

I set the newspaper down and accidentally tipped over the shadowbox frame of Mama's cross-stitch. I picked it up and rattled the small nugget of gold around on the inside. I guess I could sell it and pay off the coffee machine. I rested the box on the table, and for the first time saw the faded handwriting on the back.

Mama's cursive writing read: "Find treasure inside Papa's chest." Mama often called God "Papa Father." I put the box down, trying to remember a Bible scripture that said the same, but couldn't match Mama's writing with one. Not that I'd paid much attention in Sunday school.

I was about to dismiss the notion when I looked down the hallway, and through the open door. I noticed the Chinese chest that Grandpa had brought back from Japan after the war.

I walked to my bedroom and ran my fingers over the elaborately hand-carved chest. What an expert craftsman the artist was. I looked at the odd lock on the chest. On special occasions, Mama would open it and show us special trinkets she'd kept throughout the years or pull out the handmade tablecloth her mother crocheted.

Remembering that Mama told me to keep the key somewhere safe, I'd placed it in my underwear drawer. I dug around until I found it and slid the unique square key into the lock and opened it.

Removing the lock and opening the lid was as if Mama had entered the room. The pungent smell of antiquity, dust, and candle wax drifted from the chest. The lacey tablecloth that adorned our family table each Christmas and Easter covered the other contents, and I carefully removed it and laid it on my bed.

One corner held the stub of a six-inch diameter, faded green and white candle. It had burned for one or two hours on every December nineteenth, Mama and Pop's anniversary. Mama would indicate a foot and a half from the tabletop and laugh, "It was this tall the day we got married."

Mama continued to light it each December for the twenty-two years she'd outlived Pop. I picked it up and sniffed. I remembered how it used to fill the house with a fragrant cedar smell, but now just smelled like old wax. Next to the anniversary candle were two tarnished silver candlesticks. On the same special holidays, they'd replace the whiskey bottle. I think Mama had told us they belonged to her mother.

Mama had stacked shoeboxes under the tablecloth. I opened a few of the boxes and realized that the rest of her treasures were all photos—many of them old, in black and white. It seemed like I remembered lots of other trinkets and a few other pieces of silver, but Mama must have dispersed those to the girls. I opened and closed the other boxes to make sure I wasn't missing something of value. I wasn't in the mood for a stroll down memory lane.

I replaced the boxes, candle and tablecloth, and as I shut the lid, I noticed another note from Mama stuck in the corner of the frame.

I carefully wiggled it out from between the wood braces

and opened it. To my shock, it was not in Mama's cursive, but in Pop's blocky print.

To my son Andy,
I imagine since you have found this both your mother and I are dead, as I know you would never get in this chest without your mother's approval. God rest her soul. Hopefully, her prayers were enough to grant me entrance into heaven to be with her.

I do not understand how this all works. Maybe I am looking down on you, but you need to know I'm sorry for my failings. But since you're the smartest and strongest of will of all of us, I figure I'd leave you with the burden of the claim that I was never keen enough to figure out what to do with. You know I was not much for religion. I left that one up to your mother, but she hit me over the head with this verse from Proverbs and I now give it to you: 'How much better is it to get wisdom than gold!'

If you haven't found it by now, the family claim has produced! Your mother said we had all we needed, and that was enough. She encouraged me to bury the gold I found. She said it would destroy us and the land that we loved. There is more gold there—I am sure of that!

So son, I'm sorry to leave this riddle for you to solve. But you have what it takes to make the right decision. You were always the sensitive one.
Good luck…Pop

I turned the piece of paper over and saw that Pop had drawn a rough sketch of the claim. A semicircle represented the amphitheater, and Pop penciled in a tree at the alcove. There was an X in the spot where we'd found the buried nuggets. I brought the drawing close to examine a second X. Not exactly GPS coordinates, but it looked like he marked it on the wall of the alcove.

EPILOGUE

Father and Son

Five Years Later

The eight o'clock freight train rattled the windows of the house. I waited until it was over the Blackfoot to carve another cut into the top of the chest. I wished I'd met the man who'd carved Grandpa's trunk, which inspired me to make one of my own. I'm sure, like mine, every detail meant something to him. Simple things were the big things. The monster bull trout I caught at the fishing hole, the mountains that surround Milltown, the wildflowers I placed on Pop's grave every June nineteenth.

And this was just the top. There was still so much of life to go that would fill each side of the chest with carvings of my story.

I looked up and smiled as Abby knocked on the threshold of the door to my workshop.

"I made you a decaf caramel macchiato," she said, set it on my desk, and handed me a copy of the Missoulian.

She had the newspaper opened to a small article near the back. The title read: "Missoula Humane Society Receives Anonymous One-Million-Dollar Gift."

Abby kissed me on the forehead and gave me a seductive smile. "Don't stay up too late."

I leaned into her and lay my head on her chest. "Thank you."

"Harry is already asleep. I'll wait up." She shot me a bounce of her eyebrows.

I grinned and playfully waved her away. It was probably a good thing that Mrs. Jarvi was gone. She'd have her ear to her window, I'm sure. She'd passed three years ago, the year after I married Abby. Mrs. Jarvi had willed the rental house to us. One of her kids inherited the main house and the single-wide. I still did the yard.

At four, Harry was still too small for yard work, but someday I expected to give him that assignment, like it or not. "A little hard work won't kill you," as Pop would say. Mostly I hoped that Harry and I would fill the chest carvings with stories of grand adventures. There were many trout to catch. Harold Andrew was his full name, but we call him Harry. I just hope the kids at school won't call him Hairy Andy, or else they'd have both Mama and Papa Bear to deal with.

I read the entire article even though I figured I knew what it said. A one-million-dollar cashier's check arrived with the instruction to build a new wing of kennels and to name it "Maxi-boy Rescue." They did not know who the generous donor was or why it was given.

I bent down and picked up Max 2.0. He was a rescue dog as well and still a little nervous around us all, but seemed to mesh more and more with our family every day. He and Harry were already fast friends.

I looked up at the small wooden box I'd made for Max. We lost him to kidney disease last year. The heart carving sat on top of it. I don't care what your station in life is, the death of your four-legged best friend hits you hard.

"Miss you, Maxi-boy." I crossed myself and looked at the lit candle on the new memorial I built in the corner for Mama, thankful to God for the simple blessings of my life. "To find contentment in the life we're given is a treasure worth searching for," or so my therapist says. There was plenty to work through, but the letter from Pop was a spark that lit new meaning in my life.

I still drive Number One, and Marty treats me no differently. At least I wasn't in jail, where Willie still sat out his sentence. Carrie ended up serving one year. I'm sure the prosecutors tried for more, but they had a hard time making most of the charges stick. Abby and I saw a picture of her upon release. Prison time had changed her looks on the outside and hopefully how she was on the inside.

After finding Pop's letter, I went to the claim. It took me a while, but at the back of the alcove there were two wedges of rock that hid a small window into a vein of gold. Like many gold veins, quartz surrounded the ribbon. For the most part, I'd left it undisturbed. Like Mama, I felt I had absolutely everything I needed—food to eat, a roof over our heads, and most important, all the love of Abby and Harry.

To this day, I often sit at Pop's marker and wonder what he was thinking. He may have had plenty of his own faults and wounds, but I finally understood that most of what he did, he did for the good of the family and the Blackfoot. He could have easily taken the money and ran. He sacrificed all for Mama, us kids…for me. That's the love of a father.

Again, there was a day when the sons of God came to present themselves before the Lord, and Satan also came among them to present himself.

The Lord said to Satan, "Where have you come from?"

Then Satan answered the Lord and said, "From roaming about on the earth and walking around on it."

The Lord said to Satan, "Have you considered my servant, Andy? For there is no one like him on the earth, a blameless and upright man, fearing God and turning away from evil. He has held firm in his faith and integrity, even as you tempted him with glory, gold, and lust."

"Yes, indeed," Satan replied, "but he only succeeded because you wielded a secret weapon—his father's letter."

Then the Lord sent Satan away from his presence, saying, "The relationship between father and son *IS* my secret weapon."

CALL TO ACTION

I can't tell you how much it means to me to hear from my readers. The best way to do this is to sign up on my website: AuthorTimothyBrowne.com (I promise not to bombard you with tons of newsletters or communications!)

As a thank you, I would like to give you a free eBook copy of *Maya Hope*. Just click the button that says, START MAYA HOPE NOW to get your free copy and to sign up. I look forward in connecting with you!

Also, I hope you enjoyed reading *The Book of Andy*. I would so appreciate it if you would leave a review on Amazon, Barnes & Noble, Goodreads, and BookBub. You can simply copy and paste your review into each one. These reviews are so very important to my career as a full-time writer. Your honest reviews truly make a difference and so easy to do. Just go to the respective website:

Amazon: https://www.amazon.com/review/create-review?&asin=B096MWS6TX
Barnes & Noble: https://www.barnesandnoble.com/s/Timothy%20Browne
Goodreads: https://www.goodreads.com/author/show/15623925.Timothy_Browne
BookBub: https://www.bookbub.com/authors/timothy-browne

Thank you!

AUTHOR'S NOTE

As I wrote *The Book of Andy*, I lost my father to COVID. He was my biggest fan, and I miss him every single day. He was always the first to read every completed manuscript, and usually, after finishing, he would simply nod and say something semi-encouraging. That was just Dad in ALL aspects of life. He was not the most demonstrative in showing affection, but near the end of his life, he would tear up and tell me how proud he was of my writing. And I truly believe that. He was perhaps prouder of my stories than anything else I've done in my life, including medicine and mission work.

My Dad was an amazing man, but far from perfect, just as I am far from a perfect son or father. A reality in which most sons and fathers can relate. So, in *The Book of Andy*, I wanted to, in part, explore this perfectly imperfect relationship between father and son—this often complicated, incomplete, and at times, rocky, but an always love-inspired relationship. Frequently as children we do not know what challenges our parents face, and it is not until later in our own life that we look back with wisdom and grace.

In my younger years and even sometimes currently, I often looked at certain choices that my father made, scratch my head, and not understand why he made that decision. There are two truths that strike me: 1) He loved his family more than anything else in the world. 2) As with us all, we must make decisions based on our life situation, and use the information we have at hand to measure out the pros and cons. Then follow our heart and pray for God to guide us. And in the final analysis, we hope we have made the absolute best decision. Lord help us!

So, in the spirit of *Walter Mitty*, *A River Runs Through It*, *Forrest Gump* and other great American novels, I give you *The Book of Andy*. May you find humor, romance, the love of family, and mostly hope in these pages.

With hope of love for you…Timothy

Please visit:
    www.AuthorTimothyBrowne.com
    and sign up to receive updates
    and information on upcoming books by Tim.

facebook.com/AuthorTimothyBrowne

twitter.com/authortimbrowne

instagram.com/authortimothybrowne

IMPORTANT NOTE ON MENTAL HEALTH

The world is changing rapidly, but thank God, so is all our ability to access mental healthcare. Seeking help for life's stresses has become the norm.

If you or someone you know is in crisis, please seek help immediately. Call 1-800-273-TALK (8255) to reach a 24-hour crisis center available through the National Suicide Prevention Lifeline: https://suicidepreventionlifeline.org

Like my character, Abby, I am a strong believer, that psychotherapy can be extremely helpful in finding healing in our lives. One stream of therapy that I am very fond of is Internal Family Systems (IFS). To find more about this and working with your "parts" please visit: https://ifs-institute.com/

ALSO BY TIMOTHY BROWNE

Coming Soon: LARIMER STREET

Can you be faithful to God when your experiences don't match your expectations?

Based on the true story of the charismatic leader of the Sunshine Rescue Mission, *Larimer Street* **is the triumphant, epic tale of one man's courage and redemption through his weaknesses and failures. There is power in going through—in surviving. And in the final analysis, losing some battles but winning the war.**

Larimer Street, downtown Denver, 1907—Jim Goodheart, a tall and handsome man, loses everything. Staggering in drunkenness and desperation on a dark night in November, he decides to drink a bottle of carbolic acid and make room in the world for a better man. Jim stumbles onto the doorstep of the rescue mission on Larimer Street, Denver's skid row.

In spite of Jim's life-long battle with alcoholism, and by divine redemption, he becomes known as the captivating leader of the Sunshine Rescue Mission. Through World War I and the horrific 1918 Influenza epidemic, the mission serves the destitute in an era without safety nets or social programs.

The pain of WWI and his personal war against alcoholism brings him to the point of losing it all again, except his loving wife, Ada, and his faith. *Larimer Street* is a story of courage and redemption. It is not a story of Jim's success *over* his challenges, but a story of triumph *through* his weaknesses and failures.

Fans of *All the Light We Cannot See*, The *Nightingale*, and *Unbroken* will enjoy this riveting saga of history, faith, and love.

Available Now: THE DR. NICKLAUS HART SERIES

MAYA HOPE

A doctor stumbling through life. A North Korean bio- terrorist plot. The two collide in an unforgettable tale.

Dr. Nicklaus Hart, a gifted trauma surgeon, searches for meaning in his life. His self-reliant spirit is broken with the death of his missionary best friend, found sacrificed at the base of a Maya Temple. Going to Guatemala to fill the shoes of his friend at the mission hospital, he discovers God's redemption and peace in the smiles of the children he cares for. But his own life is in danger as he and his team stumble onto a deadly North Korean plot.

Amazon: https://amzn.to/2IkM2TU

THE TREE OF LIFE

A massive earthquake hits Eastern Turkey, the ancient area of Mesopotamia, unveiling hidden secrets and opening an epic battle between good and evil.

Dr. Nicklaus Hart has lost his moral compass. As an orthopedic surgeon in a busy trauma practice, the cares of the world overshadow what Nick knows is true about himself. With his life unraveling, he falls into his old patterns of stress relief but knows they are a poisonous cure. Nick is shaken from his moral slumber when a massive earthquake strikes Eastern Turkey, and he makes the snap decision to respond. Thrown into the chaos and devastation, Nick must face his internal struggle head-on.

Amazon: https://amzn.to/2HqXUqD

THE RUSTED SCALPEL

A pharmaceutical company promises you hope and happiness in a pill. Would you take it if it cost your relationship with God?

Dr. Nicklaus Hart returns from responding to a massive earthquake that rocked the Middle East, allowing an ISIS terror cell to enter the ancient area of Mesopotamia. Captured, tortured and blinded by the hands of the radical terrorists, Nick arrives home a broken man. He has lost everything he holds dear—his sight, independence, profession and most of all, hope. But at the bottom of the pit, God sends him a lifeline and restores his physical and spiritual vision.

Amazon: https://amzn.to/2oXuTrW

THE GENE

Following their marriage, Dr. Nicklaus Hart and Maggie Russell enjoy the splendor and passion of a honeymoon in Hawaii. They learn that their union has brought new life, but the overflowing joy of Maggie's pregnancy and their romantic getaway is interrupted by the shocking news of a genetic disorder discovered in Maggie's family lineage—that both Maggie and the baby carry the mutated gene for the horrific Huntington's disease.

Nick and Maggie travel to Poland, where the top geneticist, Emmanuelle Christianson, has founded and operates BioGenics whose mission statement is: Advancing the Human Genome. Their journey reveals more than the fight for knowledge, it uncovers a simmering evil left over from World War II. One that puts their lives in danger.

Amazon: https://amzn.to/2THnuwC

CPSIA information can be obtained
at www.ICGtesting.com
Printed in the USA
BVHW031438220721
612632BV00014B/624/J

9 781947 545229